SWING
THE FLY

ANTHOLOGY | 2023

Photo: Adrian Cortes

Editorial Team

Zack Williams	Publisher/Editor
Mitch Baker	Editor
Steve Bird	Trout Spey
Topher Browne	Atlantic Salmon
Daniel Ritz	Conservation
Rick Kustich	Great Lakes
Kait Sampsel	West Coast
Thomas Wöelfle	International
Kelly Williams	Advisor / Copy

© 2023, Swing the Fly Press, LLC

All rights reserved.

No part of this publication may be reproduced, distributed, or transmitted in any form; including but not limited to photographing, photocopying, digital, or mechanical methods, without the prior written consent of the editor.

For questions, contact editor@swingthefly.com

Swing the Fly (Print)
ISBN: 979-8-218-24054-7

ISSN 2472-3274

Swing the Fly (Online)
ISSN 2472-3282

Printed in Canada

Front Cover

Thomas Wöelfle

Back Cover

Adrian Cortes

Artists

Al Hassall
Richard C. Harrington
Greg Pearson
Tony Perpignano

*All photos unless otherwise noted within were taken or provided by the article author.

Contributors

John Alevras
John Barratt
Steve Bird
Kirk Blaine
Pete Bodo
Glenn Chen
M. Robbins Church
David Conrad
Adrian Cortes
Trey Combs
Sam Davidson
Kevin Feenstra
Greg Fitz
Sam Flanagan
Aaron Goodis
Richard C. Harrington
Al Hassall
Todd Hirano
Dec Hogan
Marty Howard
Joe Janiak
Rob Kirschner
Rick Kustich
Art Lingren
John McMillan
Bob Meiser
Jeff Mishler
Greg Pearson
Tony Perpignano
Rob Perkin
Billy Pfeiffer
Luke Probasco
Armando Quazzo
Jim Ray
Daniel Ritz
Joseph Rossano
Kait Sampsel
Marcel Siegle
Thomas Wöelfle
Glenn Zinkus

Table of Contents

Shoulders of Giants

6	*Homage to Steelhead*	Marcel Siegle
8	*Back to the Skagit*	Jeff Mishler
12	*The Legacy of Wes Drain*	Glenn Zinkus
18	*A Steelhead Story*	Greg Fitz
24	*My First*	Dec Hogan
30	*Late to the Steelhead Party*	David Conrad
36	*A Bond Between Fisher and Boat*	Kait Sampsel
42	*Recovering Steelhead*	John R. McMillan, Rob Kirschner
52	*Developing Your Own Fly Tying Style*	Marty Howard
58	*New Takes on a Classic Style*	Trey Combs
68	*Colors You Can Count On*	Kevin Feenstra
76	*Controlling Depth*	Rick Kustich
82	*Adaptability Required*	John Alevras
88	*Alo's Partridge & Peacock*	Armando Quazzo

Grand Venues

94	*Resolve*	Jim Ray
96	*Rivers*	Joseph Rossano
106	*A Bavarian Traveling Man*	Thomas Wöelfle
114	*My Daughter's North Umpqua*	Kirk Blaine
120	*Three-Eye Seeing*	Daniel Ritz
128	*Film Is Not Dead*	Aaron Goodis
134	*Chinook on the Decline*	Glenn K. Chen
142	*Travels Through B.C. with Bamboo Rods*	Art Lingren
146	*Saving the Klamath*	Sam Davidson
152	*A First Salmon Trip*	Greg Pearson
158	*Colors of Fall*	Joe Janiak

Stories to Tell

166	*After the Floods*	Sam Flanagan
168	*The Caddis, the Fly, the Fish, and the Bird*	M. Robbins Church
172	*The Long Journey*	Todd Hirano
178	*Naming Runs*	Bill Pfeiffer
182	*Tuning the Deschutes with a Nine*	John Barratt
186	*Jungle Trout & Jungle Rods*	Robert Meiser
192	*Reflections on Winter*	Rick Kustich
196	*Accommodations*	Luke Probasco
200	*The Temptation of Lilith*	Steven Bird
204	*The Tide Turns*	Art Lingren
206	*Silence of the Lamm*	Pete Bodo

$2.2 Billion Down the Drain

Over the past 20 years, the federal government has spent billions of your tax dollars propping up failing hatcheries. By interbreeding and competing with wild fish, the 5 billion hatchery fish released into the Pacific every year haven't stopped the decline of salmon and steelhead. They've made the problem worse.

There are almost 250 hatcheries from California to Alaska, and along with hatcheries in Russia, Japan and South Korea, they release more than 5 billion hatchery fish every year. The result? Watered down genetics, declining returns and wasted resources. **BEN MOON**

patagonia 50

Shoulders of Giants

Artwork: Al Hassall

Photo: Marcel Siegle

HOMAGE TO STEELHEAD

Marcel Siegle

I have seen you change your color,
seen you dance with your mate in the twilight,
I have witnessed your curious nature;
Tricking you to dance with me at times.

I have watched you disappear right in front of my eyes,
like phantoms in the evening sky.
I have seen you suddenly die;
and many times leap into the sky,
I have seen you stare directly into my eye.

You've made me wander in pursuit,
Made me lose myself into your realm,
healing me at times.

I have seen you flourish, but mostly suffer;
Yet here you are against all odds,
a brief moment to say goodbye.

Dave Pinczkowski (left) and Ed Ward

BACK TO THE SKAGIT

Jeff Mishler

All steelheaders get old. I spent my childhood reading stories written by anglers at the end of their rope and beyond. Captivated by a timeless lifestyle enshrined in angling literature, I never imagined a time when my peers and I would be approaching the end of ours. Not that I'm near death — though that could happen any day — but my river skills fade each season. Agility is compromised by wavering balance, and less-than-perfect close vision moves rocks about underfoot. Honestly, after spending a lifetime on the river chasing these critters, I feel an overall malaise. I struggle to find new portals of interest to crawl through. And as the fishing goes to shit, the feedback we seek is harder to find. At 60 years of age, I go fishing to find community.

And so, when Ed Ward noted that he and Dave Pinczkowski would be spending some time on the Skagit River this winter to fish and work with the OPST/Pure Skagit crew to create media for their brand, alas, I had something to look forward to.

In 2008 Ed and I filmed Skagit Master Volume One. At the time, it was to be the ONLY Skagit Master film. One and done. That was the plan. Fortunately, for the future of steelheading with a spey rod, no one could have predicted how many copies we would sell. And after the first one knocked it out of the park, why not make another, and another? I did.

I digress. Now, in 2023, Ed and I are just going fishing.

"I hope you're not all gung ho about this."

"Ed, I think we are on the same page."

"It takes me a while to get going in the morning. I don't think I want to fish before noon. I've got my dogs and, honestly, I'm only good for a few hours."

"Sounds perfect, Ed. I look forward to it" And I meant it.

The surrounding Cascade mountains capped in January snow define the river valley. Vivid recollections played of days spent exploring this impressive river system, memories molded in their shadows, play on as my truck worked up state highway 20 toward Concrete. Re-entry into Skagit country felt like watching my favorite movie for the 27th time.

The Bunny Ranch was now called The Glacier Peak Resort, and as I rolled my truck up the drive to the office I expected a facelift of some sort with the change of ownership. But everything remained the same, including the cabin where we filmed the fly tying sequence and round table conversation with Jerry French. It looked exactly as it did in 2008. Resort occupancy was up. Cars plugged the driveways and tenants walked aimlessly about. The bunnies were mostly gone but for a large black one greeting me at my doorstep every morning. Cabin 21 was so cozy and dialed in that I imagined selling my beach house in Oregon and relocating. However, regressing further into my hermit shell would be a most unhealthy choice considering that 2022 was a year of physical and psychological challenges: my wife of 15 years divorced my ass, I caught COVID in Alaska and thought I might die, a chimney fire destroyed the interior of my home, someone pulled an excavator trailer across the back of my truck at an intersection in Tillamook, and Taylor Hawkins died.

Swing the Fly Anthology 2023

I saw the divorce coming (how many steelheaders stay married?), but the Foo Fighters drummer's death hit particularly hard because I am a big time fan who procured two tickets to their sold out show in Bend, Oregon. Thanks to a deeply connected friend who knows Joan Jett, my son and I were hoping to get backstage passes, because Dave Grohl and Joan are friends. (How cool would that have been?) But the tragedy of Taylor's death and 2022 have passed, and at the 15-year mark since the production of the first Skagit Master, I'm back on the Skagit River.

At 11:30 I realize that the Hamilton bar is too shallow to launch my sled. The depressions to the sides of the concrete ramp aren't deep enough, and I don't feel like backing my truck into the middle of the river while water runs into the cab over the rocker panels. The Birdsview launch will have to do, though launching my 18-foot Willie boat there is an exercise in perfect trailer positioning. The unimproved boat ramp drops off into 6 feet of water with one-half extra rotation of the trailer tire. A perfect launching depth is found just before the trailer drops into the abyss. The tires are hanging on the edges of submerged concrete blocks, buried in river sand. Extracting the sled requires perfect trailer positioning and boat control, using the downstream bunk guide as a pivot point for the hull to spin on. While you power the vessel onto the trailer the river pushes against your upstream chine. The move requires the correct timing of your pivot and power. This river remains the domain of small, lightweight sleds and drift boats, though rowing down miles of slack water in an upstream wind is as much fun as a stick in eye.

Ed moves the time back to 1:00 p.m. so he can walk his dogs. I launch the sled into the fast current, toss the anchor onto the sand, park the truck and casually ready my gear. Everything needs to be changed out.

The biggest misconception about steelhead fishing on the Skagit is that you must use heavy sink tips and heavily weighted flies. If you took some of the lessons from the Skagit Master series literally, I can see why. Scott Howell, in Skagit Master Volume Two, covered presentation and used long chunks of T-14 and lead eyed Intruders. But we did not fish the Skagit in that movie. When you see this river for the first time, it is apparent that there is a lot of holding water and the fish can be in a lot of places.

Unless you are an expert at reading steelhead water, your first impression of the Skagit will be overwhelming.

"The first day I fished the river I had no idea where to fish," Ed told me while recording his podcast at the end of our third day. The Skagit is not an Oregon Coast stream where fish rest in deep slots and pools. Productive Skagit water is often slow moving. It's often less than 5 feet deep. It's often right at your feet, or just as often, way the hell out there. And this is why the Skagit is set up for the spey rod. The long bars and tailouts fish wonderfully with 12-13 feet of T-11 and a lightly, or unweighted, fly. For the occasional outside bend or boulder garden, you might need T-14 in various lengths, but I know where Ed wants to fish, so I set up my 8136 with a 26-foot Skagit head, 13 feet of T-11, and anticipate that I will change out the fly depending on the swing. It's a basic set up, and it works almost everywhere on the Skagit.

When Ed arrives at Birdsview driving a clean Toyota Tundra sporting a tonneau cover and kayak rack, there is a period of friendly recognition that it has been, in fact, 15 years. I have spent days in a Russian Arctic army tent, with this guy, waiting out a three-day snow storm while our food supplies vanished and the Russian interpreter used up all of his English. He came to the Oregon Coast in 2001, and we fished all five rivers in the area, finishing the trip with a primetime float of the big river, where we went three for five in water so high that when you jumped from the boat you couldn't see the bottom and simply trusted that you wouldn't ship water over your waders. I've written stories for multiple magazines about Ed, photographed him from every angle, drank whisky at night until way too late, listening to his ideas and reasons for committing to a casting discipline that is hard to explain, let along photograph or film. And still, after all of this, it felt like yesterday when we were here at this place, getting ready to go fishing.

The only difference is that the edge is gone.

I HAVE SPENT DAYS IN A RUSSIAN ARCTIC ARMY TENT, WITH THIS GUY, WAITING OUT A THREE-DAY SNOW STORM WHILE OUR FOOD SUPPLIES VANISHED AND THE RUSSIAN INTERPRETER USED UP ALL OF HIS ENGLISH.

The intensity or drive to be early, to beat the other angler, to spend every minute possible on the water, working out the kinks in his discovery process, has passed. Ed just seems mellow. Content.

Ed and I push away from the beach around 1:30 and spend most of our time talking about our lives and picking up rocks. Ed loves to look for jade, and apparently the Skagit Valley is full of it. I still don't know what it looks like, but I guess it's everywhere. We casually fish two spots before dark sets in. Hardly hardcore. And this is when I realize that steelheading has changed for both of us. I could care less that we only fished for two hours on a river we hadn't seen in a decade. Nor did he.

"How do you feel about how Skagit Master One turned out?" I ask before we fish the second run of the day.

"I think everything in the show is still relevant. The casting concept is for sure."

"What would you change?"

"Nothing really. I think some of the terminology was confusing and I would probably spend more time on the 45-degree thrust concept, but otherwise, it's still relevant."

This is why the show has done so well. Through time, the fundamentals of a constant motion/constant load casting style stay the same.

So, steelhead fishing for Ed Ward in 2023 represents opportunities to refine his casting technique and play with the gear that he has designed. OPST rods, Commando lines, Commando Tips and Lazar running line combine create a tangible representation of a steelheader's life. He is psychologically invested. But he is always tinkering by changing the elevation of his sweep, lowering the casting stroke to bounce the fly up under the brush on the far bank, and using the various pokes and skagit spey casts off both shoulders to test the overall versatility of the system he has created.

"Hey, let's run the boat down to this side channel I know. I want to cast my 3-weight

IN THE SHADOW OF THESE RESTRICTIONS I CAN SAY THAT THE FISHING REALLY HAS GONE TO SHIT, AND I WONDER WHY ALL OF THE OLD ANGLERS LIKE ME AREN'T MORE PISSED OFF.

micro-spey with this new line and tip combo and see if I can find some searuns."

In the middle of steelhead season, with fish in the river and time left in the day, Ed wants to go find some cutthroat. More testing. More discovery. More joy. Pure Skagit, in its many forms.

On the second day of screwing off, I hooked a beautiful chrome hen of about 14 pounds on my second cast, while waiting for Ed to finish running his dogs. Not really a cast, but more of a flip. With half of the Skagit head outside the rod tip I rolled the works out onto the water and led the fly immediately to the inside across the soft, sweet spot thirty feet away. The fly stalled. Nothing noteworthy, other than the fish ate my red fly. I set immediately and then she was away. Fast and far. In the air four, then five times. Deep into the running line, then the backing on her first blast.

Working her back slowly, the deep flex of the soft 8136 reminded me of so many other steelhead fought on this very stick. In my hands, through the handle, I could feel her working against the current and side pressure from the bellied line. Slowly, she came back to my feet and then, right on cue, rolled onto her side and I slid her into the shallows. A fresh Skagit River steelhead is amazing to see. Broad tail. Fat flanks. Clear fins and not a scale missing. The tiny head seemed to belong to a smaller fish. Egg production was this specimen's duty, and she had the reserves to succeed. The barbless hook slid cleanly from the corner of her mouth without a drop of blood. I turned her upright over a rocky bottom and with a wiggle and jerk her fins stood upright. Another flip of the tail and she returned to the river.

Back in camp that night, surrounded by the OPST production team, we toast the steelhead of the Skagit River.

"Long may they run!" Dave Pinczkowski says as we clink our glasses, and he has reason to be optimistic. The Soul Roller landed a Hoh River fish the week prior and has hooked and lost two on this trip to the Skagit. It only a matter of time for him.

But I am thinking less optimistically. These moments of celebration were common in decades past. The fly angling pioneers swung flies over larger runs with less effective gear, and still managed to bring a few to hand. I am happy to be here, with these men, celebrating a fish. Proof that steelheading has become a social event for me. Here is community. This is how clans form. Friendship flourish. Traditions solidify.

But this river will close to all fishing soon, and fly anglers will not be allowed to catch and then release a Skagit River steelhead, let alone swing a fly over fishy lies until a state agency says that enough steelhead are returning and angling may resume. In the shadow of these restrictions I can say that the fishing really has gone to shit, and I wonder why all of the old anglers like me aren't more pissed off.

Collectively, why aren't we dedicating our remaining years of frustrating immobility to an effort focused on making sure all those nature-raping mother fuckers pay for the destruction they reap?

The solution is simple, right? Fix the rivers. Fix the ocean. Fix the climate. How loud can you yell? Into the air? Into the face of the storm? Take a stand for wild things. Clean water. Healthy forests. Anything to make a difference because we are out of time.

But then again, you would be screaming at a mirror. And that is why we need these friends.

A Wes Drain-crafted steelhead fly reel; this one made in 1987. Wes Drain made a handful of fly reels from 1985 through as late as 1989 on a lathe in his garage. John Holmes, a Boeing engineer and good friend of Drain, helped with the finishing steps at Boeing. This reel was given to John Holmes in 1987. Flies tied by Sean Dahlquist.

THE LEGACY OF WES DRAIN

Glenn Zinkus

There it is: a wispy collar of purple, a neatly stacked yet sparse pinch of squirrel tail wing and that fluorescent pink body with a precisely wound flat silver tinsel rib — layered with hints of exotics in the form of a toucan feather veiling the tail and a fiery red cock of the rock feather shining through as an underwing.

The Drains 20 — perhaps the best known of Wes Drain's steelhead patterns — is an icon in the world of Pacific Northwest classic steelhead flies. Drain is widely known for pioneering the use of fluorescent materials in fly tying. During the post-war 1940s, Drain and his friends were either fashionistas or knew where to seek out the new fluorescent colors available in swim trunks. Before this material became available as spools of Gantron, they carefully unraveled the trunks to make strands of radiant threads, adding these new touches to their steelhead flies.

The Drains 20 began its life named the Pool & Rapid, undergoing an evolution of materials and appearances before becoming the bright, slender and elegant fly revered today as a steelhead fly classic. Earlier generations of the Pool & Rapid were fuzzier flies - first tied with a wolf-hair wing; the next was tied with a wing of guard hairs from the back of a badger; and a third iteration with a wing of jackal fur. Finally, there was the version we know today as the Drains 20, with the squirrel hair wing. Drain, if he had a favorite, was the badger version, with the black and white hairs that he sourced from Herter's, a huge supplier of exotic materials in the past. However, Drain opted to settle on a wing made from materials that are always on the shelf.

Wes Drain was born in 1914 in Kapowsin, Washington, lying in the morning shadows of Mount Rainier, yet a brief drive to the saline waters of Puget Sound. He was born into a family that was in the silver mining business, and he did work a stint during his younger days as a gold miner in Montana. He took his first trout on a fly on the Little Blackfoot with a Sandy Mite after his mining shift, and his first steelhead on a fly was in 1940, on the Stillaguamish — a memorable 7-pound 6-ounce hen on an orange shrimp fly.

Drain's early development as a fly fisher and fly tyer was formed under the tutelage of Letcher Lambuth. It was from Lambuth that Drain learned the craft of fly tying and the nuances of aquatic entomology. Lambuth encouraged Drain to visit Preston Jennings at his home in New York City. Drain once penned, "He (Lambuth) was in lively correspondence with Preston Jennings on many technical aspects of trout and trout food at the time and was aware that Jennings had imported the Old English Blue Gamebird strain to this country."

Drain seized the opportunity to visit Jennings on a two day leave from his South Caroli-

The evolution of the Drains 20, as tied by the fly fishing Renaissance man, Dave McNeese. This fly was originally named the Pool & Rapid by Drain, and later changed to the Drains 20 after he caught his record 20-pound, 6 ounce steelhead on the Skagit with this fly. Originally developed as a searun cutthroat fly, the first iteration on the left made with wolf hair, the second iteration in the center features a badger hair wing, and the final Drains 20 is on the right.

na army base before leaving for Europe during World War II. The Jennings visit was a landmark in Drain's fly fishing career, providing Drain a mental sabbatical during his tumultuous war years in Europe. Drain's visit cemented a lifelong friendship with Jennings. Two major takeways from the Jennings visit was the impression of just how systematic Jennings was in pursuit of all things fly fishing, and another were the theories of appearance and color in flies. The art of fly design — as Jennings wrote in his unpublished manuscript on flies for Atlantic salmon and steelhead — "encompasses the study of the laws of nature, and the adaptation of those laws to the needs and usages of man. Fly fishers and amateur fly tiers are basically artists in that they must be students of nature."

Drain also saw his first natural blue dun hackle during this visit. It was Lambuth who encouraged Drain to write Jennings upon his return stateside, to source Original English Blue Games (OEBGs) for Drain and fly tyers on the West Coast. Jennings obliged, authorizing William K. Stauffer to provide eggs and instructions to Drain. Despite the shipping challenges, and then learning to hatch and raise OEBGs, Drain successfully kept a flock at the family stump ranch near Olympia from 1945 to 1949 — at the peak having five good blues and younger ones in waiting, providing an ultra-rare supply of natural blue dun capes for his use in the Northwest.

Drain learned the intricacies of professional fly tying from tying empresario Mike Kennedy while they both worked together in the downtown Seattle Eddie Bauer store. In addition to the Drains 20, Drain developed more steelhead flies considered to be the classics from the early days of fly fishing for steelhead, including the Box Car, the Steelhead Bloody Mary, and the Steelhead Kelly. Drain's angling buddies, including Walt Johnson, an innovative tier of his own steelhead classics, together with Drain, fished their home water of the North Fork of the Stillaguamish with dry flies they developed for what was then a robust summer steelhead fishery. The Box Car, with its peacock body, white wing, and red tail with a brown hackle ahead of the wing was one of Drain's dry flies for summer steelhead.

Following the war, Drain, together with many of the Washington steelheading fraternity, bought adjacent parcels on a favorite stretch of

A historical photo with a caption originally penned by Bob Wethern: A rare, virtually non-existent, glimpse of Wes Drain in his fly tying room (he always kept the curious out by declaring it "too messed up").

the North Fork from a local farmer, on the Elbow Hole. Some built cabins to form a fly fishers' settlement. The famous Elbow Hole was described by Enos Bradner in his ***Northwest Angling*** book, although it was never named and well disguised in his prose to keep the location out of print. This enclave included the likes of Ralph Wahl, Gus Middleton, Ken Onimous, Enos Bradner, Sandy Bacon, Frank Headrick, Walt Johnson and Wes Drain, with Al Knudsen buying an adjacent parcel next to Drain. Later, Steve Gobin and Steve Raymond bought in from some of the original owners, and the McCleods also owned a cabin here.

The guys did seize opportunities to spend time at their camps, like one time when Ernest Schwiebert came to Washington to present a slide show to the Washington Fly Fishing Club (WFFC). Schwiebert had an extra day to fish, and of course, the WFFC wanted the day to be a success. It was decided that Ralph Wahl, Frank Headrick and Drain would take Schwiebert onto the Stilly for a day. Wes knew the upper river best and served as the guide. Ralph Wahl served as the driver for Schwiebert and the photographer for the outing. Frank Headrick was the chef for the après fishing steak barbecue at his cabin. Wahl, in an article for the club newsletter, penned, "I used all the alibis I could think of on the drive to the river. Too early in the season; water too high; fish not there yet, etc." All of that aside, Drain and Schwiebert donned their waders, strung up a 9-1/2 foot rod, and set out for the river. A river that, by the way, was running high but clear. Finding a place to cross, Drain led Schwiebert into a pool where Wahl spotted at least one fish from his perch above the river. After changing flies to a General Practioner, Schwiebert was into an acrobatic chromer, a fresh run hen that he revived before releasing her back into the pool, making the day a success. I'm sure those steaks tasted even better at the Headrick cabin.

The Legend of The Wes Drain Reels

Drain began work in 1950 for Penberthy, an instrumentation company. In his personal correspondence with Bob Wethern, an outdoor writer and editor, Drain laments the stress of his constant vigilance through his workday — overseeing the manufacture of super-polished glass. Eventually this particular shop went out of business. Drain was offered machinery from the shop, and he took a Clausing lathe that he loved. It was from this lathe that he turned out a very rare set of reels in his garage for handling bigger northwest fish. There are numerous stories of where these reels were fabricated, with numbers ranging from what can be counted on one hand to perhaps dozens. Those who knew Drain advise that the actual number was 12 reels, or close to 12, fabricated over a short span during the 1980s. The first example I've seen is dated 1985 — a Coho Salt reel, a beautiful deep purple anodized reel — up through the black anodized steelhead and coho reels made through 1989. Drain first made four reels, and then based on demand, continued machining and fabricating the reels for approximately two years to build perhaps eight more reels. One of Drain's buddies, John Holmes, a Boeing engineer, assisted with the final manufacturing steps including access to the Boeing anodize lines for final finishing of the reels.

Swing the Fly Anthology 2023   15

Above: Wes Drain emerging from the river, never without his camera.

Facing page: (left) A precious few items of Wes Drain memorabilia, including a holograph letter on his own letterhead from 1950, back when Drain was a professional fly tier; a Wes Drain-tied Drains 20; and a snapshot of Wes together with another tier of classic steelhead flies, Al Knudsen. Date unknown. (right) A Wes Drain-tied Drains 20. Wes pioneered the use of fluorescent materials with this iconic steelhead classic.

The Fly Fishing World's Good Fortune — The Multiple Lives of Wes Drain

We almost lost Drain as a younger man several times from the combat he saw during WWII, for which we will forever be indebted. Wes also suffered a heart attack while he was on a maniacal all-night drive from Seattle to the Dean River that first left him with two flat tires. Then there was a 1968 drift boat incident that left Drain floating down the Snake River at its confluence with the Grande Ronde River.

In Bob Arnold's account from his book **Steelhead Waters**, taken from Drain's own recount of the saga — as well as personal communications from those in the boat including Drain, Rick Miller and Dave Carlson at the oars — the boat was new to Carlson. As the boat glided into the chop where the currents converge, the boat upended, dumping all occupants and gear into the whirls. Drain, without a life jacket, drifted along the rocks at the bottom of the river. Grabbing what he thought was his Exacta camera, he emerged above the water's surface with a rock in his hand. Drain fought to stay afloat but was rolled in a maelstrom of water back to the bottom. He was finally thrust to the surface once again in an upswell, this time gasping for air in front of Bill Nelson from Eugene (and the founder of what is now Fly Fishers International). Nelson threw a life vest to the hapless Drain struggling to stay afloat. He tucked onto the vest and paddled to shore.

Outdoor films and shows were in their infancy during the 1960s, including the iconic American Sportsman, and the Drain Gang was out to film some of their own footage. Drain and all aboard the boat lost everything, including some of Drain's coveted EC Powell rods and numerous Wheatley boxes filled with both Drain-tied flies and dozens of Preston Jennings flies, as well as a ransom in cameras.

It was later when Drain gave Bill Nelson a particularly prized OEBG neck, passed onto him from Chip Stauffer, his supplier of the OEBG eggs. Drain later wrote, "I gave part of it to Bill Nelson of Eugene after he literally saved my own neck."

Perhaps the ultimate compliment his home club, the Washington Fly Fishing Club, could bestow was the prestigious Letcher Lambuth Fly Fishing Craftsman award, given to Drain in 1987. This is the club's highest honor for craftsmanship that "raised the quality of fly fishing and enhanced the enjoyment of our sport for anglers everywhere." And that is just what Drain did, leaving us with his classic flies, new fly-tying materials, a handful of reels tailored to the anadromous fish of the Pacific Northwest and memories of a fly fishing and steelhead luminary.

Photo: Joey Mara/Waist Deep Media

Conservation Corner

A STEELHEAD STORY:

The Legacy of Bill McMillan

Greg Fitz, Wild Steelheaders United

Early in A Steelhead Story: The Legacy of Bill McMillan, the new film from North Sound Trout Unlimited, the camera follows Scott Willison and Bill McMillan hiking up a tributary of the Skagit River as they search for spawning wild winter steelhead or recent evidence of redds. The narrow freestone creeks flowing off the North Cascade Mountains make for tough wading, but they provide critical coldwater habitat for endangered Puget Sound wild steelhead.

Narrating the scene, McMillan succinctly spells out the importance — and a bit of the magic — of what motivates his years of volunteer spawning surveys in the watershed. "There is personal satisfaction of coming to know ecosystems better because you're out there," he explains. "You're listening to what the fish are trying to tell you. What nature is trying to tell you."

Among steelhead anglers and conservationists, Bill McMillan needs no introduction. Among other titles, he is the author of the iconic book **Dry Line Steelhead and Other Subjects** and the creator of the beautiful Winter's Hope steelhead fly. For decades, he has been one of our loudest advocates for wild, native salmon and steelhead and the epitome of a citizen scientist and ecologist. TU members might also know him as the father of John McMillan, the former science director of Wild Steelheaders United, and a passionate advocate for wild salmonids and science-based fisheries policy in his own right.

For over a decade, Bill McMillan has conducted extensive annual spawning surveys across several key spawning tributaries in the mid-Skagit basin as an independent volunteer. His years of collected data and photographs comprise a fundamental understanding of wild steelhead populations in the watershed as the fish fight to recover their numbers in the face of a changing climate and generations of overexploitation, hatchery influence, and habitat degradation. His insights into the crucial ecological role the early-returning winter fish play in the Skagit System, especially regarding intermittent streams, is critically important for conservationists and fishery managers to understand.

Passing the Torch

To ensure a comprehensive steelhead spawning survey, McMillan committed to hiking each of the designated tributaries every couple of weeks for a six-month window of time between mid-January and mid-June. He completed 100 — 200 surveys a year. It is hard work, and for all his dedication, he recently began to realize he couldn't maintain the rigorous schedule forever. As he says in the video, he is now 77 years old.

Word of his impending retirement traveled

Swing the Fly Anthology 2023   19

fast among friends and supporters. Two things happened: First, members of North Sound TU and the Washington Council of TU decided they should find a way to celebrate McMillan's commitment to wild steelhead, the Skagit River, and angler-driven science. Along with the support of Wild Steelheaders United, they worked with Joey Mara of Waist Deep Media to make the film.

Second, Scott Willison, a member of North Sound TU and the owner of The Confluence Fly Shop in Bellingham, committed to carrying on the spawning surveys to ensure the body of knowledge provided by long term data collection would continue.

"Well, Bill keeps saying he is winding down, but I don't see him slowing down ..." Willison laughs, speaking from his shop.

"The data gathered is important and the longer we can build a record, the better picture we get of population trends and responses to environmental changes. We need to be making decisions impacting wild steelhead management and recovery based on the best science and observations available, and Bill's work contributes to that effort in meaningful ways," Willison explains.

The work also provides an important way to stay connected to wild steelhead, even when angling opportunities aren't available due to low numbers of fish and closed seasons. "Even though the surveys are long days, rough on waders and boots, and exhausting, I've found that they provide the same solitude and excitement I get from fishing for steelhead," Willison explains. "Finding a pair of wild fish spawning in these creeks is just as thrilling as hooking and landing a steelhead to me."

Photos: Joey Mara/Waist Deep Media

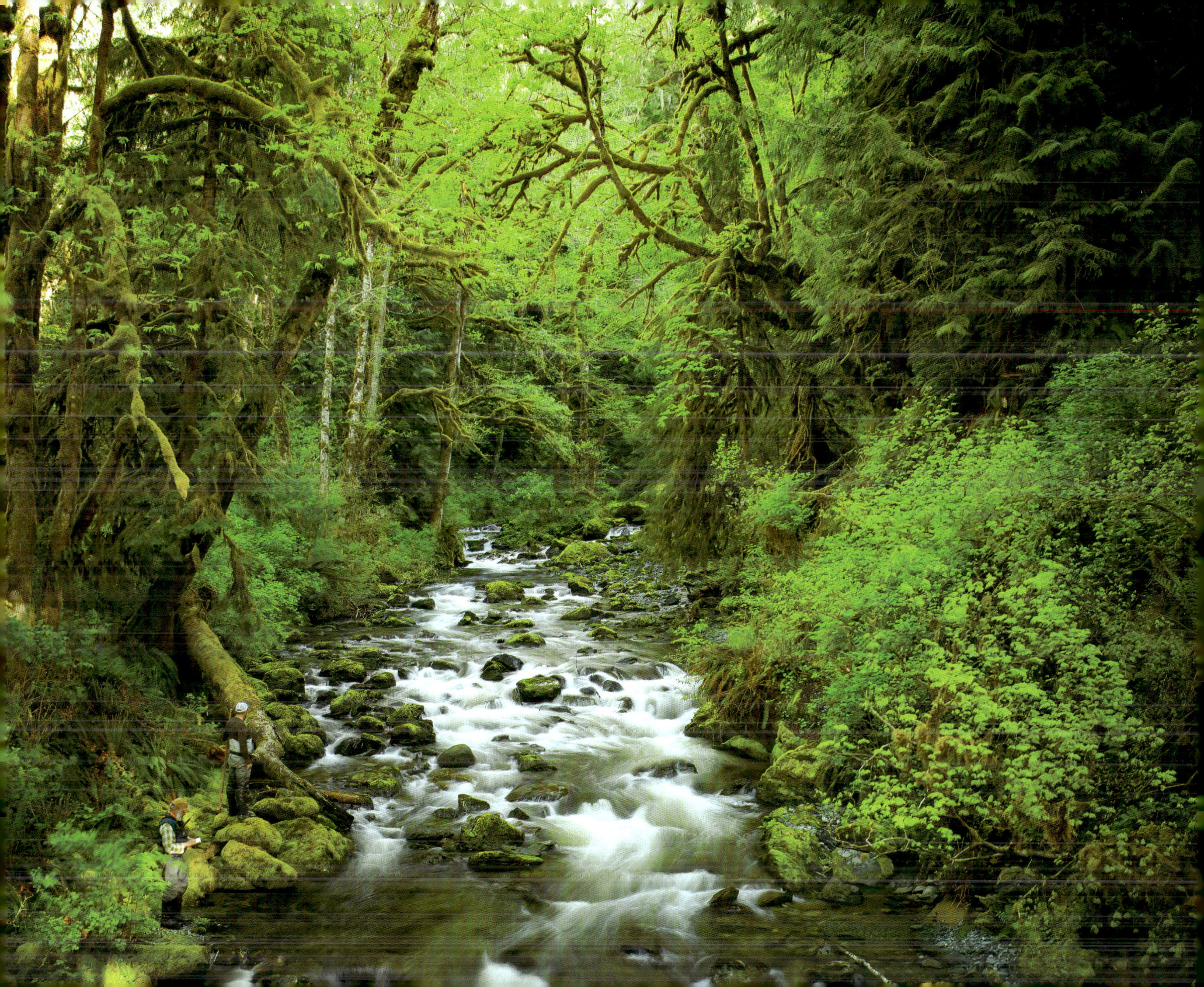

Photos: Joey Mara/Waist Deep Media

McMillan's Legacy Carries Forward to a New Generation

North Sound TU debuted the film in January at a screening at the Kulshan Brewery in Bellingham. It is now available online at the Washington TU Council's website (washingtontrout.org). Willison has been pleased with how the video has inspired interest in the opportunities for anglers and non-anglers to get involved with the surveys or even look to create similar efforts in their home rivers. "I've gotten dozens of calls since the film came out," he says. "I've been really happy to see how many younger folks want to learn more about these fish and ways they can help. They might not have understood that we have needs for more data collection, or that we still have a great deal to learn about these dynamic watersheds, but once you ignite that spark of curiosity, it is unstoppable."

"And that's a good thing! After all," he laughs, "someday I'll be Bill's age and hopefully there will be someone to continue the work then, too."

Jon Luthanen echoes the sentiment. He has served on the Washington Council's leadership team and is currently the Conservation Chair of North Sound TU. He worked as the chapter's project manager for "A Steelhead Story."

"We knew we wanted to celebrate Bill's work, but we also wanted to help educate people about how spawning surveys work and why this type of citizen science is so important," he explains. "The film has really struck a nerve and I feel fortunate to have had an opportunity to help contribute. Bill had gathered 13 to 15 years of data, and Scott is going to keep building on that. Who knows what we'll be able to learn from this work or how it will influence future decisions for the Skagit's wild steelhead? Or who it will inspire to get involved or start their own program? All of the impacts that grow from here will be the real legacy of how this project lives on into the future."

"A Steelhead Story: The Legacy of Bill McMillan" is a film by Joey Mara of Waist Deep Media. It was made possible with support from the Washington Council of Trout Unlimited, North Sound Trout Unlimited, and the Wild Steelheaders United. It is available to watch on the WCTU website at washingtontrout.org.

Everyone involved with the film production and the spawning surveys thanks Bill McMillan for his tireless work, leadership, and advocacy.

Editor's Note: Go to youtu.be/RzL1-4-8fx8 or use the QR code at the right to watch A Steelhead Story: The Legacy of Bill McMillan.

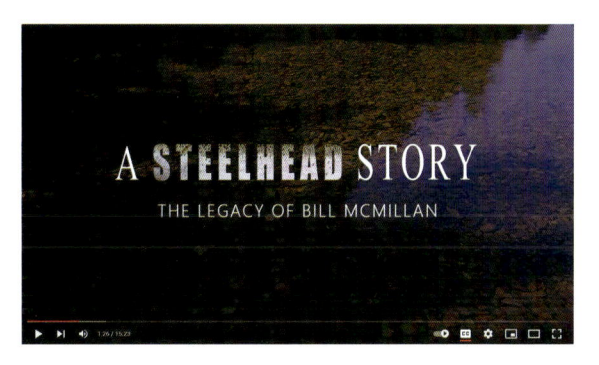

Swing the Fly Anthology 2023

CONSCIOUS OF MY UNCONTROLLABLE SHOUTS, THE WORDS I HEARD WERE CLEARLY DEFINING THIS MOMENT—ALL MY DREAMING, FANTASIZING AND VISUALIZING SINCE THE FIFTH GRADE WERE MANIFESTED IN THIS SINGLE MAGICAL EVENT.

THEN I FELL IN.

MY FIRST

Dec Hogan

The only thing unique about the story of my first fly-caught steelhead is that it's mine. Of course, anyone who's ever had the extreme pleasure of meeting freshwater's ultimate prize has had his or her own first experience. It only happens once. I've been fortunate having had the privilege of witnessing firsthand many people's first steelhead. It's one of the many perks of guiding. While I've never seen anyone upset or pissed off when playing their first steelhead, it's shocking how many times it's been a "ho-hum-that-was-nice" affair.

It always baffles me and makes me a bit sick to my stomach. I mean, I'm a drug addict and I just turned you on to the greatest high known to man — we're talkin' absolute and total euphoria that completely saturates your entire being. Pure pleasure. And then I hear, "That was pretty cool. How big was that fish?"

Bam! It's an instant shock to my system. For a moment it's incomprehensible. We should be running to the nearest and highest mountaintop to scream with outstretched arms echoing to the world of our accomplishment.

As quickly as I am overcome with chagrin, I recuperate. I know what the problem is. For every blasé first encounter I've witnessed with Mr Metal, I've see a half dozen where the dude takes my drug, is sent to blissful orbit, grabs my hand and drags me up the mountain faster than I can run.

The difference: It's all in the buildup.

For me the buildup started in the fifth grade. I was already as obsessed with fishing as is humanly possible. There wasn't a 10-year-old boy in the universe that had the passion more than me. One day at school I overheard another kid boasting about how he and his father were going steelhead fishing in northern California over Christmas break. Steelhead. I had no idea what it was, but the word alone sent a chill shiver down my spine. At that very moment my life was programmed on a path of destiny with the mystical steelhead.

Year after year I honed my fishing skills and made many memories. None of which were of the steelhead kind though. I lived in southern California for the majority of my childhood. No steelhead there. Once in college up in northern California, I came a little closer, but I was in the Sacramento Valley, and I didn't know or meet anyone who steelhead fished. Besides, for as much as I was intrigued with steelhead, there was plenty of life and sport at close hand to keep me occupied and motivated. But my steelhead dream never strayed far through it all.

College life was fun: maybe a little too fun. It was time to get disciplined and become more productive. I joined the U.S. Navy, which

Swing the Fly Anthology 2023

THEN ONE DAY I FOUND MYSELF IN THE MIDDLE OF THE INDIAN OCEAN ABOARD THE AIRCRAFT CARRIER USS KITTY HAWK. DAY AFTER DAY OF FLIGHT OPERATIONS OVER A STARK OCEAN DESERT, I WAS A MILLION MILES FROM THE NEAREST STEELHEAD RIVER. BUT I HAD WITH ME MY SMALL LIBRARY OF STEELHEAD BOOKS THAT I READ EVERY NIGHT AND A MODEST FLY-TYING KIT.

fortuitously brought me to the steelhead's doorstep. I was given orders to Naval Air Station Whidbey Island, Washington. Smack in the heart of steelhead country! Of course, once there I realized that my shipmates were from all parts of the country and wouldn't know a steelhead if it tail-whipped 'em upside their buzz-cut heads.

I fished locally in lakes for trout as well as in the saltwater of Puget Sound for anything that swam. But I knew the steelhead were close by. And like a teenage boy who is confronted by the cutest girl in class, I found myself intimidated. By reading everything possible about this noblest of game fish, I lived vicariously through tales of great steelhead anglers of the Pacific Northwest. I became increasingly enamored with river lore, flies, techniques and literally everything associated with steelhead fly fishing. It was a true obsession before I ever touched a steelhead rod.

Then one day I found myself in the middle of the Indian Ocean aboard the aircraft carrier USS Kitty Hawk. Day after day of flight operations over a stark ocean desert, I was a million miles from the nearest steelhead river. But I had with me my small library of steelhead books that I read every night and a modest fly-tying kit. Mimicking photos in my books, I taught myself to tie steelhead flies. It kept me close to my dream. Gazing at a finished fly transported me to crystalline waters and glacier-clad mountains as I imagined chrome ghosts holding behind boulders in wait of my dancing fly.

In a blink my Naval tour was over. I was free to pursue my dream of being a steelhead fly fisher. I purchased a complete steelhead outfit from Ed's Sports Shop in Mount Vernon, Washington. Yes, a no brainer — after the Navy I made Washington my permanent home. A shiny new 9 1/2-foot, 8-weight with a matching reel in hand, I had no clue where to take them.

One day while I was loitering at the fly bins at Ed's Sport Shop, this small bald dude comes up to me an introduces himself. "Charlie Gearheart," he said with an outstretched hand and a hillbilly twang to his speech.

He then immediately asks me, "You do any steelheading?"

I felt myself tense up. I really didn't want to say no.

"Well, I haven't yet, but I've got all the gear and I've been reading about it. It's something I really want to do," I replied. "How about you?"

With a big smile and a chuckle, he said, "Oh yeah, it's mainly all I do. Caught a real nice one last night — 'bout 12 pounds. She took a purple marabou."

My mind instantly took me to the river, seeing my new friend Charlie kneeling at river's edge just before dark, releasing this big chrome steelhead. Charlie was all smiles yet all knowing. I could sense his experience. I was in awe that I was finally in the presence of a real steelhead fly fisher.

After an hour of listening to Charlie, I mustered the nerve to ask him if he would point me in the right direction. He must have taken a liking to me because he told me in remarkable detail about a small slot on the North Fork Stilliguamish River that always held a steelhead. If I went there and fished it properly, he said, I'd catch one. Those words of confidence were almost too much to handle. I was off and running, headed to the Stilly with my new rod and some purple marabous. Charlie's last words to me were, "Let me know."

Once on the river, Charlie's directions led me right to the spot. It was a big, wide, shallow flat — featureless water between two runs. He said there was a deep, narrow slot on the far side. I literally ran down there and started looking for the magic spot by wading in at the top of the flat. As I started wading downstream, I didn't see anything, so I worked my way across farther and farther. Stepping along and peering at the far bank for any sign of deeper water, I began to doubt that I was in the right place. Finally, the water began to deepen a bit. I guessed this must be it. Nervously I sent my purple marabou on its first cast. My line swung around. I stepped and made another cast — just like my books and Charlie had said.

I kept working down, but my instinct told me something wasn't right. The water didn't feel "fishy" to me. I kept fishing. Who was I to say what fishy was? This was my first time steelheading!

Suddenly the water deepened dramatically. The place reeked of fish. My heart started racing. And I remember saying out loud, "This is it." I slowed my pace to a crawl and brought all my powers of concentration to bear. For the moment I forgot that I'd never done this before. I was finally fly fishing for steelhead.

I pounded the tiny piece of water for too long; nothing but my ignorance kept me at it. Charlie said I would catch one, and I believed him. I

> WORKING DOWN THE RUN I COULD SEE THE TIP OF MY GRAPHITE ROD QUIVERING AS MY ADRENALINE-LOADED TORSO TRANSMITTED ITS SURPLUS THROUGH MY HANDS.

kept casting and casting to what appeared the most likely section of the slot. On one of my endless casts-and-swings, my line stopped. I didn't feel anything particular. The fly simply stopped. I pulled up on the rod and felt weight. It started to move away, taking my line with it. I panicked and pulled back hard with the rod. I felt terrific power and weight. It's a fish! This can't be! And then it was gone.

Oh, how I wanted it back. But wait a minute: I just hooked a real steelhead. On a fly. On my fly. On the storied North Fork Stilliguamish. Under snow-capped mountains in the Pacific Northwest. This is how it feels. This is how it's done. I was fishing now, baby!

I fished the slot for another half hour with dimming confidence. I couldn't keep my mind off what had just happened and desperately needed to tell someone. I called my buddy Scott O'Donnell. I met Scott in the Navy. He was from Massachusetts. The guy would do anything and go anywhere. But mostly he liked do the things I liked to do: fish and hunt. I got him hooked on fly fishing and immediately created a monster. He and I were constant companions. We fished and hunted ducks and explored together like wild men.

That night I talked Scott's ear off for an hour. The next day when I got home from work, he was waiting for me, insisting we head up to the Stilly and my secret slot. Who was I to argue? We loaded up and headed out. I cannot recall what kind of gear Scott had at the time, but I'm sure he didn't have any proper steelhead equipment yet. No matter, he would have fished a 2-weight that night.

We hoofed it down to the river. Once on the water, I excitedly explained to him where I hooked up the previous evening. He stopped my jabbering and said, "Well, what are you waiting for? Go for it. Go catch your steelhead!"

I waded out well above the spot and started to cast. Working down the run I could see the tip of my graphite rod quivering as my adrenaline-loaded torso transmitted its surplus through my hands. I was bursting, thinking how thrilled I was to be right in this spot on this very day when . . . WHAM! I was hit so hard I could almost hear it. It felt like thunder and moved like lightning. I was stunned as the big fish peeled line off my reel faster than I ever thought possible. Then it exploded out of the river well below me. I was awestruck. I started screaming to Scott, "I'm doin' it, I'm doin' it!" Conscious of my uncontrollable shouts, the words I heard were clearly defining this moment — all my dreaming, fantasizing and visualizing since the fifth grade were manifested in this single magical event.

Then I fell in.

Fish still attached, camera thoroughly dunked and presumably dead, I stood up, took a deep breath and continued reveling in my good fortune. The steelhead made a few more runs and soon I had her in the shallows. What I saw amazed me — transparent, she circled around in less than a foot of water. The most visible thing I could see was the purple marabou hanging off the side of her jaw. Then she rolled on her side revealing absolute platinum brilliance from head to tail. She was spectacular. Her missing adipose fin let Scott and me know she was of hatchery origin. It was her only blemish. I could have kept her, but there was no possibility of killing my first fly-caught steelhead, irrespective of her birthplace.

Pictures! A photo shoot of the miraculous event was in order. My heart sank when I remembered my camera went for the big swim. Holding the fish by the tail with one hand, as its head and shoulders stayed submerged, I slung the still dripping camera from around my shoulder with the other hand. I switched it on hoping it somehow survived. Nothing. It was dead.

There wasn't a thing I could do about it. A small knot in my stomach appeared and began to expand, but nothing was going to ruin this moment. That's when Scott started digging around in his vest and pulled out a sandwich bag harboring dark plastic-looking contents.

"Dude, I have a camera," he said. "But I doubt it works. I fell in last week myself."

We both chuckled.

I anxiously said, "Awesome! Give it a try!"

Scott's camera was a 110 Instamatic. A crappy camera with film the size of a 10-year-old child's fingernail. It was a camera to record the moment nonetheless — I was grateful and optimistic that it would work. I held my platinum prize up, and Scott said, "Well, here goes."

"Click" went the camera. I wasn't impressed with the dim, cheap sound. But Scott smiled enthusiastically exclaiming, "Hey, waddayaknow, it works!" It did indeed work. For one

Swing the Fly Anthology 2023 27

shot, then it went dead.

"Oh well, we'll hope for the best," I said.

The business of photography was quickly over, and my heart was still racing, "Holy shit, I did it! I did it!" I was staring at this beautiful, mystical, deity of an animal as she regained her strength trying to free herself from my grip. I slowly opened my hand.

The steelhead that was mine for a moment was now free as she swam back to sanctuary, disappearing into the brown, olive mosaic of the Stilly's rocky bed.

Scott and I looked at one another, knowing we had just encountered something so privileged, so top secret — an ethereal feeling consumed us both. We were momentarily speechless. Then we simultaneously erupted in a gigantic bear hug. We both started talking loudly over each other, describing the instant emotions we both felt about what had just happened. A half-hour later I hooked and landed another — this time a colorful wild buck still in the river from last winter. This was fishing on a different plane. I had found Nirvana.

Oh, and the photo? Yep, I got my trophy. A single dark, out of focus, grainy frame, complete with Scott's blurry fingertip covering the lens. It was the most beautiful photo I had ever seen.

**Shaped by rivers,
Driven by connectivity,
Dedicated from first cast to last**

Humble Heron
FLY FISHING & FINE ART

Rogue North Umpqua Southern Oregon Coast

www.humbleheronflyfishing.com

Unmatched Craftsmanship. Unrivaled Performance.

SINCE 1959

WALKER 16'6" #9-10

BRUCE & WALKER
NORTH AMERICA

BruceAndWalkerNorthAmerica.com

Gene Oswald | phone: 253-279-5115 | email: bruceandwalkerrods@gmail.com

Photo courtesy WSC

Conservation Corner

LATE TO THE STEELHEAD PARTY

David Conrad, Wild Steelhead Coalition

There are historical accounts of fishermen lined up shoulder-to-shoulder on the bank of the Puyallup River in Washington. There they would wait patiently, smoking and talking, rods at the ready until someone would call out the fish were on the move. Sure enough, moments later, hordes of sea-bright steelhead would come rushing through the run by the hundreds. The anglers had a field day with it.

I'm a late arrival to steelheading. Not fashionably late, but "the party is nearly over" late. If this were a high school kegger, the cops would have come and gone. The only people left would be a few drunk jocks and their cheerleader girlfriends insisting the party was still going even though there was no booze to be found.

It was 2017 when I first I paid any attention to steelheading. I was fly fishing a lot during those days – mostly on smaller western Washington rivers and creeks – when one of my employees came in and said he'd gone steelhead fishing over the weekend. At that point steelhead were an obscure fish pursued by fanatics in absolutely miserable conditions.

I eventually embraced the challenge in 2018 and took my first guided trip on the Olympic Peninsula. I hooked a fish on the third cast (it spit the hook half-a-second later), and my father landed a gorgeous wild hen later that day.

First impressions are powerful and I quickly slid down the rabbit hole. I built up a stockpile of second-hand gear on the cheap. At the time it didn't occur to me it was all so cheap because people were giving up on it. I subscribed to the hash-tags and followed all the old-school heroes on social media. I bought the books and subscribed to the magazines.

I was all in.

Now feels like the right time to say that I'm certainly not on the VIP list for this party. I tend to fish spots where no fish would consider hanging out. I blow most of my anchors. I step when I should swing and swing when I should step. I trout set.

But, from the moment I arrived, I knew this was the best party I'd ever been to. My tardiness has, if anything, strengthened my resolve to both encounter and protect.

By most measures, Washington state is the birthplace of steelheading. The historical accounts of the great steelhead rivers of Washington are legendary. As a new arrival I dove into the legends. I'd stood in the storied waters of the Skagit and the Skykomish. Swung from the banks of the Hoh and the Bogachiel and the Sol Duc. Spent days floating the Grande Ronde.

Awash in such legacy and lore, one would expect, at least hope, to prosper.

Even so, as seasons came and went, I grew increasingly discouraged. I was putting in

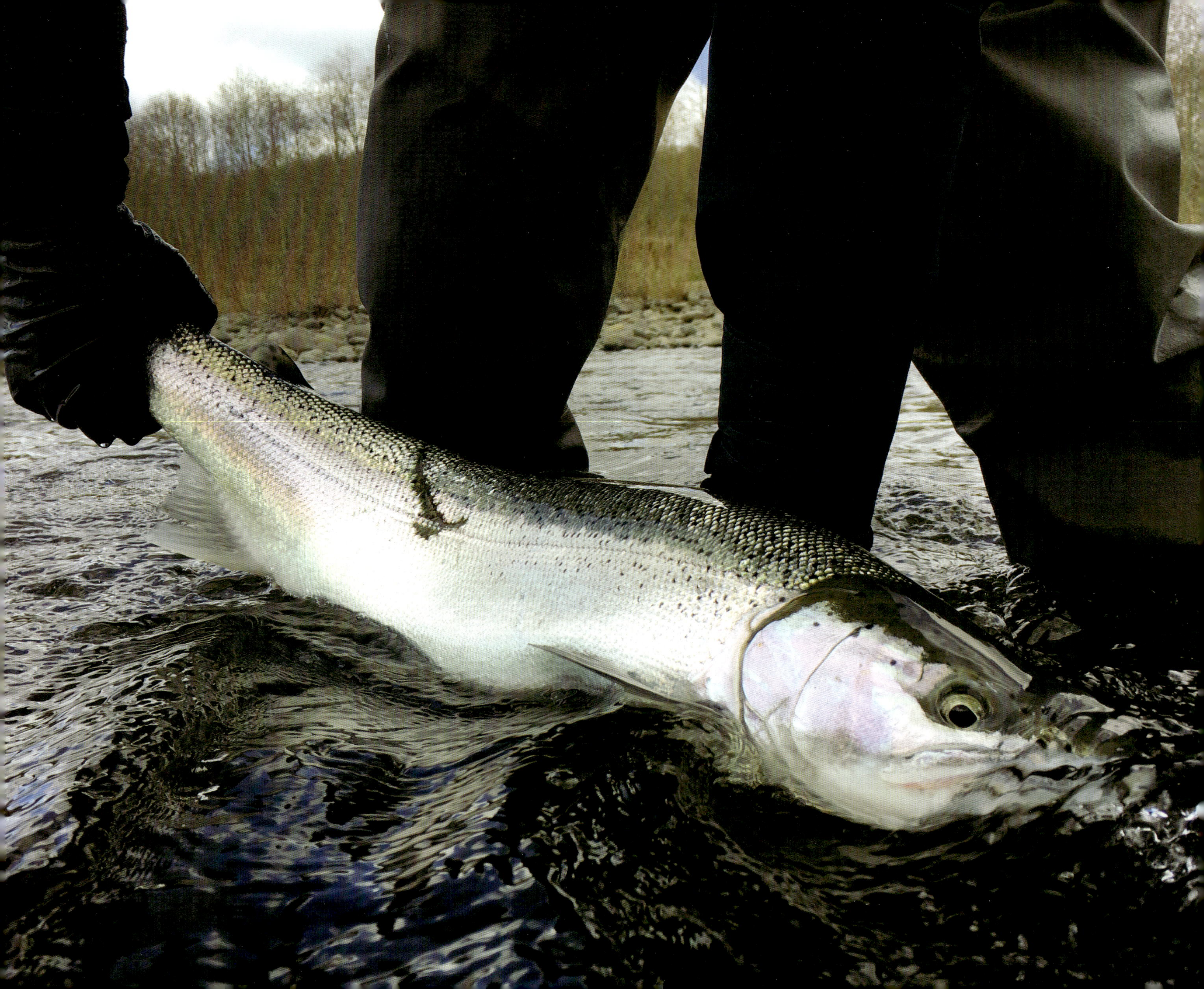

dozens of hours each year without bringing a fish to hand. There were grabs that could have been were it not for the aforementioned trout setting. There was the B-run fish that took me nearly into my backing before breaking the running line, circling back, jumping about 50 yards downriver — slowly extending a middle finger while airborne — before swimming away with my scandi head trailing from his mouth.

Our Current Dumpster Fire

The problem with today's steelhead party is the narrative surrounding it. The reality of it is not the same. It's taken a few seasons of multiple trips without bringing a fish to hand and thousands of dollars into gear, boats, guides, and conservation donations in search of for the reality to become clear.

As I grew more committed, fish are only increasingly difficult to find. I just got here and it seems like the party is already ending. What the hell happened?

The fact is, despite modest bumps over time, the return numbers continue to decline compared to historical averages (leading to an insidious shifting-baseline mentality). In response to pressure from conservation groups — and in some cases, listings under the Endangered Species Act — regulations continue to tighten around when, where and how you can fish. Whenever you have resource scarcity, you are likely to find polarized — and at times, hostile — communities. Steelheading is no exception. A friend told me how, on a recent trip, he pulled over so he could remove the Wild Steelhead Coalition sticker from his truck. He was concerned about getting his tires slashed by locals who take issue with conservation groups for fear their work will have catastrophic economic impacts on the local economy. Fish going extinct will have an even greater impact, but either way, steelheading has become a hot-button topic of discussion.

Volumes have been written about the old guard and their pursuit of wild Washington steelhead, and the booming multi-million dollar industry born from it. This cultural legacy is engrained not only in Washington's state identity (it's the state fish), it is a part of the lore of fishing around the world.

Reading those volumes I'm often left resenting the old guard who failed in such a way at "guarding" something they cherished. Anglers have refined and innovated the art of steelheading over the last century, taking and taking with little giving back. I wonder if they hadn't been so nonchalant about the bounty they pulled from the rivers, maybe I'd still have a chance to swing up a fish on the Skagit. I wonder if they hadn't had so much to say about catching steelhead without a word on protecting them, maybe the OP wouldn't have become a case study in divisive management policies.

Surely I wish it was as it used to be, with enough fish that we didn't need to give it a second thought. Of course, that was the problem — we did need to give it a second thought.

The New Steelheader

My continued reflection on that past still leaves me shaking my head at the tales of a resource squandered at our hubris in thinking such a good thing could last without taking care of it.

When you have rivers that are lousy with fish, why worry? Just keep partying.

Of course, I appreciate that hindsight is 20/20 and we do the best we can with the information we have at hand. Historically, the information either didn't exist, wasn't very

Photos: Dave Conrad

THE FUTURE OF STEELHEADING, MY STEELHEADING, WILL BE A DIFFERENT PARTY – THAT'S FOR SURE – BUT WE STILL HAVE A CHANCE TO MAKE THIS PARTY SOMETHING THAT WILL LAST. IT'S NO LONGER A PARTY FOR HOBBYISTS – IT'S A PARTY FOR ACTIVISTS, BUT IT CAN BE JUST AS SPECIAL.

solid, or we weren't paying attention to it.

When you're late to the party you are subject to all the decisions that took place before you arrived. Someone didn't buy enough beer; someone else burned the hamburgers. Somebody put hatchery fish in a pristine, healthy river or logged too close to the riparian zone. Another person allowed the fishing season to overlap too closely with spawning time.

In the end, it's on us, now. It's on us to figure out if we can keep this party going.

Looking around I don't find a lot of people taking meaningful accountability. What I do see is a lot of people pretending everything is fine, or worse, denying the science behind the situation. When someone does go out on a limb to identify the scarcity issues the responses are often swift, personal attacks.

If you can't fish for steelhead and talking about fishing for steelhead presents risks to your tires, or worse, what's a budding steelhead fisher to do? For me, it has required me to redefine what "steelheading" is in order to find ways to stay connected to it.

For me, the new steelheading is about finding ways to stay connected to the fish and the culture around it even if I'm not on the water. It's embracing the tension in being a member of a community defined by its ability to put a hook in the mouth of a fish on the brink of extinction. It's finding ways to ensure future generations have opportunities to encounter those fish.

Yes, steelheading for me is still the stoke of the grab, and gear and the beautiful flies. But it's also worrying. It's writing letters — so many letters — pleading with politicians to help protect the resource. It's writing checks to conservation groups desperately trying to put a dent in the problems. Then, yes, watching more committee meetings on Zoom and then writing more letters.

Keeping the steelhead party going will require mindfulness from everyone on the guest list. That includes the government, the commercial fishing industry, land developers, big timber, fish and wildlife management, agriculture, and yes, guides and recreational anglers.

It will require understanding that none of us are entitled to these fish.

It will require all of us together shifting from an exclusively "taking" mindset to a priority "giving" one.

This is not to say that people should stop fishing. I firmly believe if people stop fishing, they will stop caring about the fish, and then we will be in truly dire circumstances. But to ensure that's even possible, we do all have to find ways to contribute to rebuilding sustainable fisheries if we hope to pass this pursuit on to future generations.

Nature has proven that it can rebound and recover if given the chance. But, between high-efficiency angling, population growth, the associated human development impacts on habitat, and our incessant need for technologies that change the climate and the waters these fish swim in, the opportunity to rebound is slipping away quickly.

The future of steelheading, my steelheading, will be a different party — that's for sure — but we still have a chance to make this party something that will last. It's no longer a party for hobbyists — it's a party for activists, but it can be just as special.

We all want the party to keep going but that will require us all to start finding ways to care for a resource that needs us now more than ever.

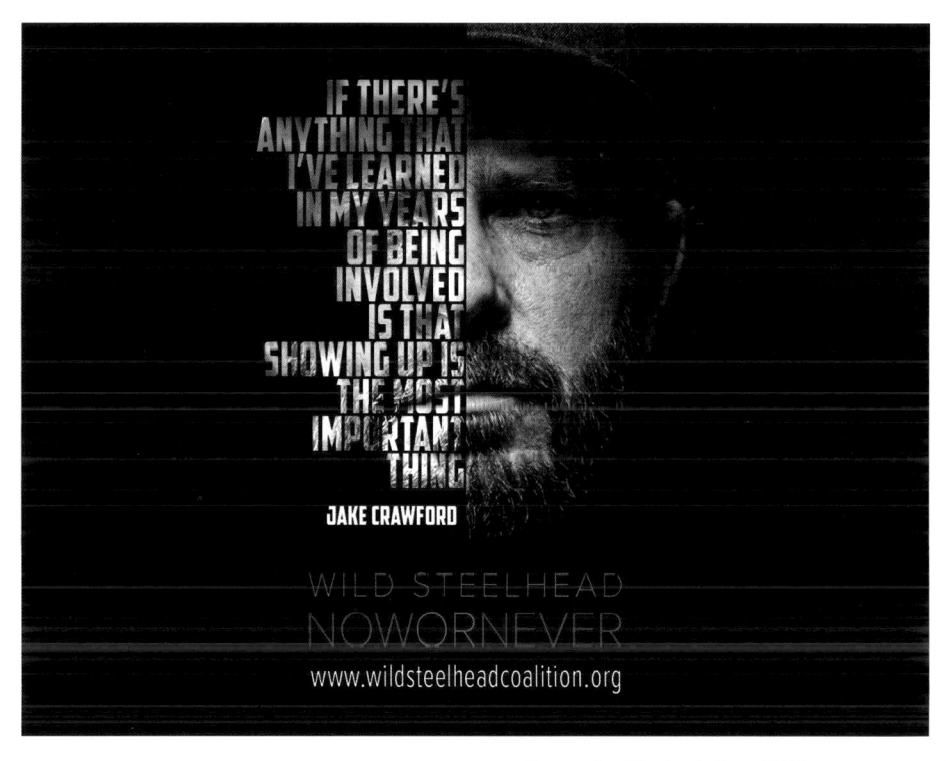

Photo: Dave Conrad

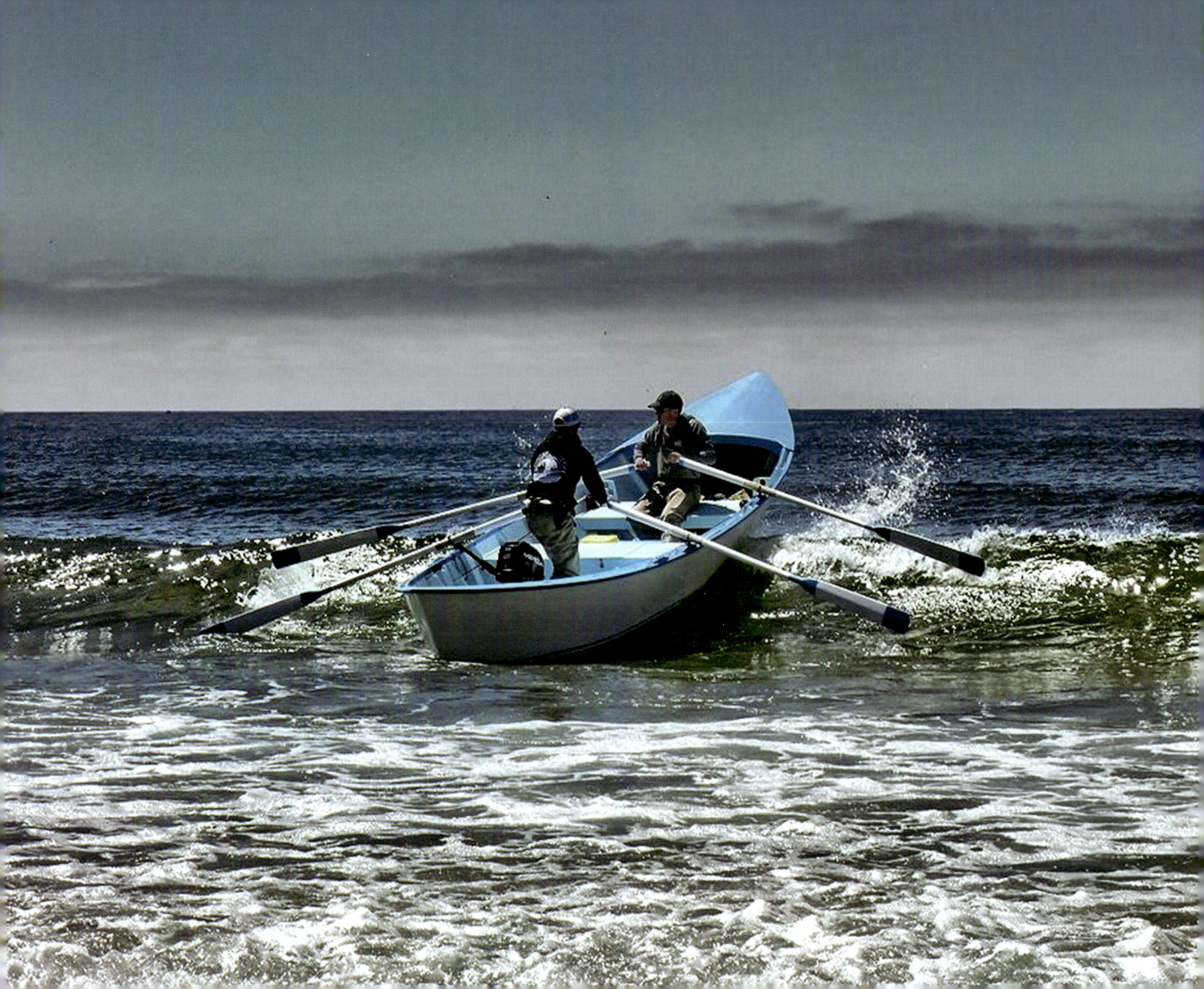

A BOND BETWEEN FISHER AND BOAT

Kait Sampsel

This story isn't your typical "swing" of things story. Rather, it is a journey about one determined man's desire to continue his family's heritage and deep-rooted, historic method of fishing — a bond between fisher and boat.

Captain Rob Perkin is a third generation Dory man with 35-plus years of experience. He is a man focused on education and stewardship at Connect Outfitters. The sandstone headland of Cape Kiwanda, Oregon, is at the heart of it all.

On any given day in the coastal town of Pacific City, Oregon, dory boats can still be found scattered along the beach. This dory community has been here for over 100 years. But not many people even know what a dory is and or why they are imperative to this small town.

Unparalleled fishing is touchable within a half mile off the beach at the Cape, but due to a shallow, dangerous bar in the Nestucca River, a larger surf boat needed to be designed and launched in the lee of Cape Kiwanda. Thus, the dory was born. The effort these dory fishermen have made to fish in this area is remarkable.

Dories are flat bottomed, open hull boats that are known for being extremely stable and capable of hauling thousands of pounds of fish. They only become more stable the deeper they sit in the water. Cape Kiwanda offers protection from common summer northwest winds and swell. There are prime reefs and salmon fishing just offshore — this new fishery was ready to be explored!

Origins of the dory can be traced back as far as the early 1900s and are closely tied to the surf dories and Nestucca River gill net boats that sold their fish to the salmon cannery established in 1887 near the mouth of the river. Commercial fishing in the river was taking a huge toll on the fisheries, so a bill was passed in 1927 limiting commercial fishing to the open ocean.

Many loggers, teachers and local farmers who used fishing to supplement their income had to change course — and thus looked to the natural protection of Cape Kiwanda as their only alternative.

Cape Kiwanda lacked roads in the early 1900s, so supplies for boats were taken to the Cape via horse. The first dory boats were assembled on the beach and kept above the high tide line all summer. Without outboard motors, these first dories were double ended boats that were the size of a large drift boat. This is the boat that Rob learned to navigate with as a young boy, and he still has that original to this day.

The boats had two rowing stations for one or two people to row. Many of the fisherman would row 7-8 miles north in the morning and use the current and mid-day northwest winds to fish their way back to the Cape.

Today's boats have evolved a lot from those first versions. The average dory is 22-24 feet

photo courtesy Rob Perkin

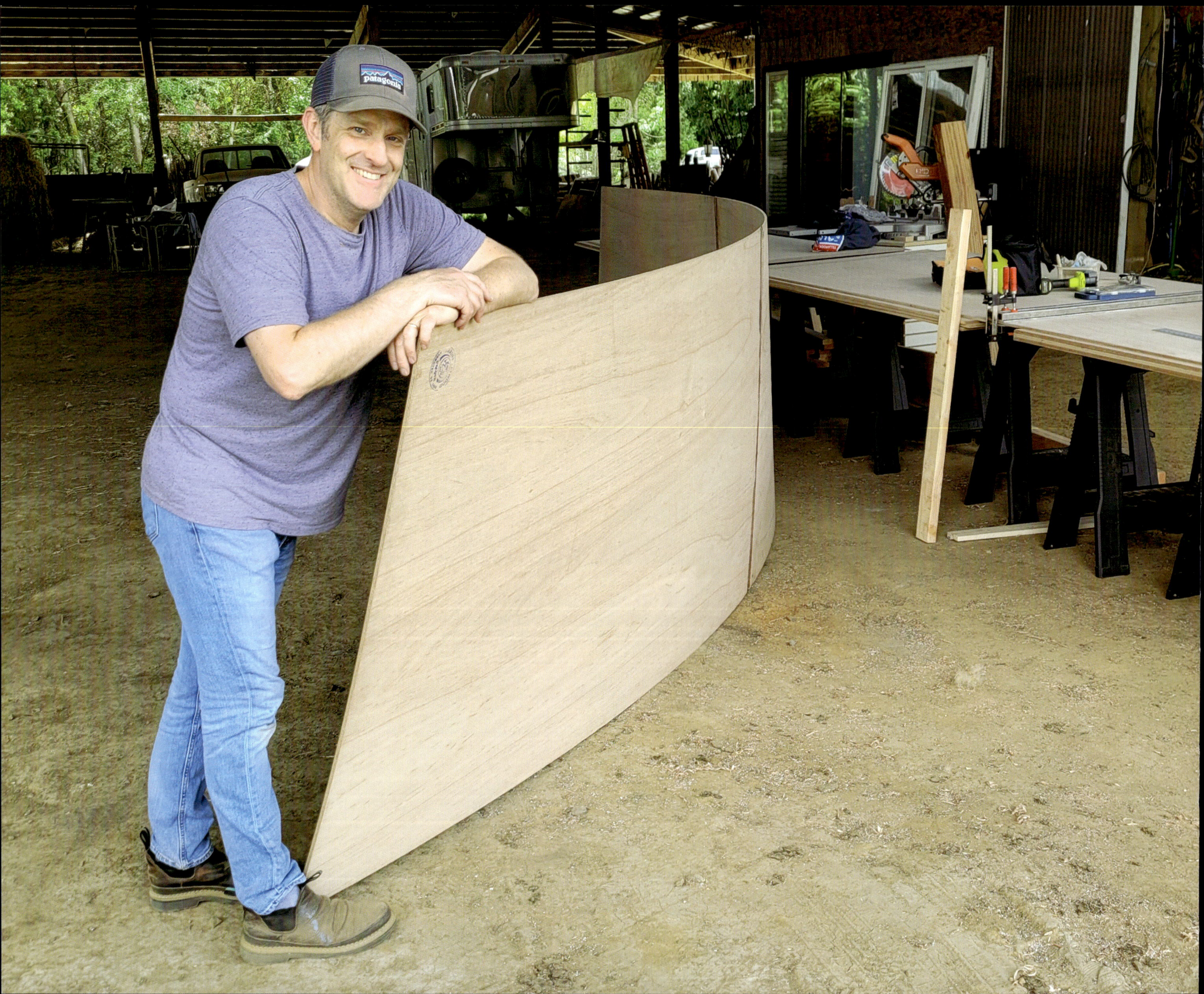
patagonia

in length, and while many captains still carry oars, the primary source of power is a 75 to 150 horsepower outboard motor.

Nowadays a unique Dorymen's Association flourishes in the area and currently is celebrating 26 years with roughly 200-plus captains contributing. It's a nonprofit organization where charter, commercial and recreational captains work together — not just in finding fish but in keeping everyone safe on the ocean. With no Coast Guard station nearby, they take it upon themselves to help their neighbors and intertwine past with present.

From the time Rob could walk, he was interested in water. Being born and bred in Canby, Oregon, it was always nearby. Some of his first memories were meeting his grandfather and dad on the beach when they would return from a morning of fishing.

He drove his parents crazy, always asking when he would be able to join them on the boat and explore the waters off Pacific City. At the young age of 10 he was deemed old enough to head offshore in a dory and fish with his grandfather and dad.

Rob's tenacious attitude and determination did not stop there. By the time he was 14 he had saved up to purchase a Greg Tattman 16-foot drift boat kit, which he built with his grandfather. But having a boat before you can drive can only get you so far — his coaxing and bargaining skills were sharpened when he had to ask his dad for a ride to the coast every Saturday to go fishing with his buddies.

On the ocean, Rob learned quickly from family members how to navigate their old double ended dory and the more modern square ended dories. Rob will tell you, "You never stop seeing new things and learning on the ocean. There is so much magic on the water, and the open ocean is like stepping into a different world each day."

For Rob, his outlook is different from many ocean anglers; he not only harvests fish but also catch and release angles on the ocean — and with a fly rod at that!

The idea of targeting salmon and rockfish in the ocean with a fly rod started for him after reading Les Johnson's 2006 publication, *Fly Fishing for Pacific Salmon*. The book focused on fishing Puget Sound, but the tactics seemed like they should work off the Oregon coast just as well. He decided to bring along his single-hand 8-weight fly rod on the next trip.

While his family had fly fished for trout and steelhead in the rivers, the thought of catching salmon on the fly in the vast Pacific was met with great skepticism by his dad and brother. Fortunately, it didn't take long to prove the effectiveness of flies.

The introduction that my husband James and I made with Rob and his wife Erin was pleasantly unusual. Rob — being the steward

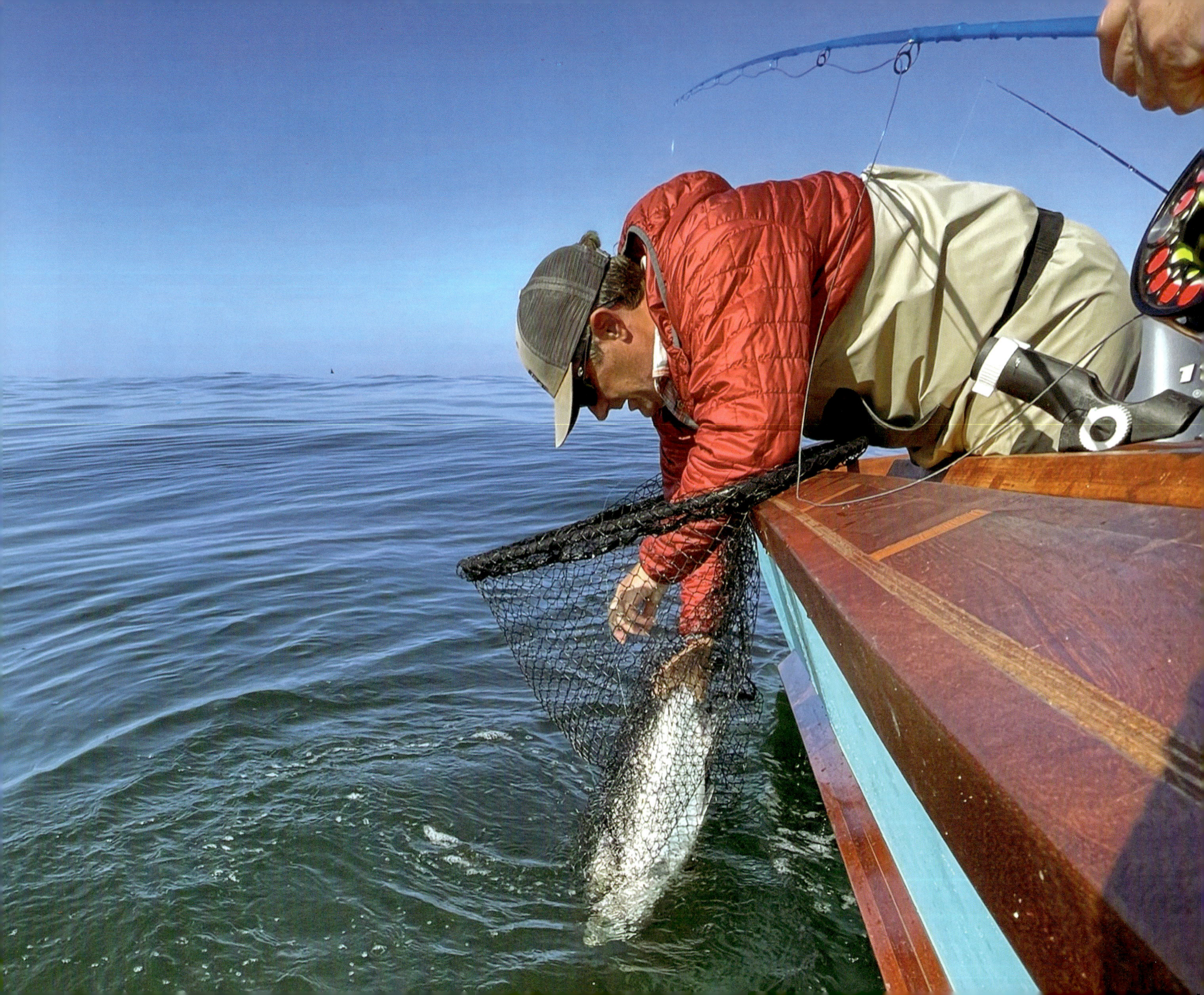

he is — bid on a Native Fish Society trip that we (Humble Heron Fly Fishing) donated, and he called to book the trip. We knew nothing other than they knew their way around a two-handed rod, but neither of them had fished the Rogue before. James told Rob to meet him at the local boat ramp, and the trip would start from there. It was dark at the put in and the boat ramp of choice had been deteriorating over the years, making the drop of the boat less than ideal.

This very average day of fishing turned eventful when Rob, showing up early, was getting ready to put his own beautifully hand-built Ray's 17-foot Rogue wooden drift boat Stella into the water. Rob was accompanied by his better half, Erin, and a small chihuahua named Cooper, in a puffy coat topped with a PFD,

James remembers vigorously laughing with surprise that someone would show up with their own boat for a commercial guide day. "Just doesn't happen all that often!"

Rob followed James down the river in Stella and on his third run of the day caught his first Rogue River steelhead. After that we quickly became friends with the Perkins, and now are happy to call them family.

Rob was then working in experiential marketing for 10 years — in the real world with a real job. He talked about one day wanting to become a fishing guide to honor his true passion and family heritage.

Late, he finally demoted himself to pursue happiness over career, creating Connect Outfitters in the process. I hear of fishing guides changing professions all the time for better financial support, but not many people quit a good job to be a fishing guide! Rob did so with tact and responsibility to the fishery and the community.

Erin and Rob started their adventure into outfitting in 2021 — their first stop was to fine-craft and build a 24-foot traditional PC Dory named "Vison." They had built other drift boats together in the past but nothing of this caliber or size, and did it on a tight deadline to have it seaworthy by guide season. It took them four months with help from friends, never having built an ocean-going dory before.

Rob puts in more work than most guides I know. I quickly came to understand why Rob was fueled with such passion to do all of this when he invited us into his dory.

For us it was an anniversary trip, one we now try and do every year. Rob picked us up and headed down the beach with a stiff smile. "Fishing from a dory begins and ends before you ever pick up a fly rod," he said.

Photos courtesy Rob Perkin

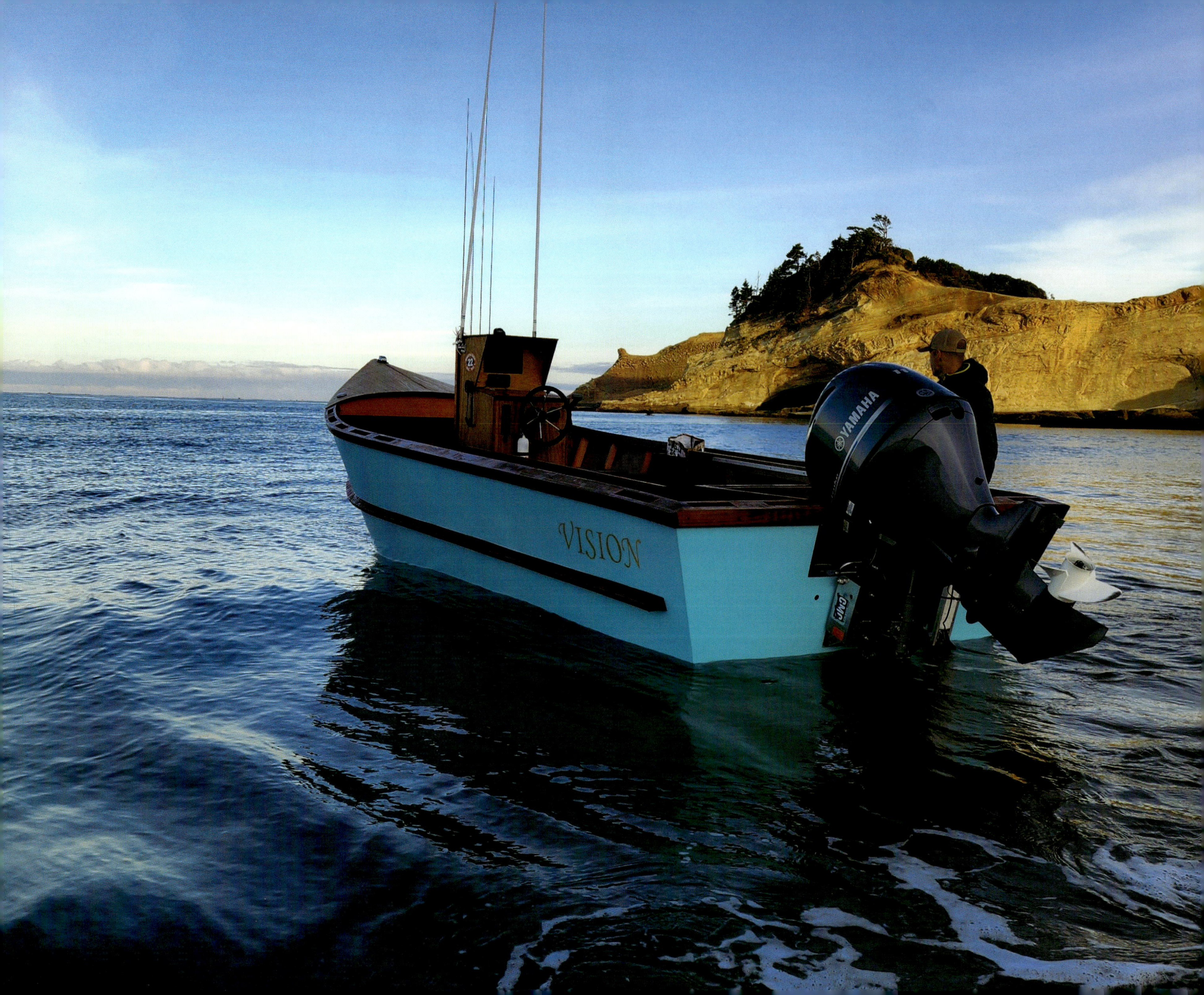
VISION
YAMAHA

THE DORYMEN'S BOND WITH THE FISHERY, THEIR BOAT, AND COMMUNITY IS WHAT MAKES THIS TOWN OF 1200 INDIVIDUALS THRIVE – A FISHING TOWN LONG BEFORE IT BECAME THE SURF AND VACATION DESTINATION IT IS TODAY.

"Launching a boat off the beach and through the surf is something that must be experienced, and I can't think of a better way to finish off the day than running a dory back through the surf and sliding up onto the beach." James and I looked at each other, for we had no idea what to expect. We were completely out of our element, but Rob calmed our nerves and told us how to participate.

Launching a 24-foot dory boat that weighs anywhere from 2500-4500 pounds is no simple task, and one that requires a choreographed dance between boat, fisher, vehicle and tide — all timed to perfection. A huge key to making the whole thing possible, explains Rob, "is a good, galvanized trailer that has a tilt bed with rollers. This allows the flat bottom dory to easily slide off the trailer and into the surf when launching and makes it possible to back right under the boat for easy loading at the end of the day."

I laughed and said, "Rob, it sounds like you don't even need a captain then?" Rob blushed and said the gear makes it look easy. A modest man, Rob.

He awkwardly turned with a smile and hopped in his truck, backed up his dory and pushed on the brakes, sending the dory out into the surf. James turned the boat around while Rob parked his rig, and I climbed into the boat. Rob quickly piled in as well to get the motor in place; he gave James a thumbs up to hop in, started the motor and off we went.

Flying through the breaking waves I placed my full trust in Rob. There were no "oh shit" moments, just this sense of surfing at one with the ocean, which I had never felt before and quickly realized I could do again and again — the excitement and the adrenaline taking over. I turned to look at Rob who was meticulously calculating the timing of the waves looking back and forth; Rob's demeanor changed out on the ocean. At that instant I saw him as a guide returning to his beloved salmon fishing grounds, like an old friend who he hadn't seen in some time.

By June, Rob is yearning to see the salmon returns. This year, 2023, promises to be a good coho salmon season. Rob has slowly seen the decline of salmon in the area, and he is open about sharing knowledge with guests in his boat. He has studied these fish over the years and understands their habits, what depths they like best, where their food supply is based on the currents. This is no easy feat to accomplish with migratory fish. He fishes for rockfish, lingcod, cabezon, coho and chinook salmon and albacore tuna.

Rob fishes for these above species with 9-foot single-hand fly rods of various weights and reflects on his steelhead guide season talking about the difference of styles; "I love taking a two hander and swinging for anadromous fish. This is not that fishery. This is your chance to play with a single hander for salmon and practice the same "let 'em eat" principles you will need later in the summer and fall when you're targeting steelhead."

His style of fishing in the ocean is called "bucktailing" — the primary way to locate salmon. This involves trolling flies in the propwash with a 9- to 10-foot, 7- or 8-weight rod. The technique is an exciting way to watch coho grab flies close to the boat and take off on tail-walking runs across the water.

Once a good school of salmon are located, guests can set up and cast off the stern of the boat, enticing grabs sometimes within a few feet of the boat. Albacore tuna are also caught in much the same way that he targets the salmon, except he uses a 12-weight fly rod for these vicious fighting fish.

Rob bucktails with flies at a quicker speed for salmon and can use multiple rods per person. The goal is to get multiple rods hooked up, and throw bait to the fish in order to draw them closer to the boat where guests can then cast flies into the school.

The rockfish he targets with the fly are primarily black, blue, deacon and tiger rockfish, all with a 9-foot, 6- to 7-weight rod. Many of these rockfish species are found off Pacific City's shallow reefs anywhere from 40-feet deep to the surface. Rob uses everything from heavy sinking lines with Clousers to floating lines and poppers when the rockfish are feeding at or near the surface. To target lingcod and cabezon he uses extremely heavy fly lines with heavy flies using 9-foot rods, 8- and 9-weights. These fish are located on the bottom of the local shallow reefs, so you need to get down 40 to 50 feet quickly and stay there.

To be able to experience and witness this magical dance of launching and fishing from a dory is something I would not have experienced had it not been for Rob. I am grateful for his determination and love for the fishery in Pacific City. The dorymen's bond with the fishery, their boat, and community is what makes this town of 1200 individuals thrive — a fishing town long before it became the surf and vacation destination it is today. The residents work together as a team out in the ocean for a common goal of not only fishing but also to continue a historic tradition. This is what keeps this small coastal town living in unison with the rivers and ocean.

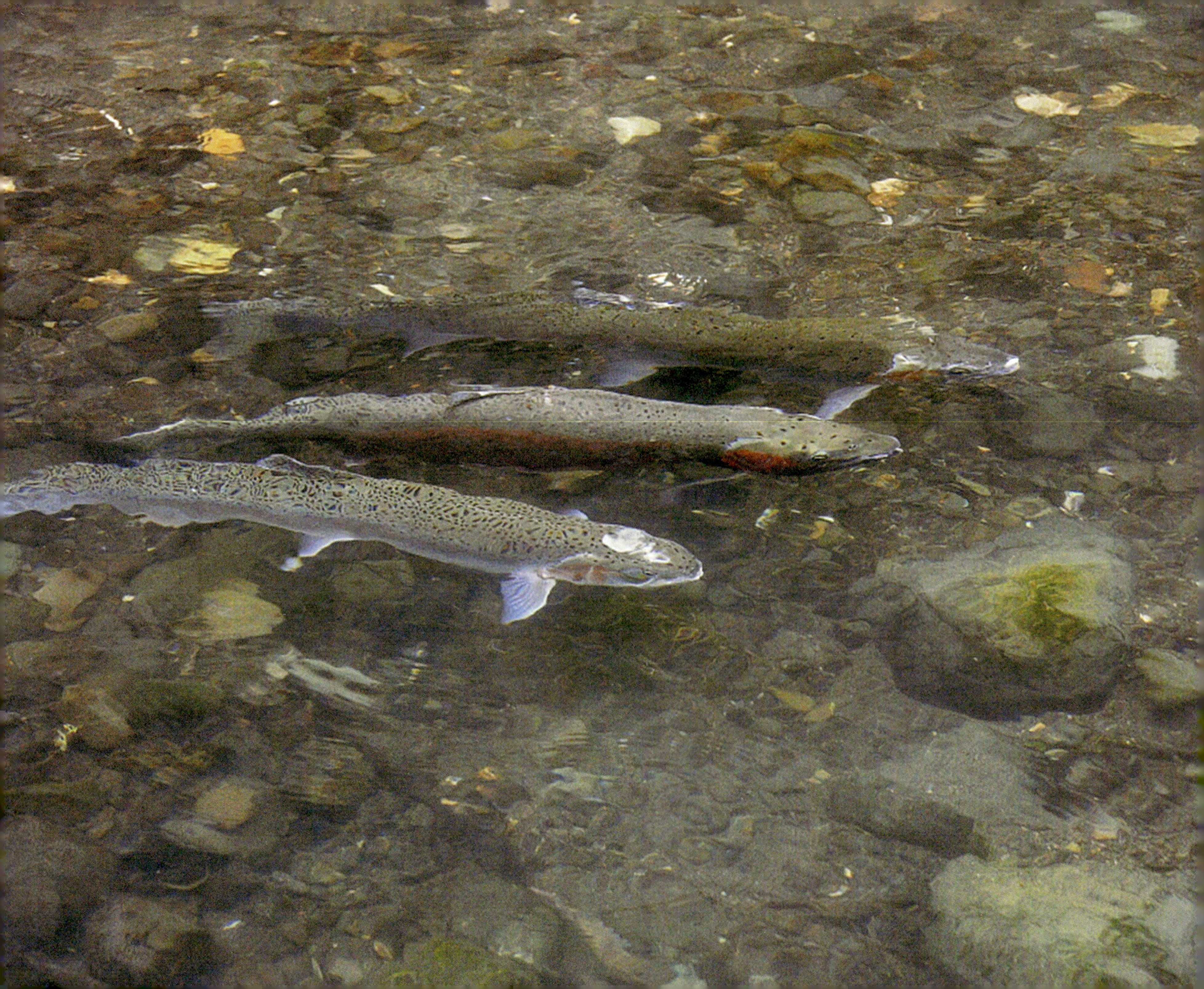

Conservation Corner

RECOVERING STEELHEAD

By Improving Synergy Amongst the H's and Rethinking Fisheries

John R. McMillan and Rob Kirschner, The Conservation Angler

From coastal rainforest streams to high desert rivers, the Pacific Northwest was once home to the most abundant populations of steelhead anywhere, which is why the region has such a long tradition of steelhead fishing.

That tradition is at greater risk now than at any time in history. Most populations are listed under the Endangered Species Act and remain in poor shape. For example, fishery managers estimate that only 20,700 wild steelhead will return to the Columbia River Basin this year. If the projection holds, it would be the smallest annual run size passing Bonneville Dam since records began in 1938 (Figure 1).

The good news is we are heavily invested in salmon and steelhead recovery thanks to ESA listings and billions have been spent to restore habitat conditions, remove barriers, and improve hydropower operations. The fish would likely be in a far worse situation if not for these listings.

The bottom line, however, is that steelhead are struggling throughout a substantial part of their range, raising two questions: (1) Why are recovery efforts not producing more fish?; and (2) Is there anything we can do as anglers to improve the odds for future runs of steelhead?

Here we'll discuss a few of the overarching, large-scale reasons we believe recovery efforts have not been as effective as hoped. We will also dive into the future of recreational fisheries that anglers, as individuals and as a community, have the most influence over. This list is not exhaustive, and some actions are so obvious that they don't need more explanation. For example, fisheries experts agree that the four lower Snake River dams must be breached to save and recover Snake River steelhead, and every conscientious angler should advocate to breach those dams with the same energy and conviction that helped the angling community and others stop Pebble Mine.

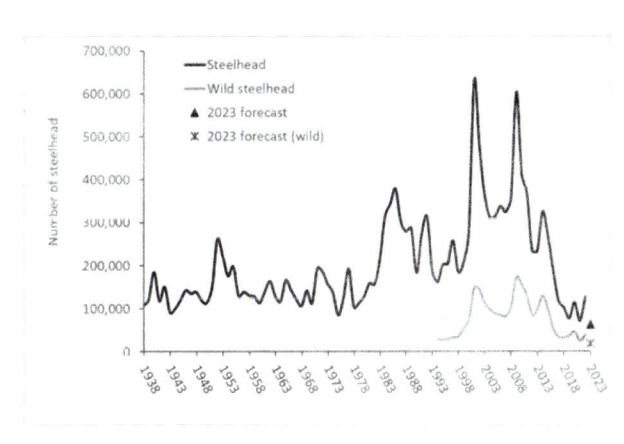

Figure 1. Annual number of summer steelhead passing Bonneville Dam in Columbia River from 1938-2022, and the projected 2023 forecast for all summer steelhead and wild summer steelhead.

Photo: John McMillan

Balancing Recovery Efforts with Better Synergy

One reason recovery efforts have lagged is we usually don't truly prioritize an all-H approach (habitat, hydropower, harvest, and hatcheries). Actions have mostly focused on habitat and hydropower, while we've only nibbled around the edges of harvest and hatcheries, perhaps because they are more socially challenging.

Which is why Oregon Coast coho salmon are so interesting. It is one of the few places where we've truly implemented and documented an all-H approach.

After coho salmon were listed under the ESA in 1998, the Oregon Department of Fish and Wildlife virtually eliminated harvest to increase adults on the spawning grounds, drastically reduced the number of hatchery fish to minimize risks of hatchery fish spawning with wild fish, and implemented several habitat restoration projects (see Falcy and Suring, 2018). Additionally, Pacific Power restored fish passage at Soda Springs Dam on the North Umpqua River. Once marine survival improved, the abundance of wild coho salmon sharply increased and peaked at levels not seen in over 30 years. Annual run sizes have varied since, including some poor returns, but overall, the status has improved to the point where whispers of "de-listing" are occasionally heard, a rarity among salmonids in the Lower 48.

It is difficult to parse out the marine survival improvements from other actions across the whole Oregon Coast, but the large reduction in harvest was clearly important. And finer-scale research in one of the Oregon Coast streams (Salmon River) found the abundance and productivity of wild coho salmon increased and spawn timing expanded and moved closer to the historical timing after hatchery releases ceased. Based on these changes, the authors concluded that hatchery closure can be an effective strategy to promote wild recovery (see Jones, et al., 2018).

Harvest: Manage for Ecological Relationships and Evolutionary Strengths

Natural, pristine rivers in the PNW are beautiful, but they are often pretty darn unproductive. That is why the former abundance of salmon was partly built on the brick-by-brick contributions of spawning and dying salmon. Pacific salmon are keystones. Their eggs and carcasses help subsidize growth and survival of many species of juvenile salmonids, along

Photo: John McMillan

with a multitude of other animals, trees, and plants. Steelhead spend 1-4 years in freshwater as a juvenile before migrating to the ocean, and they need a sufficient supply of food, especially going into and through winter when natural productivity is lower. Eggs and flesh from fall and winter spawning Chinook and coho salmon — as well as the insects entrained by redd excavation — help fill that food gap.

Accordingly, we can restore and reconnect habitat, but recovering steelhead to any semblance of former abundance will also depend on rebuilding the nutrient supply.

Further restricting, or even closing, non-tribal mixed-stock ocean fisheries for PNW-sourced Chinook and coho salmon and allowing most or all those fish to reach the spawning grounds would be bold. Even if harvest doesn't appear to be a statistical problem, a lot of fish are killed, and evolution is like a biological game where those additional fish aren't purely surplus — they are stores of energy that bring critical ocean nutrients to freshwater and fertilize the future of steelhead. Tribal fisheries, most of which occur in terminal areas, could fill the commercial market gap, which seems appropriate given their treaty rights and cultural standing in the region.

Although wild steelhead fisheries are not harvested commercially to the extent of salmon and most recreational fisheries are non-retention, past and current harvest can still influence traits that are fundamentally important to resilience and viability.

Run timing of wild winter steelhead in the Hoh, Queets, and Quillayute Rivers on the Olympic Peninsula, for instance, now peaks 1-2 months later than it did historically, and the breadth of migration timing has contracted by up to 37 percent (see McMillan et al. 2022). The shift aligns with the onset of and expansion of hatchery steelhead programs on the OP, which were selected for early-entry from late-November through early-January. Fisheries were then structured to be most intense early in the season so that fishers — sport and commercial — could harvest the hatchery steelhead at the highest rate possible.

A protracted run timing is important for many reasons, including accessing different habitats at different times, but critically, it also allows steelhead to respond to climate change.

Winter runs enter and spawn several weeks to a month or more earlier in southerly areas compared to more northerly ones. As glaciers melt and the OP becomes warmer and drier, the run timing of winter steelhead will need to shift to keep pace. That will only be possible if harvest and hatchery practices allow the populations to re-express their former diversity.

Harvest has also likely affected other aspects of steelhead diversity, such as age and size, and rates of repeat spawning. Diversity is especially important to steelhead. It's frequently mentioned in recovery documents, but it's rarely prioritized. Even where monitoring efforts are better, fisheries are usually not structured to sustain diversity (Idaho A- and B-run being an exception).

Habitat can give rise to great diversity in fish, but sustaining that diversity also depends on sufficient food and steelhead being able to express the traits that make them so unique.

Hatcheries: Too Many Fish That Are Less Productive and Diverse

Hatcheries once provided the promise of salmon without healthy rivers. Now, after a century of artificial production and research, we know hatchery salmonids have a myriad of negative ecological and genetic effects on wild salmonids. Despite that knowledge, rather than undertake large changes as with Oregon coho salmon, most actions have been minor. Examples include increasing the proportion of wild fish used for broodstock, rearing juveniles at more natural growth rates, and maintaining or setting aside a few rivers for "wild only" production.

Some of those small steps are indeed valuable, but here are three reasons we need to think bigger and act bolder with hatchery releases.

First, hatcheries released approximately 5.5-billion juvenile salmon/steelhead into the North Pacific in 2019, compared to only 0.6 billion hatchery juveniles in the 1960s. Pink salmon predominate among those releases, and it appears they have triggered a trophic cascade in the North Pacific. The abundance of hatchery pink salmon has been linked to adverse effects on growth, age-at-maturity, survival, and abundance of sockeye salmon, Chinook salmon, coho salmon, chum salmon, marine fishes, and seabirds (see Ruggerone et al. 2021). More recently, unpublished analysis has correlated the abundance of pink salmon with poor returns of some steelhead stocks in Idaho, British Columbia and Washington.

How are we to realize our vast investments in habitat and recover wild steelhead when hatchery pink salmon, and chum too, are eating the ocean out of house and home?

We can't directly change the hatchery pink salmon releases from Japan or Russia. We can advocate for closing the hatcheries in Prince William Sound and other areas in Alaska (which account for 39% of total hatchery pinks) to reduce ocean impacts on ESA-listed stocks in the PNW.

Second, hatchery salmon and steelhead predominate in many watersheds. While they may disperse and access restored and reconnected habitats, they are almost always less productive than wild fish. A review of early-generation hatchery salmon and steelhead derived from wild fish found that hatchery adults, on average, produced about half as many offspring as wild adults (see Christie et al. 2014). Which pair of fish would bring the best return on our habitat investments? Obviously, it's not hatchery fish.

Last, we are trying to "climate proof" habitat by protecting cold water areas but have not discussed climate proofing fish populations. Hatchery fish are often less diverse than wild populations and interbreeding with hatchery fish can reduce productivity and alter the ge-

Swing the Fly Anthology 2023   47

netic structure wild salmonids evolved over millennia. The habitat will change, and salmon and steelhead will need to adapt. Whether they can do so partly depends on their genetic capacity for change. Large-scale, hatchery-free zones could increase those odds by rebuilding the genetic structure and diversity to prepare steelhead for the next step in their evolutionary history.

Recreational Fisheries and Uncertainty about Sublethal Effects

Recreational fisheries are often the last fishery steelhead face before they spawn and it's the recreational impacts that anglers have the most control over. In that sense, we are the guardians to the spawning grounds.

Given poor returns, fishery closures, climate change, and emerging science on sub-lethal angling effects, now is the time to evaluate potential recreational impacts more thoroughly. It's a difficult subject to broach because most fisheries require wild steelhead release. However, since the inception of catch-and-release (CnR) fisheries in the 1980s, anglers have become increasingly efficient, and now, it is not uncommon to CnR every steelhead in a river, on average, more than one time (see Bentley, 2017). In some years and rivers, every fish is caught twice on average (see Bentley, et al., 2015).

Although we know CnR mortality in steelhead is low when temperatures are cooler, we don't know if CnR mortality rate varies when fish are caught multiple times. We don't know how a combination of warmer water and multiple encounters influences survival. Additionally, we are just starting to understand sublethal effects — such as, but not limited to, effects of changes in blood chemistry, elevated levels of stress hormones, and fungal infections — that can result in a fish surviving but with reduced capacity or altered behavior.

Several publications have examined sublethal effects of CnR on fish physiology and behavior. We found only a handful of studies on steelhead and Atlantic salmon (which display similar CnR mortality rates and patterns as

Photos: John McMillan

steelhead) that evaluated effects of angler capture on reproductive success and behavior.

One steelhead study in Idaho reported the number of eyed eggs produced by females did not differ among fish that were CnR versus those that were not (see Pettit, 1977). More recently, another found that fight time and air exposure did not affect survival or reproductive success of hatchery steelhead (see Whitney, et al., 2019).

Those findings don't necessarily mean there isn't an effect, however, because the Idaho studies only tested production of eyed eggs and survival from egg to fry. More recently, a study in Oregon tracked survival through the juvenile and adult life stage (see Johnson et al. 2023). Like Idaho, they didn't find an effect at the eyed egg stage, but there was a strong negative effect on fry to adult survival in fish caught by anglers (see Johnson et al. 2023). Specifically, steelhead caught by anglers and hauled to the hatchery produced 46-53% less offspring than those that swam into the hatchery voluntarily. Because steelhead caught by anglers were also held in the hatchery for longer periods than those that entered voluntarily, however, it is difficult to isolate stress effects from CnR and extended captivity.

One study on Atlantic salmon found a 27% reduction in reproductive success of females that were CnR by anglers (Bouchard, et al., 2022), which is about half the fitness loss documented in the Oregon steelhead study. A prior study on Atlantic salmon found reduced reproduction of juveniles by larger females (Richard, et al., 2013). In contrast to the steelhead research, another found females exposed to stressful exercise produced fewer eggs (Papatheodoulou, et al., 2021).

While the effect on reproductive success in steelhead is not yet clear, a large body of research on many fish species suggests aggres-

Swing the Fly Anthology 2023   49

> FLY ANGLERS IN WASHINGTON, OREGON AND IDAHO PLAYED KEY ROLES IN ADVOCATING FOR AND SUPPORTING THE PARADIGM SHIFT. THEY WERE, AND ARE, OUR FOREFATHERS THAT *SWING THE FLY*.

sive, bold individuals are more vulnerable to angling, and aggression and boldness are partly heritable. Consequently, repeated capture and stress may not only alter reproductive success of larger fish but could alter the genetic frequency of bolder and aggressive individuals within populations (see Koeck et al. 2018; Prokkola et al. 2021), which is concerning if bolder individuals are also the fittest fish (see Sutter, et al., 2012).

Given the uncertainty and high encounter rates coupled with declining runs, the fish and anglers need agencies to take the lead and conduct research to evaluate sublethal effects, just as they did with CnR mortality rates.

Today's Fishery Contributes to Tomorrow's Future

Conceptually, there are several ways to modify fisheries and still allow opportunity while reducing overall steelhead encounters.

For example, don't allow fishing from boats. Boat anglers consistently have higher encounter rates than bank anglers, and eliminating boat fishing has reduced encounter rates on OP rivers, like the Hoh. Although encounter rates on the Deschutes River — where boat fishing is not allowed — are still relatively high, they would likely be much higher if the rule wasn't in place.

We can also manage our best remaining steelhead fisheries like hunting seasons, including gear and timing restrictions, and/or limited entry. Seasons could be longer for anglers who fish the least efficient methods, as often happens with archery, and shorter for those using more efficient tactics. The number of boats, guides, and total anglers could also be limited to a number per day or week, or a season could be open only during certain days of the week.

Alternatively, some rivers could be managed using very restrictive regulations, such as the North Umpqua River steelhead fishery. Catch and release limits could be enacted on more, if not all, rivers.

Personally, we prefer longer and more consistent fishing seasons that include all necessary science-based safeguards. One way to reduce likely risks, while agencies accumulate data on sublethal effects, is to voluntarily reduce our efficiency and encounters. Over the longterm, once the research is settled, we can modify fishery restrictions based sublethal effects data and viability models. In the meantime, anglers should carry the risk of uncertainty, not the fish.

Right now, we don't know whether the impacts are negligible or if they shave a significant portion of reproductive potential from fish that are caught. Nor do we know how those effects may vary based on run type (summer vs. winter) or size. This is why we are concerned about high encounter rates when steelhead populations are struggling to replace themselves.

Change is never easy. The battle to eliminate catch-and-kill and shift to catch-and-release in the 1980s was fraught with disagreement and heated arguments. There are numerous challenges beyond those we have listed here. Nonetheless, fly anglers in Washington, Oregon, and Idaho played key roles in advocating for and supporting the paradigm shift. They were, and are, our forefathers that *swing the fly*.

Decades later the burden of conservation still rests upon our shoulders. Some challenges are large-scale and daunting, but others, such as our recreational fisheries, can be resolved through research and advocacy as they were before. It's time to give back to the fish just as we did back in the 80s because today's actions determine tomorrow's future.

We at The Conservation Angler look forward to the test and will continue to push the envelope of conservation to try and give the fish and future generations the opportunity to experience swinging a fly for wild steelhead.

References

Bentley et al. 2015. Evaluation of recreational steelhead catch in the South Fork Toutle and Washougal Rivers, 2011-2014. Washington Department of Fish and Wildlife. Olympia, Wash-

Photos: John McMillan

ington FPT 15-06.

Bentley, K. 2017. Evaluation of creel survey methodology for steelhead fisheries on the Quillayute and Hoh rivers. Washington Department of Fish and Wildlife. Olympia, Washington. FPT 17-03.

Bouchard et al. 2022. Effect of catch-and-release and temperature at release on reproductive success of Atlantic salmon (Salmo salar L.) in the Rimouski River, Québec, Canada. Fisheries Management and Ecology 29, 888– 896.

Falcy, M.R. and E. Suring. 2018. Detecting the effects of management regime shifts in dynamic environments using multi-population state-space models. Biological Conservation 221: 34-43.

Johnson et al. 2023. Can angler-assisted broodstock collection programs improve harvest rates of hatchery-produced steelhead? Environmental Biology of Fishes. DOI: 10.1007/s10641-023-01401-5

Jones et al. 2018. Population Viability Improves Following Termination of Coho Salmon Hatchery Releases. North American Journal of Fisheries Management 38: 39-55.

Koeck et al. 2018. Angling selects against active and stress-resilient phenotypes in rainbow trout. Canadian Journal of Fisheries and Aquatic Sciences 76: 320-333.

McMillan et al. 2022. Historical Records Reveal Changes to the Migration Timing and Abundance of Winter Steelhead in Olympic Peninsula Rivers, Washington State, USA. North American Journal of Fisheries Management 42: 3-23.

Papatheodoulou et al. 2021. Simulated pre-spawning catch and release of wild Atlantic salmon (Salmo salar) results in faster fungal spread and opposing effects on female and male proxies of fecundity. Canadian Journal of Fisheries and Aquatic Sciences 79: 267-276.

Pettit, S.W. 1977. Comparative Reproductive Success of Caught-and-Released and Unplayed Hatchery Female Steelhead Trout (Salmo gairdneri) from the Clearwater River, Idaho. Transactions of the American Fisheries Society 106: 431 435.

Prokkola et al. 2021. Does parental angling selection affect the behavior or metabolism of brown trout parr? Ecology and Evolution 11:2630– 2644.

Richard et al. 2013. Does catch and release affect the mating system and individual reproductive success of wild Atlantic salmon (Salmo salar L.)? Molecular Ecology 22:187-200.

Richard et al. 2014. Telemetry reveals how catch and release affects prespawning migration in Atlantic salmon (Salmo salar). Canadian Journal of Fisheries and Aquatic Sciences 71: 1730-1739.

Ruggerone et al. 2021. Did recent marine heatwaves and record high pink salmon abundance lead to a tipping point that caused record declines in North Pacific salmon abundance and harvest in 2020? North Pacific Anadromous Fish Commission Technical Report No. 17: 78-82.

Sutter et al. 2012. Recreational fishing selectively captures individuals with the highest fitness potential. Biological Sciences 109:960-965.

Whitney et al. 2019. Effects of Fishery-Related Fight Time and Air Exposure on Prespawn Survival and Reproductive Success of Adult Hatchery Steelhead. North American Journal of Fisheries Management 39: 372-378.

I OFTEN HEAR, ESPECIALLY WITH STEELHEAD FLIES, "THE FLY DOES NOT MATTER." I FEEL SORRY FOR THOSE WHO TAKE THIS APPROACH AT THE VISE.

DEVELOPING YOUR OWN FLY-TYING STYLE

Marty Howard

Developing a personal style as you progress through the learning curve of fly tying is inevitable. It matters not the type of fly you are tying; whether steelhead, trout, salmon or even saltwater, the end product will take on characteristics relative to how you perceive its construction.

Trying to mimic someone else's creations is one of the most difficult tasks I have encountered in fly tying. No matter how extensive the effort, there is always a slight variance in the final appearance of the fly. Luckily the fish I pursue are tolerant and willing to reward my efforts at the vise.

When I am handed a fly, any fly, we will use a steelhead fly as the example, the first thing I look at is the tip, tag and tail. If any of the three are not in harmony with the style of the hook, I know the rest of the fly will appear off. I have always said, "Your hook, no rules." But there are key elements, such as proportions and placement of materials, that bring balance to a fly. The slight variances on how and where materials are secured on the hook is where we begin to see one's personal style develop. It is also important to note not everyone will come to the same assessment when judging the appearance of a fly. What I like in design and balance may not be the same as what you like and that is more than OK. The key is having confidence in what is tied to the end of your line.

Every fly tyer will go through several stages as they develop their own style of fly tying. Before this can happen, like any learned skill, you must master the basic skills, such as thread control, selecting or high grading materials and the all-encompassing proper proportions. How fast you progress is determined by the amount of effort you place in each skill level. Learning the basics and being able to apply what you have learned enables advancements into the more complex techniques. The simple move of securing a tail or adding a tip and tag must be honed before moving on to the next step. A perfect body will not shadow a less than perfect tail. If one part of the fly appears out of balance, the fly will as well.

From the tip, tag and tail, my eye gravitates to the head of the fly. Back when I first started tying flies, there was no emphasis on how the head was finished. The heads on the trout and steelhead flies I was tying were massive. Dozens of unnecessary turns of thread where applied, not only to the head but throughout the whole construction of the fly. The thought was more turns of thread added durability.

My desire to learn how to tie classic Atlantic salmon flies changed my whole perspective on thread control. Less is best, not only the placement and number of securing wraps but the actual amount of material to use, was the rule. Transferring the lessons learned into trout and steelhead flies changed the appearance of my flies. Even better, they improved the durability of the fly.

It is common to get in a hurry when learning how to tie flies. Failing to recognize the importance of mastering each stage of construction can lead to poor performance in the final product. No matter what the fly looks like, if there is a breakdown in any part of the construction, the durability and how the fly functions can be affected.

From the first turn of thread to the application of head cement, attention to the details of each step of construction will ensure a positive outcome. One of the best lessons I learned is, until you whip finish the thread, you can always remove and start over at any stage of the tying process. Hooks are expensive, and a sharp blade can come in handy.

I often hear, especially with steelhead flies, "The fly does not matter." I feel sorry for those who take this approach at the vise. It is true in some circumstances, no matter what fish you are pursuing, the fly plays a minor roll in seducing a take. "You can catch them on your car key," or "A piece of yarn works just as well," are phrases that are often interjected into the conversation. It might be true, but the whole essence of "fly fishing" is lost when thoughts travel those paths. The fly is your connection to the fish. The effort in tying a well-dressed fly, whether it be a Hare's Ear nymph or a married wing steelhead fly, brings greater reward to the process. Finding balance at the vise will produce a more enjoyable experience.

When I teach a beginning fly tying class, the first actual tying instruction is how to apply the thread to the hook. Learning how and where to apply the first turns of thread starts the whole process of finding balance. Every turn of thread is a key component in how the fly will turn out. Starting the thread at the eye of the hook, a very common move, is not always the perfect approach. Each turn of thread will impact how the next step of construct will turn out. For instance, bulky and unruly turns of thread on the shank of the hook, will transfer into the shape of the body. If you want a perfectly flat floss body, the under-body of thread needs to be perfect.

My first assumption when learning how to tie flies was, the more turns of thread the stronger the durability of the fly. It did not take long to learn this is not true. Less is best is one of the hardest lessons to learn at the vise. Learning how to work the thread has multiple understandings. I use 6/0 Danville Fly Master thread for 90% of my fly tying. With all the options of thread on the market it is easy to get confused on which thread is best for any given application. The reason I use the Danville thread is because I know it well. I have learned just how much pressure I can apply before it will break. I know how to take the twist out of the thread to get it to lay flat on the hook. I like the color choices and I can find it in most fly shops.

Getting to know the thread you are using is very important. It can be quite frustrating if the thread is not behaving well as you tie the fly. As you progress through the learning curve of fly tying, thread control will become mechanical. Very little thought will go into how the thread is working; the thread becomes the glue that binds everything together. Speaking of glue, super glue and head cement can be applied to the thread at anytime during the construction of a fly. It is not cheating. I use a fair amount of glue when constructing one of my foam hoppers. Wax is also a valuable aid.

One of the best lessons I learned, with bobbin in hand, is thread can be unwrapped just as easily as it can be wrapped on the hook. Nothing is final during the tying process. Three turns of thread can secure most materials. Taking a turn of thread off before securing the next material will minimize the amount of thread used. The color of the thread you use can effect the appearance of the fly when it gets wet. Black thread under a hot pink floss will turn the floss black when wet. I use a primrose colored thread when I want to protect the color of the material I am securing to the fly.

Once you have mastered the art of thread control, securing materials becomes more instinctive. Less thought goes into how to secure the material. It becomes more of a how much material and placement thought process. In the following step-by-step I am going to take you through each part of the construction of a steelhead fly. From the tip, tag and tail to the last turn of thread.

When I began my fly-tying adventure, I was tying trout flies, dry flies, wet flies, nymphs and streamers. Long story, but I started tying steelhead and classic Atlantic salmon flies for the fun of it. Learning how to tie steelhead flies changed the way I tie trout flies.

The lessons in this step-by-step can be applied to any fly tied at the vise. For the fun and love of fly tying, I have not chosen a specific pattern. I am going to start the thread and go from there. Finding balance in a fly does not come from the color or nature of the material.

My rule, that there are no rules, gives me freedom of choices as I tie a fly. However, I will always give credit to those who have inspired my fly tying. Some would say, I am freestyling at the vise, but this is not true. Simply changing the color or a slight variance in the material does not make it a freestyle. It may be my style, but to take credit for coming up with something new is a reach. You will find once you have mastered a style of a fly, full feather wing as an example, you will find there are no limits as to what you can use to construct a fly. Learning how to substitute material, adding a slight variance to a standard pattern, and changing the color and texture of a fly is the greatest part of the process. Tying a fly that you will fish with confidence is the key.

Step 1. 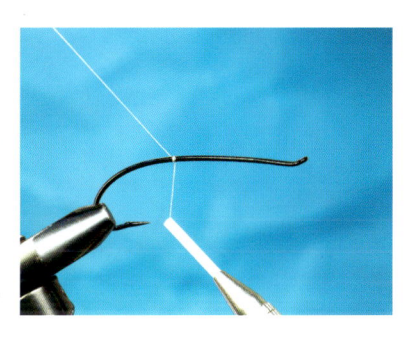
Secure the thread to the hook using three firm wraps. The starting point for this fly is on the flat portion of the shank directly ahead of the start of the bend. This is where I start the thread when I am tying a steelhead fly on a hook. The starting point may differ when I am tying on a tube or a shank. A lot happens at this starting point. The tip tag and tail all meet at the start of the bend of the hook. Finding the start of the bend can be difficult on hooks such as this Alec Jackson. It is easy to tell if you have hit the mark. If the tail is in line with the shank of the hook, you have found the flat portion of the hook. There is where thread control starts. Remember for most materials it only takes three or four firm wraps to lock them into position.

Step 2. 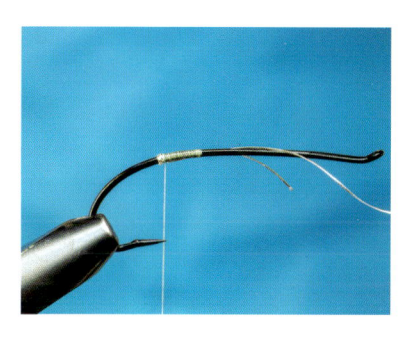
I use oval tinsel for the tip. The oval tinsel creates a dam, stopping the floss from unwinding down the bend of the hook. Secure in a length of oval tinsel to the back side of the hook. I use size small tinsel on hooks ranging is size from 3 to 3/0. The options are endless when it comes to tinsel. I prefer Lagartun tinsels because of the metallic properties. Metal tinsel does not stretch, which is important when firm wraps are necessary, bringing the ribbing through seal dubbing as an example. Wrap the thread down the bend of the hook, trapping the tinsel as you go. The tinsel will migrate around the hook, work to keep it in line as you make the securing wraps. Gauging where to stop is a part of finding the balance in the hook. It is better to have a shorter tip and tag. Going too far down the bend gives the tag a saggy appearance. I use the hook as a guide. When the thread is hanging between the point of the hook and the start of the bend, I know I have hit my mark. Take three or four turns with the tinsel, butting each turn tightly against the last. Wrap the thread back to the starting point, trapping the tag end of the tinsel as you go. The thread is creating the underbody for the tag. Any bumps or bulges will transfer into the tag. Consistent wraps and keeping the tinsel in line is the goal.

Step 3. 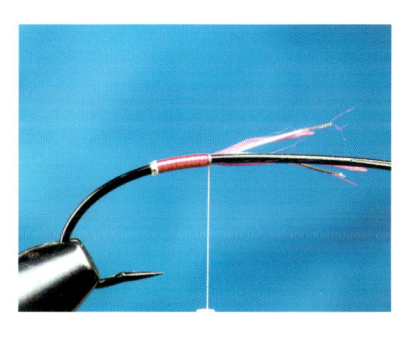
Adding a tip and a tag to a fly is not always necessary. I use the tip and tag as a contrast or hot spot addition to the pattern. Using tinsel as a tag is also a viable option. Secure a length of floss to the hook. I prefer silk floss, but any floss will work. One of the reasons I like silk is, you can split the floss into a smaller diameter. Not a rule, but less is always best. Wrap the floss down the bend to the tag, butting each turn tightly against the last. Once the floss reaches the tip, return the floss to the tie-in point and secure. Remember thread control, take two turns of thread off before securing the floss. Every turn of thread at the tie in point will affect the next step. Too many turns will cause the tail to ramp upwards. Keep it flat.

Step 4. 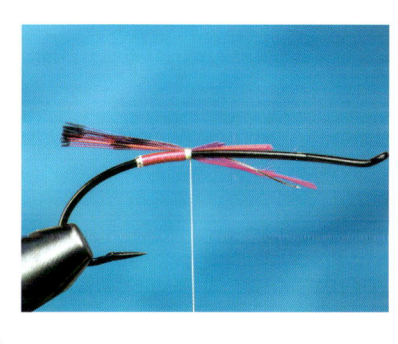
I use three basic materials for the tail - Golden Pheasant crest, and tippet and barbs from a saddle hackle. Golden Pheasant crest feather simply stated are a pain, but they look great. My favorite is the tippet feather. I have tippet dyed in a few colors, making it possible to match any color combination. Tippet barbs are easy to set and stay straight. To get started, clip off a clump of barbs from the feather. Gauge to length, using the end of the hook. I place the tippet in right at the end of the hook. Too long or to short in the tail's length will throw off the balance. Using the different part of the hook as a reference for placing materials makes it easier to hit the correct securing point.

Step 5. 
Adding a rib to the fly adds contrast and durability. For this fly I am using both types of tinsel, metallic and synthetic. I will never have enough tinsel in my collection, but then I am kind of that way with all fly tying materials. There is no reason to limit yourself, but I do find I use more flat or oval silver tinsel than any of the other options. I do like mixing tinsels such as what you see in this pattern. For this pattern I secure the ribbing materials in at the tail joint. The first rib to be wrapped forward is the last rib to be secured to the hook. For this fly the flat Mylar rib will be wrapped first, so I will secure in the oval twist first.

Swing the Fly Anthology 2023

Step 6. 
Build a dubbing loop using the tying thread. Load the loop with dubbing and give it a spin. Wrap the dubbing forward and secure. I use Velcro to release the fibers of dubbing that were trapped as the dubbing loop was wrapped forward. Do not crowd the eye of the hook. Knowing where to stop the body material comes with practice. The stopping point may vary, depending on the wing material and the hackle used for the collar. I use seal dubbing for my steelhead flies, but there are a few good substitutes on the market.

Step 7. 
Bring the ribbing material forward making open wraps. Five wraps is the standard I use, but as you can see with this fly, four wraps looked best to me. I like fewer wraps, depending on the size of the hook. Six wraps would be the maximum number of open turns. Velcro the body material to release the trapped fibers. Do not clip the tag ends of the tinsel until you are sure the ribbing is tight - it will loosen during the brushing process. Remove a few of the securing wraps, tighten the tinsel, then reapply the securing wraps. The tighter the rib, the more durable the fly will be.

Step 8. 
Add a collar by wrapping hackle around the hook. I use schlappen and guinea for most collar work. There are a number of tricks to get the barbs of the hackle flowing rearward. You can pinch the barbs together prior to wrapping the collar or pull the barbs rearward as you make each turn. The length of the barbs and the mass of the collar is key to the balance of the fly. Too long is a better than too short and too much is better than not enough. This is one spot on the fly where less is not best. Add enough collar to balance out what is on top of the hook.

Step 9. 
For this fly I have chosen hair for the wing. When I first started tying steelhead flies, hair winged patterns made up the bulk of the flies used to catch both summer and winter steelhead. You can use calf tail, buck tail and bear hair to construct a wing. I prefer the look of a stacked wing, meaning all the tips of the hair are in line. Not a rule, just the look I like. The amount of wing is key to the balance of the fly. The wing keeps the fly tracking broadside during the swing. The wing is gauged to length then clipped before securing. I add a drop of head cement to the hair just prior to securing it in. The head cement softens the hair, making for better compression against the hook. The head cement binds both the thread and the hair for better durability.

As you progress through the learning curve of tying flies, you will find many different ways to create a fly with style and balance. Keys to remember are: thread control, material selection, correct proportions and placement management. It's very difficult to replicate certain fly tiers' styles, and keeping this in mind will lessen frustration at the vise. With each fly you tie, you are working on your own style. Good luck at the vise, and enjoy the journey.

Craftsmanship | Beauty | Performance | Perfection

R.B. Meiser Fly Rods LLC

www.meiserflyrods.com | rbmeiserflyrods@gmail.com | 541-770-4766

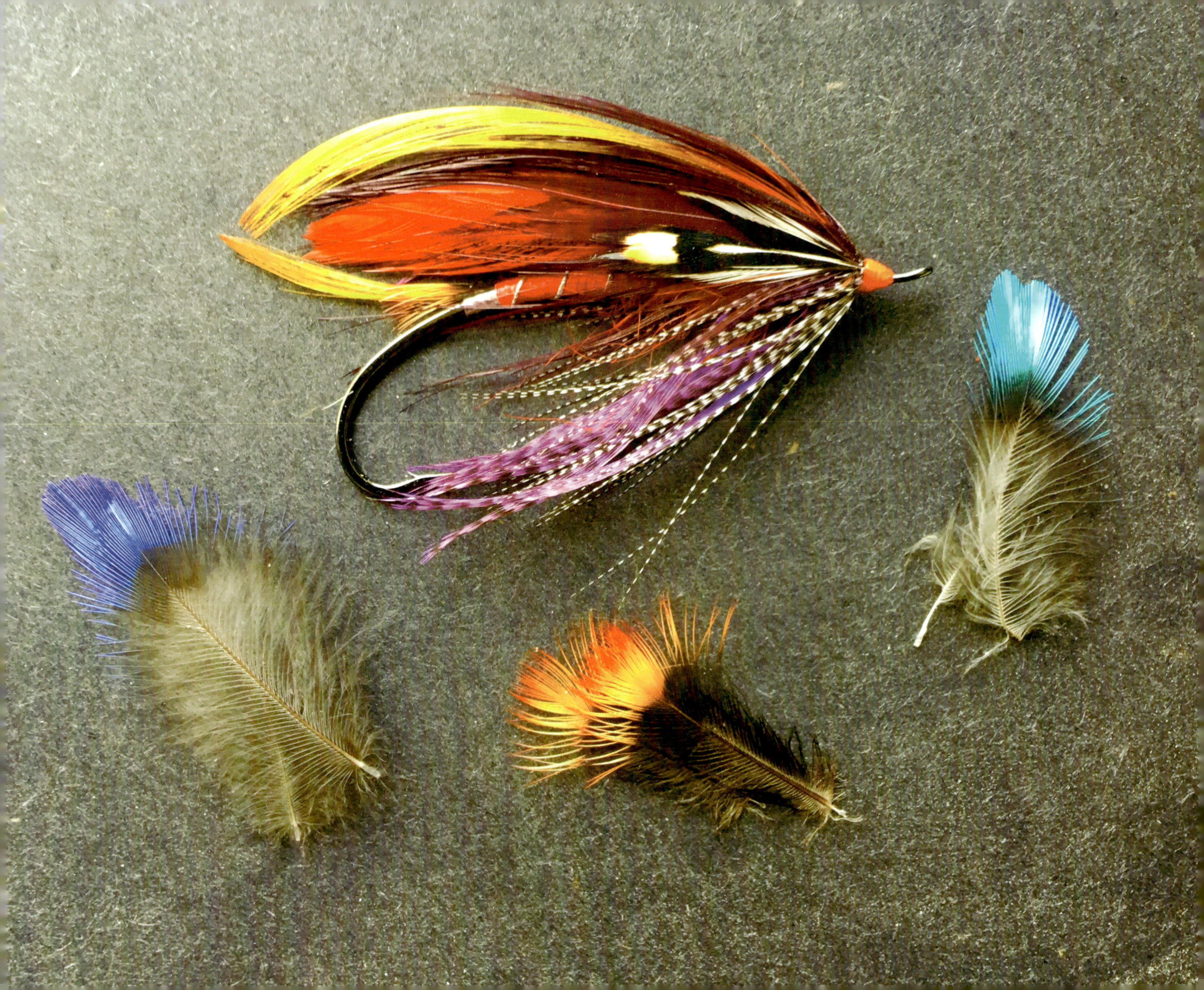

NEW TAKES ON A CLASSIC STYLE

Dave McNeese's Original Steelhead Flies

With A Fine Twist Of Class

Trey Combs

Late one afternoon, Dave McNeese tells me he's packing for a trip to a remote canyon in Oregon where he plans to capture one of North America's rarest butterflies. Dave is a serious lepidopterist, his private collection the envy of small museums. He's searching for an insect known to taxonomists — with a genus-species name in Latin to prove it. Scientists don't know where the butterfly lives; Dave does, and he's happy to keep it that way.

McNeese industriously occupies an alternate universe a place so foreign to my frame of reference that our conversations frequently have me stammering to stay up to speed. I find myself separating the fascinating stuff that I don't want to ever forget, to his more mundane knowledge of how to match the hatch for Deschutes redsides, or to how to stalk a high-country bull elk. I've long known that his grasp of fly-fishing history is so vast that sometimes I find it quicker to call Dave than surround the question with Google searches. The collateral nuggets of information drop like little bombs and messes with my concentration. Often I hang up forgetting why I was prompted to call Dave in the first place.

Typical of Dave's far ranging pursuits, he designed and built a line of custom fly reels with the largest model for big-game offshore speedsters—billfish, tuna and wahoo—fish that I'd seen fry reels famous for being bomb proof. He gave me one of these models to test drive on one of my long-range fly-fishing exploratory trips that departed San Diego several times a year. (Called "long range" because much of the hull serves as a gigantic fuel tank; some boats are capable of motoring from California to New Zealand.)

I was the lone fly-fishing charter master for Shogun and Royal Star for 11 years and several dozen charters. My charters were for up to three weeks at sea, and as far away as French owned Clipperton Atoll 10 degrees north of the Equator. I kept "forgetting" to ship Dave's workhorse reel back to him and the one trip turned out to be dozens. His reel never failed, the sealed drag silky smooth without ever being lubricated. I'd just rinse the reel off in freshwater — or asked a guest angler to do so — and it would be ready for the next marlin. During these years I'd assign the reel to at least one new angler per trip. The reel's amazing performance left me wondering how such a marvel of engineering came out of a fly tier's imagination.

I must add that many clients were so anxious to get a marlin on a fly they didn't fish "legal," i.e., 12-kilogram maximum or about 26 pounds breaking strength for the class tippet under the rules of the International Game Fish Association. As a result, I had anglers fish 80-pound-test leader from fly line to fly. Dave's reel was set on full drag and that was it. Again, it never failed. I did, however, go through a case of Rio's big-game fly lines that I'd designed with Jim Vincent. The weakest connection was that between the fly line and the 50-pound test Spectra backing. I learned that Dave's ceramic drags and the ceramic heat shield on the space shuttle were the same material. I thought, *of course, had to be, and just how did Dave come by the material? Maybe not knowing would be easier to understand.*

When I first met Dave, I'd driven to his home in Salem, Oregon to talk about steelhead flies. But first he told me that he'd just shot a record antelope, with a pistol. I'd already heard that, as a kid, he'd made walking money from winnings in sporting clays professional trap shooting. I can't remember a time when Dave wasn't the most knowledgeable person in the world on organic fly-tying materials. I once read to him from my book on South African birds, and though he came at the subject as a collector of fly-tying materials, he was amazingly knowledgeable about the myriad species. But his skills at the fly-tying table are what has brought Dave such attention as an exhibition fly tier.

Like the man in the Dos Equis beer television commercial, Dave is the most interesting fly fisher in the world.

My Flies

Dave worked for a lumber company in the late 1960s while remaining obsessed with hunting and fishing. His wife encouraged him to take the leap and open a

> MCNEESE INDUSTRIOUSLY OCCUPIES AN ALTERNATE UNIVERSE—A PLACE SO FOREIGN TO MY FRAME OF REFERENCE THAT OUR CONVERSATIONS FREQUENTLY HAVE ME STAMMERING TO STAY UP TO SPEED.

fly-tying materials mail-order business they called "My Flies." Dave became the first person to export dyed Arctic fox to Europe and Scandinavia. Almost overnight, the material replaced bucktail among steelhead fly tiers. I vividly recall the transition. The ease of tying wings, the shape they took, their superb action in the water, the super small head — all promoted a more professional look to my flies.

There was also the Glasso-look that was taking steelhead fly tying by storm.

Dave set up a homemade eight-burner stove in his garage. He bought commercial-sized pressure cookers and purchased quantities of dyes from both Keystone and Herter's. Almost from the start of his research, he discovered the value of first dyeing all the materials with fluorescent white before repeating with solid colors. This gave red, orange, even black a rich depth that had never been achieved.

The pressure cookers were used to deeply infuse colors into hard guard hairs on Arctic fox, otter and other furs. "When I first started," Dave says, "I'd open a pressure cooker and find a mess." The furs were blasted to pieces by excessive heat under pressure. He soon mastered the techniques that guaranteed international success for his new business.

Dave traveled to upstate New York to visit Harry and Elsie Darbee, where he offered to trade Elsie a box full of valuable dyed hackle and 50 wood duck flanks in exchange for lessons on how to tie their iconic style of Catskill dry flies. During his stay, Dave went to New York City and the Hudson River Valley to visit a host of celebrity fly fishers that included Sam Melner, Ted Neimeyer, Eric Leiser and Poul Jorgensen. Dave and Poul had common interests; they immediately became friends.

Sam Melner, who owned Fly Fisherman's Bookcase, one of the first large-scale mail-order companies in the field, was so impressed with the quality of the materials Dave had given the Darbees that he booked a flight to Eugene and purchased Dave's entire "My Flies" inventory. Jorgensen also came west where Dave guided him to his largest-ever trout on Oregon's Williamson River, and then to his first steelhead. Dave had ample opportunity to study how Jorgensen tied Atlantic salmon flies from Poul's 1975 book, *Salmon Flies: Their Character, Style, and Dressing*. McNeese adopted many of Jorgensen's methods, another rung on the ladder on Dave's endless quest to learn everything he could related to fly fishing. Dave soon graduated to Victorian built-wing salmon flies and membership in Atlantic salmon tying guilds.

As Dave prepared to return home, Elsie Darbee packed up four dozen fertilized Andalusian chicken eggs from the rare strain of Andalusian chickens that they'd selectively bred for generations. The shade of blue dun neck hackles from these chickens were prized by traditional dry-fly tiers. The four eggs crates were in Dave's lap on the long flight home. All but one egg was successfully hatched, the chicks taking their place in Dave's fly-tying aviary. Their progeny continues to thrive under Dave's care.

McNeese booked a flight to New York City and visited Levin and Sons, a business that wholesaled furs, materials that Dave's bleaching and dyeing would turn into exotic fly-tying materials never seen before. Not surprisingly, McNeese's Fly Fishing Shop—the new business that Melner helped fund — became a mandatory stop by many of the world's most skilled and discriminating fly tiers.

When I first visited the shop, Mark Waslick — a tier with world-class credentials for tying full-dressed Victorian-era salmon flies — was commanding a workshop that Dave had brought together. Dave's vitality and his own skills attracted such masters — learning one-on-one from the very best. He brought the finest fly tiers to his shop to tie, instruct and entertain. and they would tie with the best materials the world had to offer.

Dave still maintains a busy mail-order business for feathers and furs. His book-writing project about Syd Glasso, now years long, will give readers insights into the father of modern steelhead fly tying, a private and even reclusive man who matched up with the finest fly tiers in the world. Dave has had hundreds of original Glasso steelhead and Victorian-era Atlantic salmon flies professionally photographed for the book. This will become must reading for serious fly tiers of both steelhead and modern Atlantic salmon flies.

Dave's Original Dressings

During the late 1970s, Dave McNeese's favorite "west-side" river was Oregon's North Santiam. The river then supported a strong run of hatchery summer-run steelhead and hatchery rainbow trout. Like so many fly fishers at the time, Dave was enthralled with Syd Glasso's Spey flies, particularly the Orange Heron and Brown Heron, lovely Scottish Spey-style ties incorporating orange and hot orange.

"On every cast a trout was hooked and the steelhead were put down," Dave says. "When the trout quickly tore up these labor-intensive examples of McNeese fly art, he turned to a purple fly — a color that put off trout, but a known attractor for steelhead. The result was

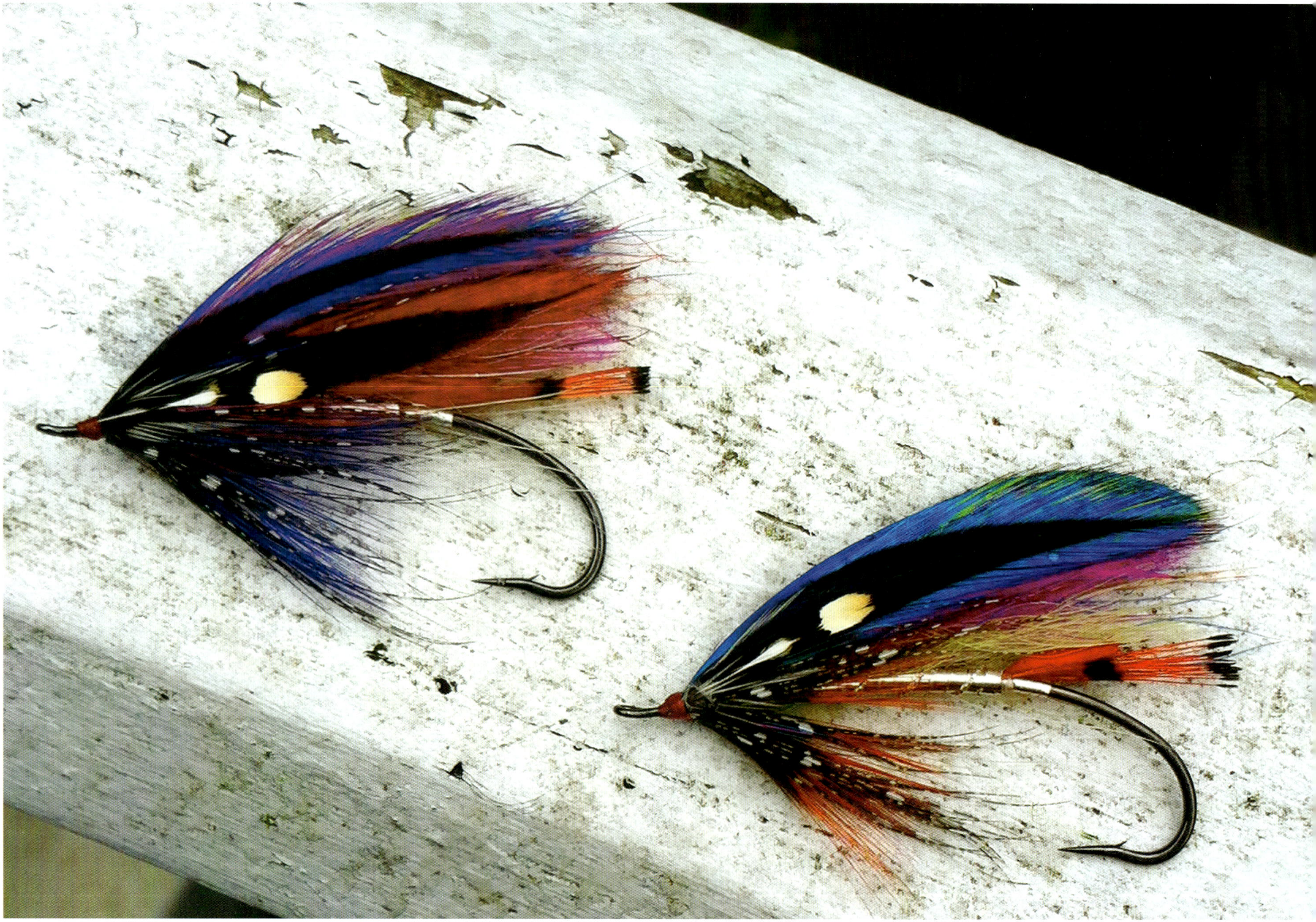

the Purple Spey. When Dave and Keith Mootry first baptized the fly on the South Santiam, Mootry took six steelhead while Dave landed four plus a silver salmon. The two steelhead killed were full of October caddisflies, "trouty" steelhead at their finest.

Purple Spey

Tag: Fine flat silver tinsel.
Tail: Fluorescent orange golden pheasant crest.
Body: Rear third fluorescent orange floss over flat silver tinsel; front two-thirds purple seal. Rib entire body with narrow flat silver tinsel.
Spey hackle: Heron dyed deep purple or black from the second turn of tinsel.
Throat: Long teal flank or natural guinea, two turns.
Wing: Hot purple neck hackles, size 10 dry-fly hackles, four to six hackles total.
Cheeks: Jungle cock, drooping down below body.
Head: Hot orange Danville 6/0.

"Dave Inks and I were tying flies together at a sportsmen's show, McNeese adds. "As he was tying a No. 4 Purple Peril, I got out my box of materials and pulled out a patch of fluorescent white polar bear. We replaced the brown wing with white and then purple polar bear. On the spot, this became Ink's favorite steelhead pattern, a fly that proved deadly in low light. Thanks to Dave Inks for teaching me how to tie a great steelhead fly. Oh, how I loved that man."

Pale Pearl (1975)

Tag: Flat silver tinsel.
Tail: Golden pheasant crest dyed hot purple.
Body: Flat silver tinsel ribbed with fine oval tinsel.
Hackle: Hot purple guinea, three turns.
Wing: Fluorescent white polar bear topped with fluorescent purple polar bear, one-third and two-thirds.
Cheeks: Jungle cock, tied in as a shoulder.
Head: Danville 6/0 fluorescent orange-red.

Dave recalls that during a mid-February float down a south Oregon coastal river, a heavy rain temporarily discolored the river: "As the rain became sprinkles and the water level dropped, I could see many steelhead and caught several. The next day I saw several hundred steelhead — many with wounds from seal bites. My largest, a 20-pound buck, had a six-inch cut just below its dorsal fin, yet the fish still hit my fly, the Crawdad. I fish this fly both dead-drifted or stripped back when leading the fly."

Crawdad (1975)

Tag: Fine flat silver tinsel.
Tail: Golden pheasant crest dyed hot orange.
Body: Hot orange seal, spun loose, rib with wide oval silver tinsel (medium width on flies sizes 4 to 8.)
Hackle: Bronze mallard. Strip one side, and wind from second turn of tinsel.
Wing: four to six stacked golden pheasant crests dyed fluorescent orange.
Head: Hot orange seal.
Cheeks: Jungle cock, drooping down below body.

Fifty years ago, "secret flies" were common among those of us who tied our own. Apparently, we kept the killer flies secret because if all fly fishers had the fly and unleashed its dreadful powers on an unsuspecting river full of steelhead, the slaughter would bring the run to extinction. This old-time stuff, however sweetly archaic, was fun and innocent, a relic of simpler times when discoveries in steelhead flies were occurring daily.

Dave found the Purple Matuka fly so effective that he fished it privately, a "secret" shared only with a couple of friends, and never displayed on his clipped sheepskin "fly of fame" hung in his office. Nevertheless, news of the hot new fly quickly spread, no doubt boosted when word got out that Dave had hooked more than 60 summer steelhead on the North Santiam. That kind of success doesn't stay quiet for long. And then Mike Bogdan (relative of Stan of reel-making fame) allegedly took 200 to 300 steelhead in a year, the majority of these on this Purple Matuka. Dave claims this "wore his reel out." Regardless, Dave's Matuka — a rare design in steelhead fly inventories — now had a permanent place in our sport.

Purple Polar Bear Matuka (1978)

Tag: Flat silver tinsel.
Tail: Fluorescent purple polar bear to length of body.
Body: Hot purple seal. Rib with flat silver tinsel followed by fine oval tinsel.
Wings: Fluorescent polar bear tied equally in four small bunches up the body.
Hackle: Purple, tied over wings.
Head: 6/0 red.

Dave says: "Enos Bradner was my hero in my younger years. I met with him several times and he shared with me many fly-fishing stories. His signature fly, Brad's Brat, became a favorite of mine. I ultimately began to alter the original to honor the 'King of Steelhead.'"

Starting in 1947, Enos Bradner was the outdoor editor of the Seattle Times for over a generation. I cut my teeth on his popular book, *Northwest Angling* (1950), and spent many a day tying steelhead flies illustrated in the book, especially the Brad's Brat. Years later, when I was tying a specific fly dressing to be set in a slipcase limited edition of *Steelhead Fly Fishing* (1991), the dressing selected was the orange and white Brad's Brat.

The original was tied as follows: Tip: Gold tinsel. Tail: Orange over white bucktail. Body: Rear half, orange wool; front half red wool.

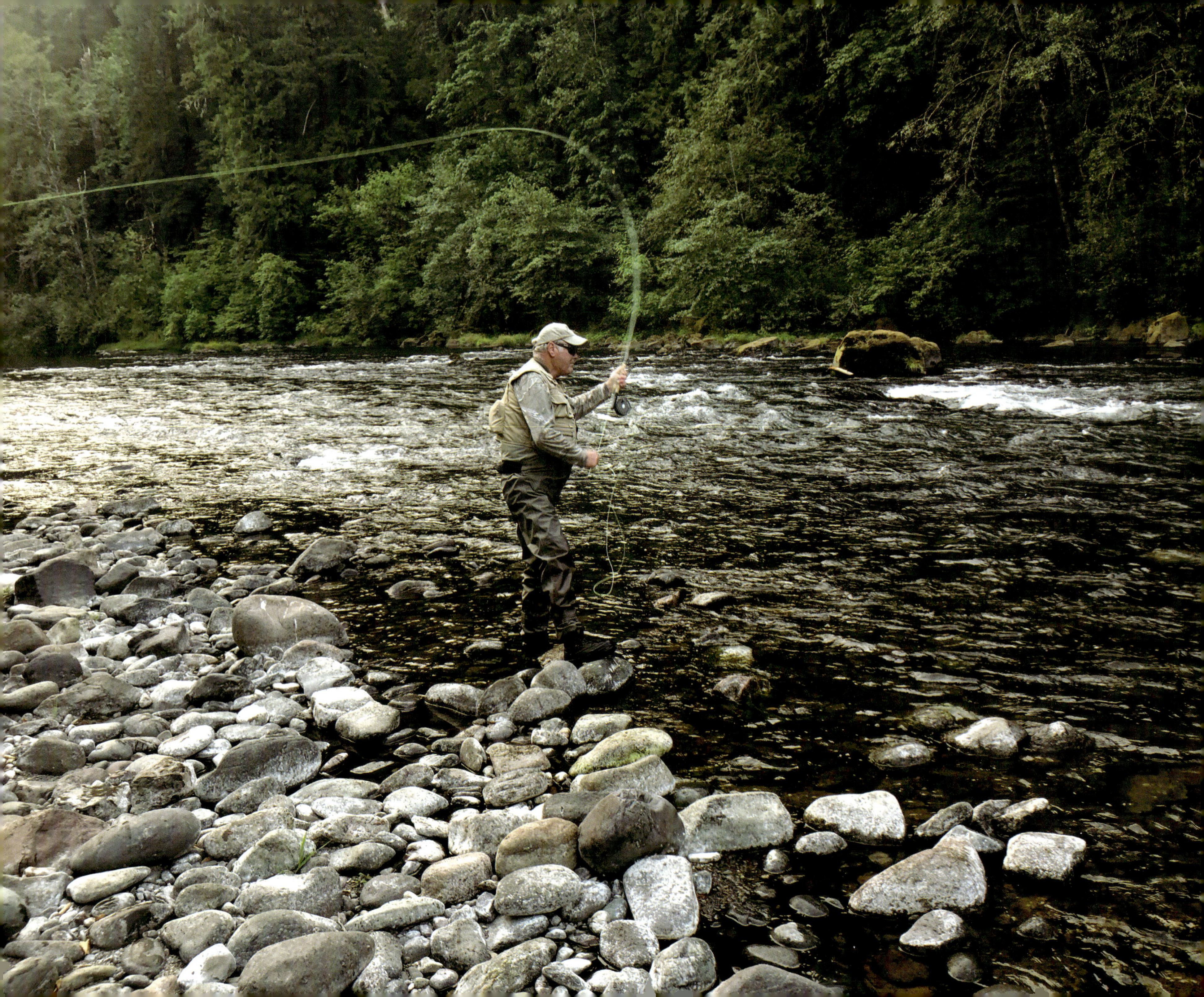

Rib body with flat gold tinsel. Hackle: Brown. Wing: Orange over white bucktail, white dominating, but the orange more than just topping.

When Bradner first tied his signature fly, fox tail wasn't available. If going organic, I much prefer fox. Today the vast variety of synthetic materials can be incorporated for tantalizing results.

Dave's Purple Brat

Tag: Flat silver tinsel.
Tail: Golden pheasant crest dyed fluorescent hot orange.
Body: Rear half divided evenly, fluorescent orange and fluorescent red floss. Front half, hot purple seal. Rib entire body with medium oval silver tinsel.
Hackle: Long mallard flank dyed fluorescent purple. Add a turn or two of natural teal.
Wing: Hot orange topped with with fluorescent purple polar bear.
Cheeks: Jungle cock tied as a shoulder.
Head: Red.

Bronze Brat

"I've used the Bronze Brat to take steelhead, Atlantic salmon, and sea-run browns," Dave says. "This is one of my must-have flies for fishing anywhere in the world for anadromous fish."

Tag: Flat fine silver tinsel.
Tail: Golden pheasant crest dyed hot orange.
Body: Rear third hot orange seal; balance red seal. Rib with flat silver tinsel.
Hackle: Two turns bronze mallard followed by two turns of teal.
Wing: White then orange polar bear. Top with bronze mallard.
Cheeks: Jungle cock.
Head: Hot orange.

Deschutes Madness

Dave's Deschutes Madness carries all the right colors. I really like the underwing of clear Flashabou. He has fished this well-known pattern for steelhead in British Columbia and in the Great Lakes.

Tag: Fine flat silver tinsel.
Tail: Fluorescent hot orange golden pheasant crest.
Body: Rear third, fluorescent orange floss over silver tinsel; front two-thirds hot purple seal, thin. Rib with narrow oval silver tinsel.
Hackle: Fluorescent purple.
Wing: Polar bear dyed fluorescent white over five to six strands of clear Flashabou.
Cheeks: Jungle cock.

Green-Butt Hilton

Tag: Fine flat silver tinsel.
Tail: Pintail flank.
Body: Rear third fluorescent green seal; balance, black seal. Rib entire body with oval silver tinsel.
Hackle: Long, to hook point, teal flank.
Wing: Four or six grizzly hackles depending on hook sizes 1/0 to 6.
Cheeks: Jungle cock.

Dave believes that the green butt and long wispy flank fibers have vastly improved the effectiveness of this pattern over its traditional predecessor, the Silver Hilton.

Murray's Fly

Dave first tied this new and still obscure fly with a red polar bear topping. The fly was a dud on the Deschutes. When a fiery brown polar bear topping replaced the red, the fly attracted many steelhead. The fly best performs in small sizes, 6 and 8. The fly honors a successful Deschutes fly fisher, Murray McDowell.

Tag: Flat silver tinsel.
Tail: Hot red golden pheasant crest.
Body: Rear half divided equally: fluorescent green and hot orange or red floss or seal. Front half, deep fluorescent purple seal.
Hackle: Deep fluorescent purple.
Wing: White polar bear over a few strands of pearl Flashabou.
Topping: Fiery brown polar bear.
Cheeks: Jungle cock.
Head: Hot red.

McNeese Madness (1981)

Dave McNeese considers the Madness the best pattern he's ever developed for the Deschutes, and neighboring summer-run rivers. The fly has continued gaining in popularity for a quarter of a century, from Oregon to the Skeena's legendary tributaries. The fluorescent purple has "pop" because it begins with bleached-out polar bear dyed fluorescent white.

Tag: Fine flat silver tinsel.
Tail: Fluorescent, red or orange floss, thick, with a few strands of clear Flashabou.
Body: Purple plastic chenille ribbed with fluorescent red or orange floss, and counter-ribbed with blue wire.
Hackle: Hot purple; add a few strands of clear Flashabou on top.
Wing: Purple Flashabou mixed with fluorescent purple polar bear.
Cheeks: Jungle cock.
Head: Hot orange.

Purple Hilton

Dave remains confident that this purple version of the Silver Hilton fishes more effectively than the original.

Tag: Fine flat silver tinsel.
Tail: Golden pheasant crest dyed fluorescent red (or substitute red floss).
Body: Rear third, orange floss over flat silver tinsel. Front two-thirds, two turns of hot orange seal; balance hot purple seal. Rib with flat or oval silver tinsel.

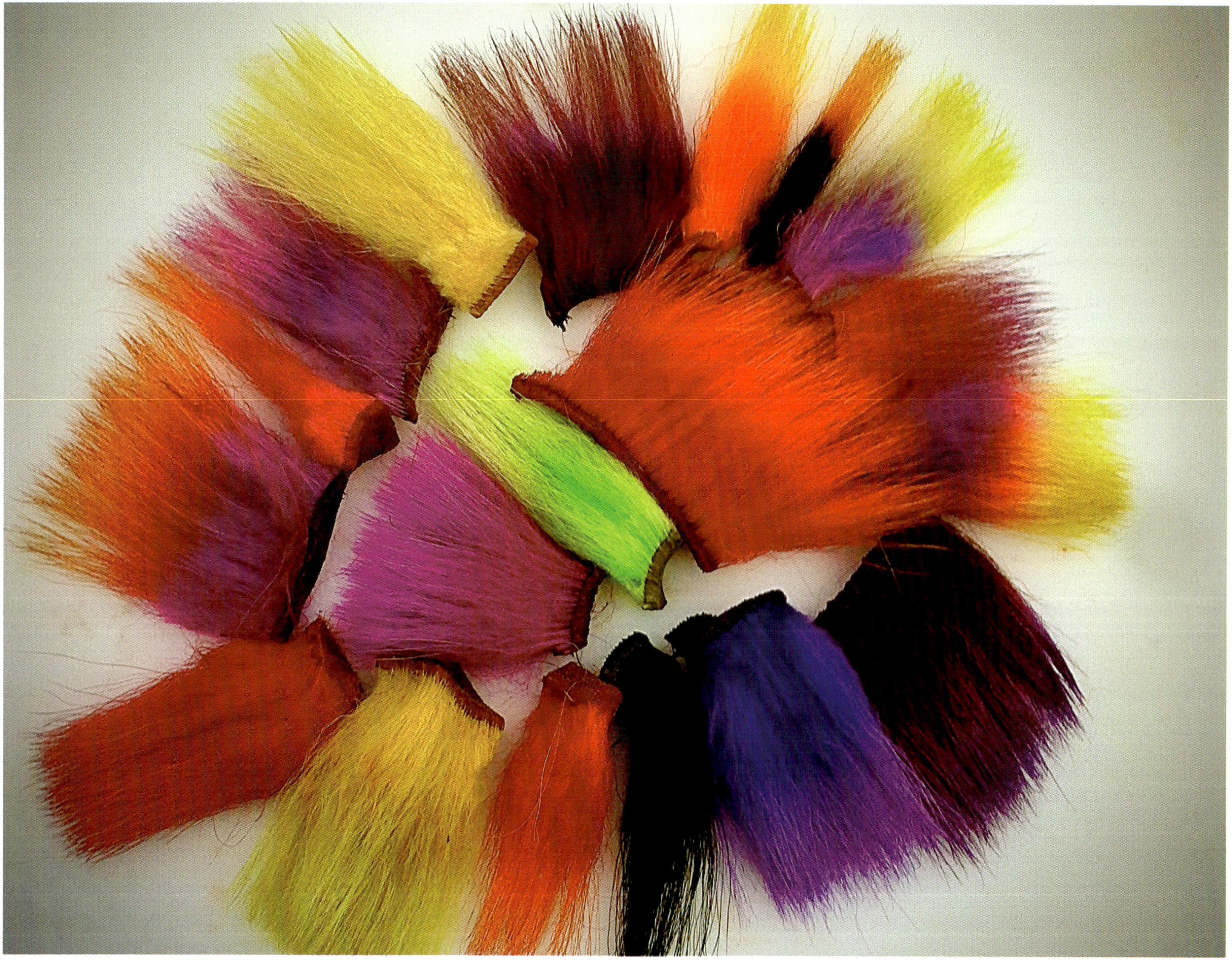

Hackle: Hot purple mallard flank.
Wings: Four matching hot purple hackle tips at hook end.
Cheeks: Jungle cock set low.
Head: Fluorescent orange.

Dave's Mistake (1987)

Dave comments: "I was tying two dozen Surgeon Generals to fill an order for a customer heading for British Columbia's Skeena. I tied these in No. 1 and 1/0, but I unknowingly got the colors backwards. The customer didn't know the correct scheme either. Two weeks later he returned to the shop with several chewed-up leftovers. When the fly fisher made his annual trip to the Skeena, he ordered more of the still unnamed flies. I finally named the fly and kept a bin filled with the pattern for local fly fishers in the Salem area. It always sold well."

Tag: Fine flat silver tinsel.
Tail: Golden pheasant crest dyed hot purple.
Body: Hot red seal.
Rib: Medium to wide oval silver tinsel.
Hackle: Fluorescent purple/blue. Dave custom dyes for this color; the tier can use a mix of purple and blue dyes.
Wing: Fluorescent white polar bear. (Note: Polar bear may be illegal to purchase. I would substitute a stiff craft fur, such as Sculpting Flash Fibre.
Cheeks: Jungle cock, large.
Head: Red.

Purple Prince (1981)

This dressing, neither Spey nor built-wing "gaudy," is an example of a steelhead fly at its most complex and beautiful. After more than 40 years Dave still becomes lyrical over the flies he's tied.

"How I love to fish flies of great beauty!" Dave says. "When fishing this fly I put either hatchery summer or wild winter steelhead on the beach. Last year I took a chrome hen from fast pocket water with this fly on my September birthday—my life in perfect harmony."

Tag: Flat fine silver tinsel.
Tail: Golden pheasant crest and Indian crow (see fly pictured for proportions).
Rib: Medium oval silver tinsel.
Body: Rear half, fluorescent red floss over flat silver tinsel; front half fluorescent hot orange seal. (Author's note: I like to wind flat silver tinsel down and back on any fly with a colored floss body. This prevents the black hook from bleeding into the wet body and ruining the dressing.)
Hackle: Hot purple pintail flank starting from the third turn of tinsel.
Throat: Pintail or teal flank, natural.
Underwing: Four fluorescent hot orange hackle tips ending just short of hook bend.
Overwing: Hot purple golden pheasant flank, two sets of two; one set to hook point, the other set to bend.
Topping: Two or three golden pheasant crests.
Cheeks: Jungle cock.

Spawning Purple (1976)

Dave comments: "Denny Hannah invited my wife and me to a three-day guided trip on Oregon's Elk River, a water now famous among fly fishers for its run of huge Chinook salmon. As we were leaving Hannah, he called to tell us that the river was blown out from heavy rains. We went ahead and made the drive and waited out the rain. By midweek the rain became a sprinkle, and the Elk began to clear. At first light I tied a few of the Spawning Purples, a new fly, and on that March day enjoyed incredible fishing. I took steelhead of 19 pounds 15 ounces, one of 11 pounds, and several in the nine-pound range. Denny had the big steelhead mounted and he displayed it at Ed Rice's International Sportsman's Exposition in Eugene."

Tag: Fine flat silver tinsel.
Tail: Hot fluorescent orange polar bear length of hook shank.
Body: Use fluorescent orange floss to form a dubbing loop and spin fluorescent orange seal. Keep turns to a minimum to form a ragged, easily picked out chenille.
Hackle: Hot orange guinea.
Wing: Four to six grizzly hackle tips dyed hot purple.
Hackle: Guinea dyed hot orange with one or two turns of teal over.
Head: Fluorescent orange tying thread.

This essay is excerpted with permission of Wild River Press from the magnificent new book "Flies For Atlantic Salmon & Steelhead: A History of the World's Most Elegant Fishing Flies" by Trey Combs.

Find additional Dave McNeese patterns from this chapter within that book.

In addition to standard and signed limited editions, a deluxe leather-bound edition comes with a museum-caliber framed set of nine flies telling the encapsulated story of the evolution of salmon and steelhead flies.

This "who's who" of contributing master fly dressers from around the anadromous world are: Will Bush (full Victorian salmon fly of your choice), Stuart Foxall (Willie Gunn), Joe Howell, (Green-Butt Skunk), Brett Jensen (Klamath Waker), Dave McNeese (Orange Heron), Jerome Molloy (Picasse), Jay Nicholas (Blue Dawn Intruder), Peter Ohlsson (Temple Dog) and Steve Silverio (Bomber).

To obtain your copy of Trey's new book go to wildriverpress.com

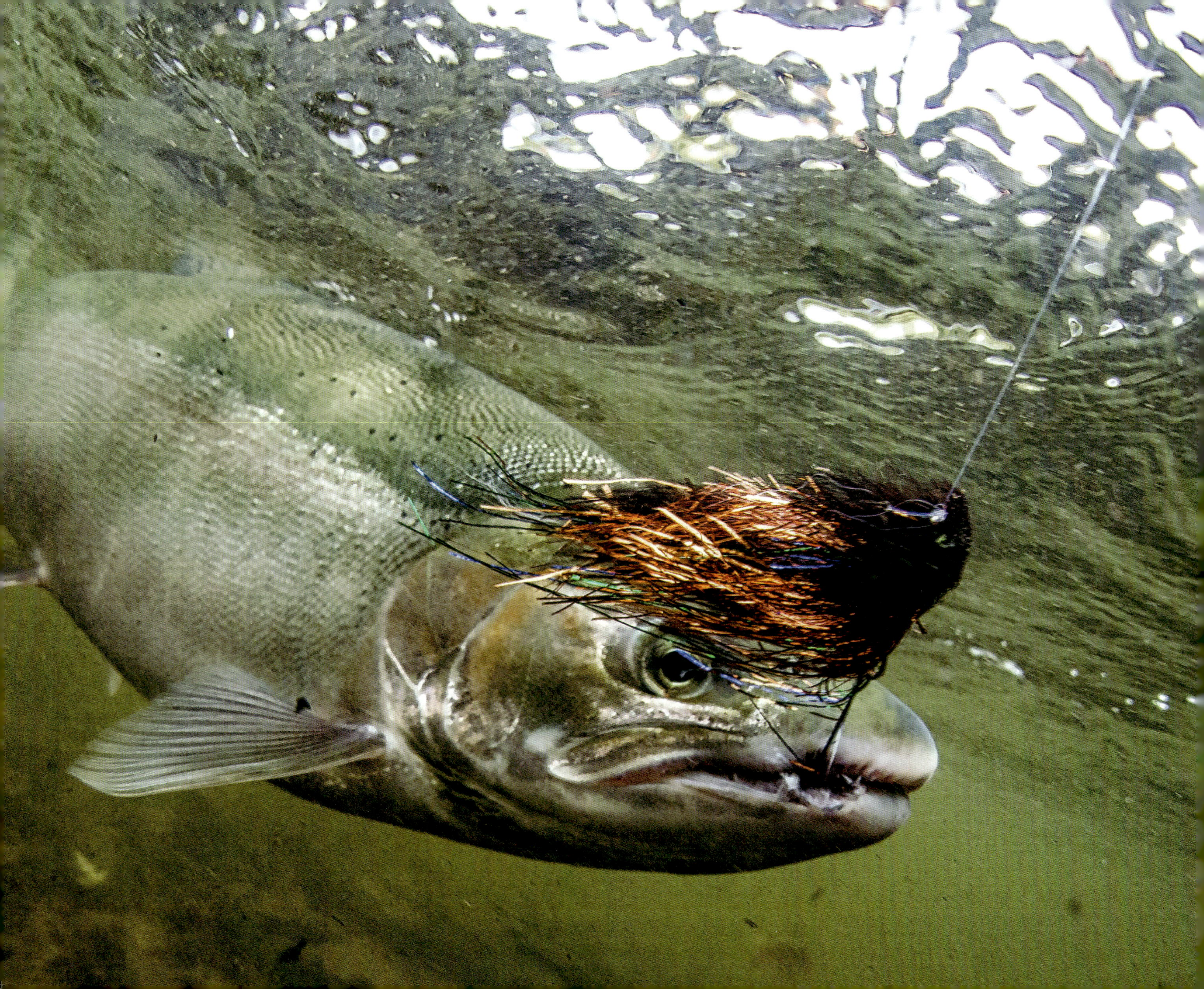

COLORS YOU CAN COUNT ON

Kevin Feenstra

As spey fishing on our Great Lakes tributaries has evolved over the last 30 years, the angling has become more refined. The gear has improved, the fly lines have improved, and so have the flies. Numerous fly patterns are at your fingertips on the internet, and there are a lot of good options out there when you hit your local river.

Yet when I discuss flies with my friends (mostly guides who are also avid spey fishers), the conversation doesn't usually revolve around just the pattern or the style of fly. Rather, the talk often revolves around the color or flash color used in the pattern. Steelhead react well to color — sometimes out of sheer aggression, but also because it may imitate a food in nature. This article covers some of my favorite color combinations, each of which represents a unique fishing scenario.

Copper mixed with black, green or red

When I was 12 to 15 years old, times were different than they are today. Often, I would get out of school and disappear for hours along a local stream. I would fish lures, and one of my favorites was a copper Super Vibrax spinner. This lure turned a lot of heads due to its flash and vibration.

When I started to swing flies, most of my patterns were drab and imitated natural things like sculpins. Yet it was always in the back of my mind that steelhead will go ballistic on metallic colored things. As time went on, bits of flash and color would be added to patterns in the form of tinsel. But I needed a way to cut the learning curve.

There was a fix to this, and I started talking to some of the plug fishermen. At the time, pulling plugs was one of the most common styles of fishing. Many of these anglers were gurus in knowing which colors to use depending on water clarity and lighting. Most commonly, they would say black and gold was the best color combination on a given day. Thus, I added black and gold flash to flies — with mixed results. However, when I looked at my flash, the gold flash in lures more closely resembled the copper flash in my fly-tying room. Flies were tied with black and copper, and it was immediately successful and has become a mainstay in my box for fall steelhead to this day.

Copper is a dominant color. Overall, the flies used are typically black, green and copper for larger leeches and sculpin patterns. As the water cools, black, red and copper is great on smaller patterns.

Green, holographic yellow and red

In the early fall, the days are a bit longer, the sun is high, and the fish can be skittish at best

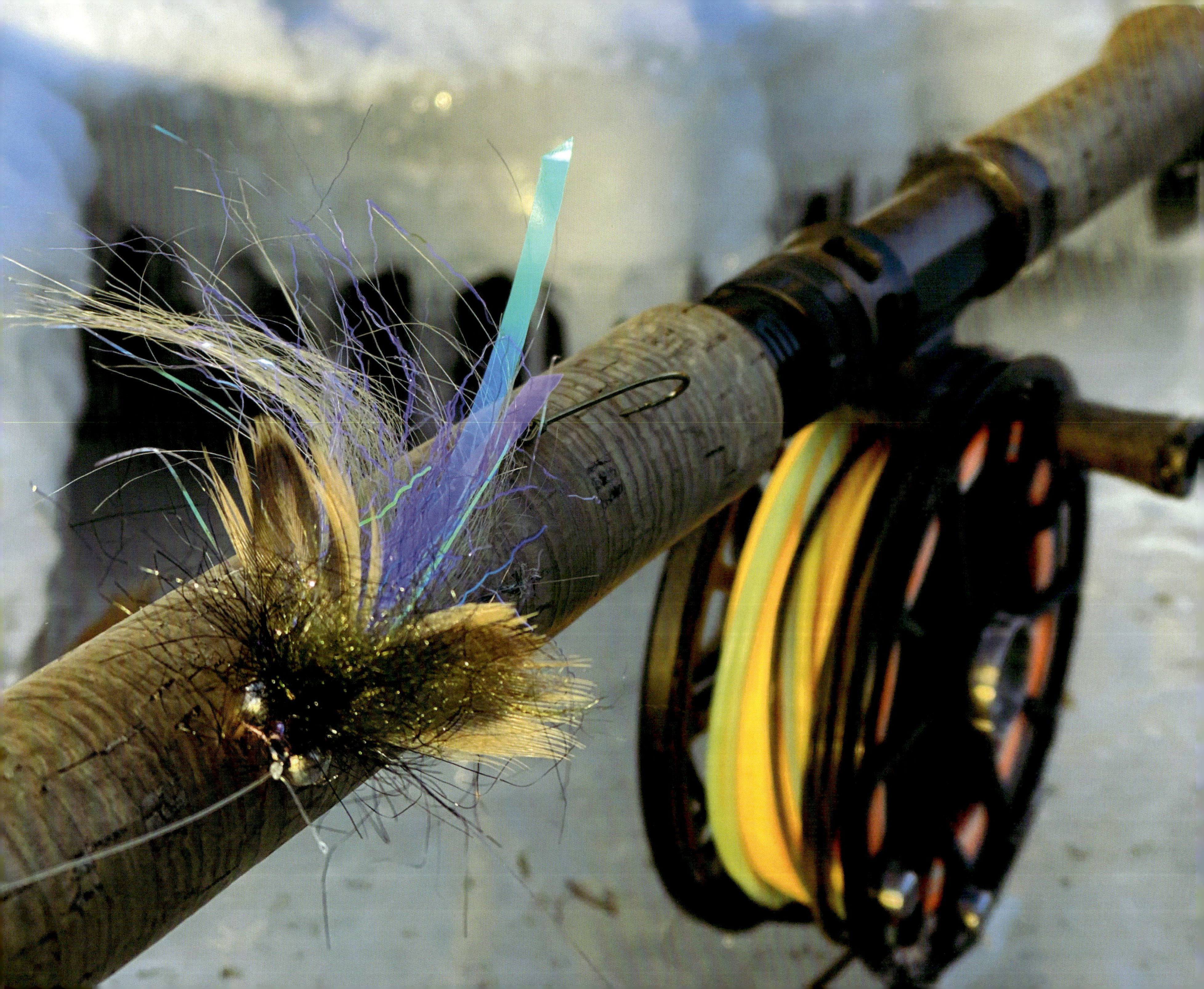

on a busy day. One approach to catching fish in these circumstances is to fish subdued patterns on longish leaders to get a wary fish to bite. Fall fish are aggressive, and so I tend to go in the opposite direction during this time. On a bright day, I use the biggest and brightest flies. Green, yellow, and red are the brightest. If you use a fly like this one, make sure you fish it all the way to the end of the run. Fish will move in front of it and finally strike when they are pushed to the tailout.

Blue

As winter approaches, and water temps drop into the 30s, a curious phenomenon happens. Often I have two clients swinging flies out of my boat at a time. When the water temps are warm, the fish will often prefer warmer colors, such as black and copper, etc. However, as the water temperature falls, inevitably I will see the fish preferring cooler color combinations that incorporate blue. I can't scientifically say exactly why this happens. The days are shorter, and there tends to be more blue light as the brunt of winter approaches. Furthermore, some baitfish lose their color in the winter months and appear more blue.

Regardless of the reason for this shift in color preference, the flies that contain blue usually are best with a black base and blue flash over the body. Other patterns that are successful during the cold months have a variety of colors, but blue is always a component. In short, if you fish in the winter, don't overlook blue.

Full spectrum

In the fall and winter, lighting conditions may change rapidly as fronts move in and out. During that time, flies that use a wide gamut of colors of flash work very well. These flies often contain colors that work well in bright conditions, such as green and gold, as well as colors that work in cold or dark conditions, such as blue and copper. My favorite fly is called a Kitchen Sink Leech, which incorporates all of these colors of flash as well as chartreuse, orange, and pink body materials. When in doubt, use all of the best attractor colors in your region and something good should happen.

Pearl and UV blue

Throughout their life cycle, steelhead feed on a variety of baitfish. In the Great Lakes, these can be alewives, sticklebacks, shiners and more. Many of the baitfish — especially those that live in the upper parts of the water column — reflect light off their shiny sides. If ever there was a food source that can be imitated well with flashy fly tying materials, this would be it.

Flies that incorporate pearl and iridescent colors are deadly and really fit this bill well. Often they have a grey or light olive colored body, and these flash colors are incorporated into the tail and the wing of the fly.

Another material that really works well incorporated into many minnow patterns is UV blue materials. The best of these materials that

Swing the Fly Anthology 2023

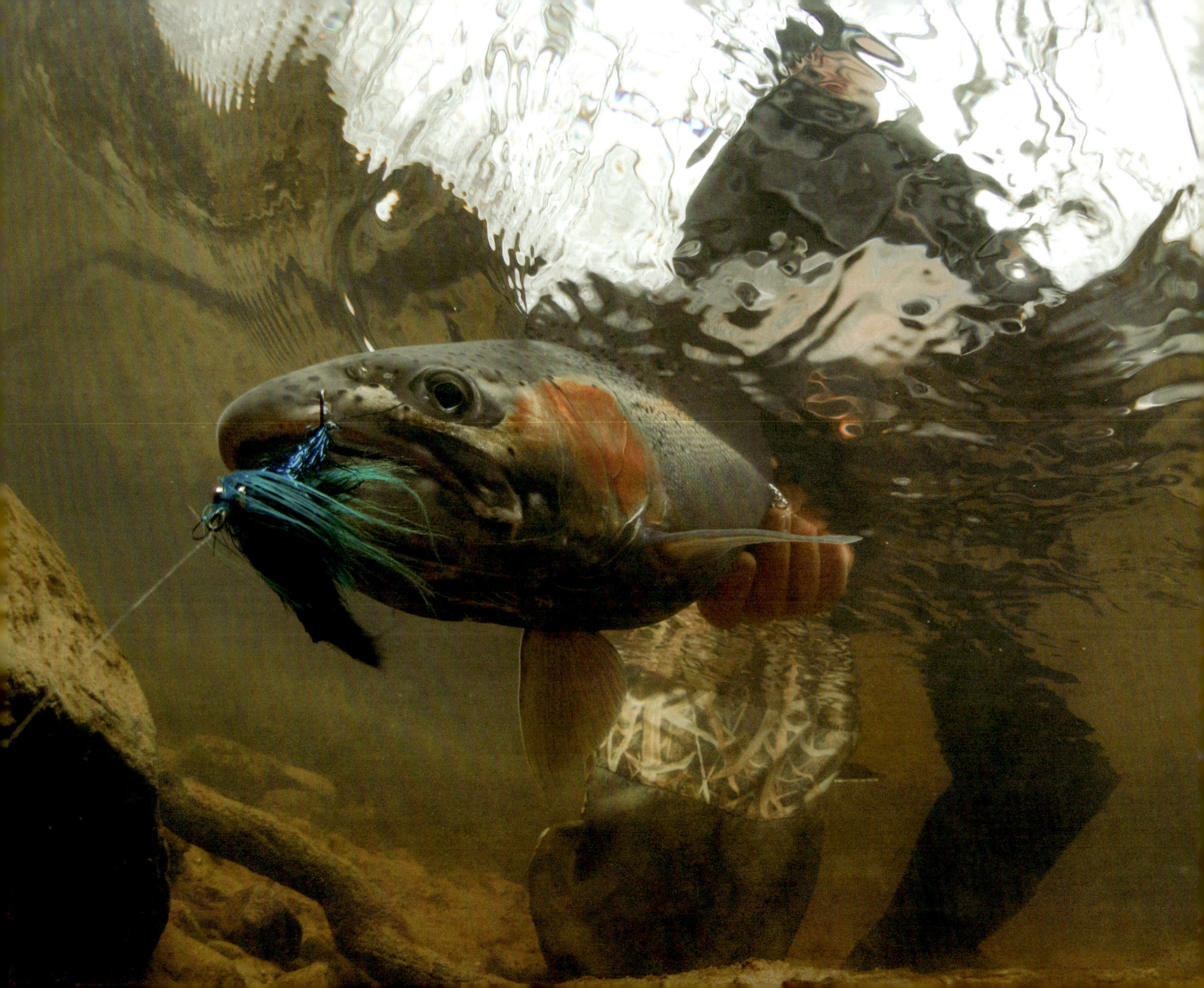

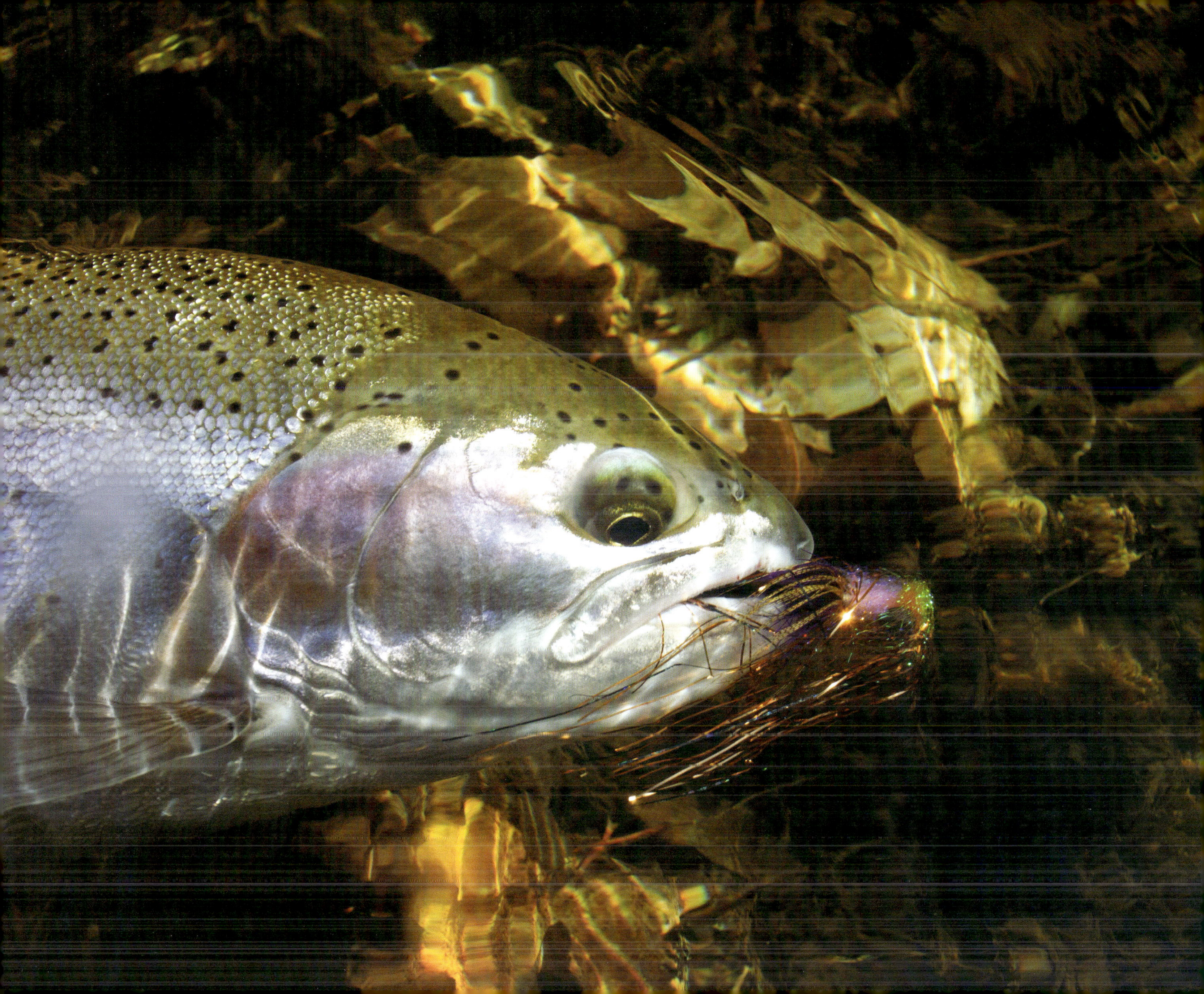

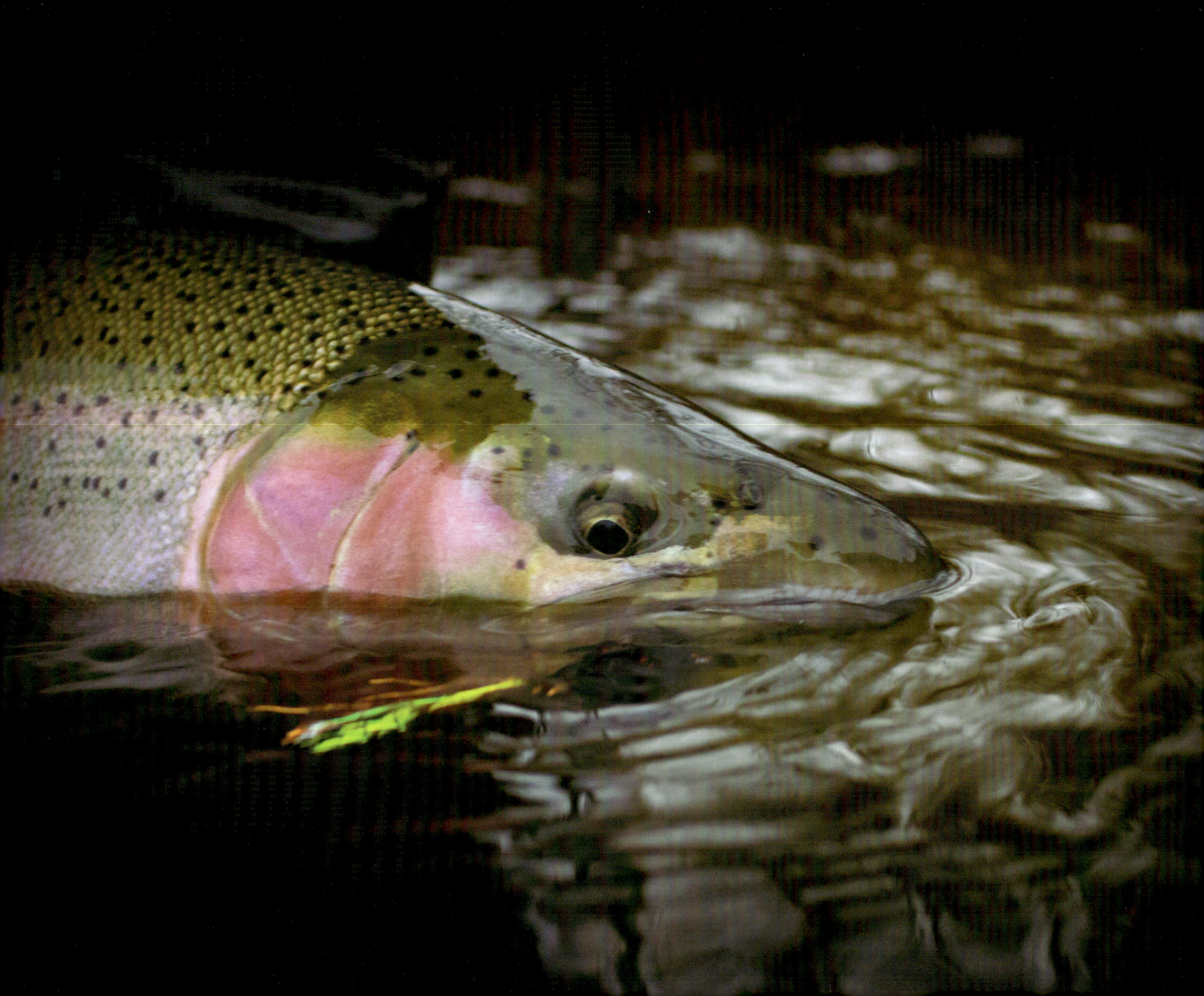

I have worked with is Hareline Ripple Ice Fiber in UV blue, but there are others as well. This material, in conjunction with other types of flash, really takes a good baitfish pattern over the top.

Slender baitfish patterns take migratory fish throughout the fall, winter and spring. However, I use them the most during the winter months. It is during the winter that many of our fish settle in and become more acclimated to the food sources in the river. At this time, they may feed on the baitfish that are always present, including shiners and other minnows.

Dark olive and cranberry

This unlikely color combination is one of the most reliable in the fly box on a day-to-day basis. I carry two boxes in my boat during the swung fly season, one of which is devoted to attractor flies. The other one carries the baitfish. When I look at the baitfish box, two-thirds of the flies have some variation of this color combination.

Many of the food sources in our rivers reflect the color of the bottom of the river, usually olive and tan. Of these earth tone colors, I always prefer olive. Many of the bottom dwelling minnows have a reddish edge to their fins, and this is particularly true of sculpins. To give the right touch of this reddish color, I started to look for a mahogany-colored flash, and cranberry holographic Flashabou does the trick.

Through much of the fall and through the winter, this color combination is good. However, in late winter, as the tip of our spring run starts to approach, fish really attack it. It could just be that the large olive and cranberry pattern presents the meal the fish are looking for. This may seem like a strange idea, but male steelhead take on an olive and dark red appearance in late winter, and become aggressive toward each other. I believe that this aggression toward this color combination may add to the success of these patterns in the late winter and early spring.

Pink and rainbow crystal flash

As I put the final touches on this article, I am off the river today because my home river, the Muskegon, was very high today and the trip was cancelled. However, there are many times when clients are coming from distance and we are confronted with fishing in high or stained water. This is common in the spring, when we have spring storms and snowmelt for a double whammy.

During high water times, a dense, colorful fly can really save the day. During the spring months, one of the primary sources of protein for migratory fish is salmon and steelhead fry. Fry are typically an inch or two long through much of the spring in my region, so I tie a pattern with a very heavy tungsten head, pink and rainbow flash, all over a gray craft hair body.

This type of fly can be fished through any typical run. It also will pick up steelhead and resident trout as they feed behind migratory trout species and suckers.

The color combinations mentioned in this article provide a solid base for fishing in my section of the Great Lakes. Migratory fish have regional preferences for the color and shape of your flies. This is true of the attractor flies but is also reflected in the baitfish that are present in your area. If you find a color that works, build on that color and begin adding other colors to it. Learning how to use flash is a key to success both in building flies and catching fish.

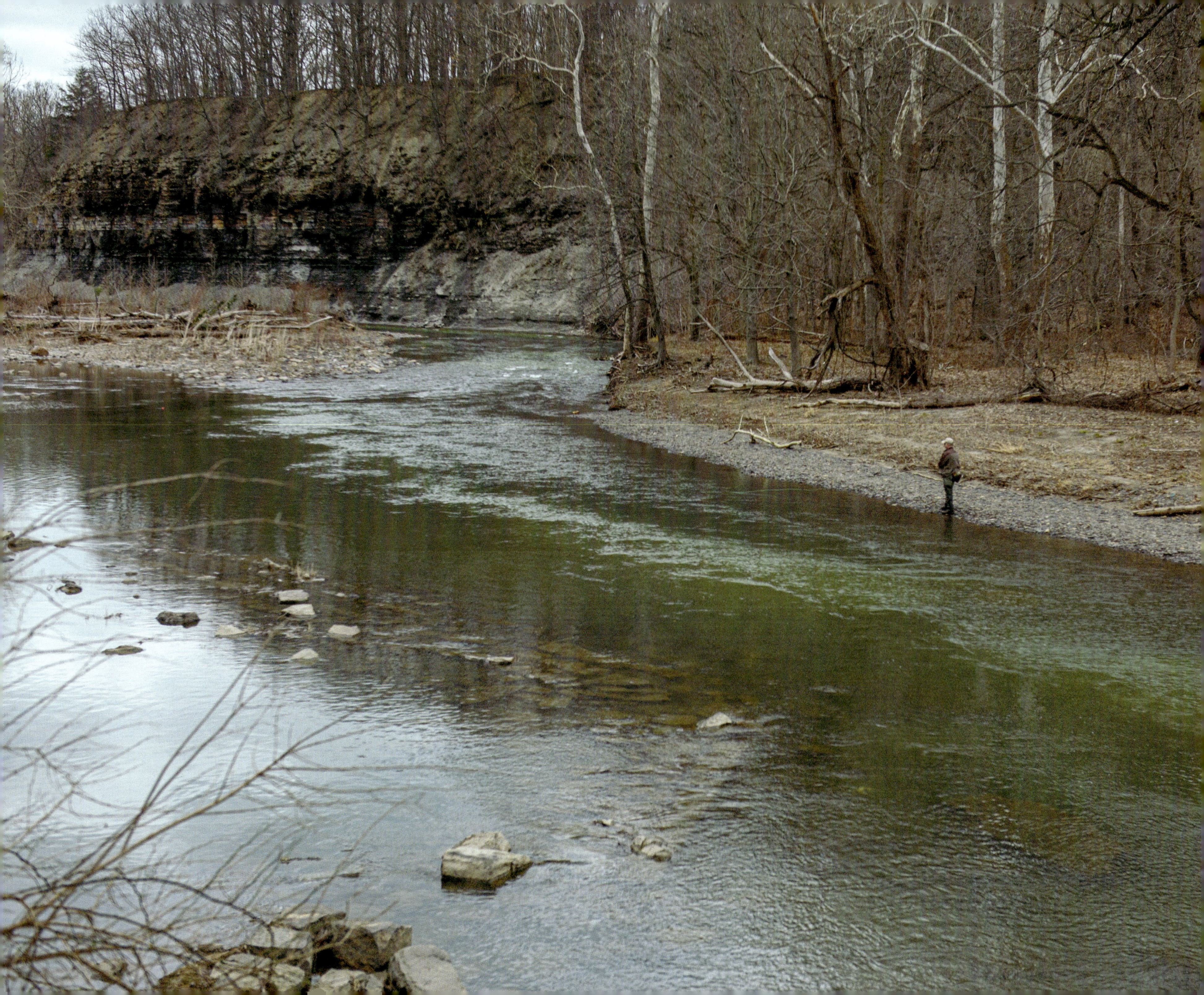

CONTROLLING DEPTH

Rick Kustich

While I'll always enjoy spey casting, both as a separate activity or integrated into fishing activities, quite often I find more of a challenge and satisfaction in the presentation of the fly.

In spey fishing I strive for connection to the fly — truly envisioning its path and speed. Is the fly swimming and behaving in a manner that will entice interest or trigger a predator? Being able to control both speed and depth allows for adjusting to the conditions and various water types or simply allowing the fly to be fished in accord with a personal preference.

Controlling the depth to fish the fly can be accomplished using various strategies, often in combination. Rigging, casting, and line manipulation can all play a part. My own approach to fishing the desired depth begins with rigging and then fine-tuned through casting and fishing tactics.

Surface

In its simplest form depth can be about no depth at all. At times fishing the fly on or just below the surface is both productive and creates an exciting visual when a fish rises to intercept or even explode on the fly. For surface fishing, rigging with a floating Scandi head or floating mid-range to longbelly line with a leader the approximate length of the rod allows for efficient casting and presentation. The leader can be constructed of a piece of level monofilament, but a tapered leader allows for a smoother turnover of the fly.

Fly patterns that represent rodents, injured bait, and various large insects can be used to entice and fool resident trout or smallmouth bass. More suggestive patterns are typically used when surface fishing for migratory steelhead, trout and salmon.

Some highly buoyant flies, such as a mouse tied with a large amount of foam, generally ride well on the surface with a straight knot to the fly. However, adding a riffle hitch is required to maintain a surface position for most patterns. The riffle hitch is an additional knot added after the fly is secured with a standard non-loop knot such as the improved clinch. The riffle hitch is basically two half hitches tied onto the front shank of the hook and even over some of the front materials. With the eye of the fly pointing upstream, the tippet should run from the fly at a side angle toward the near shore or casting bank, pulling the fly to the surface. The hitch even allows wet flies to ride on the surface or just in the surface film. An up-eye hook works best with the riffle hitch.

An alternative to the riffle hitch for surface fishing can be found using fly patterns tied on a plastic tube. The tippet is then inserted into a hole created on the side or underneath the tube using a hot needle instead of feeding the tippet straight into the tube. This provides the same side pull as the riffle hitch.

An effective approach for the surface is to wake the fly. The wake refers to the slight V created by the fly as it moves across the surface. The V allows you to see the fly and creates a slight disturbance that can attract a fish. The rod is held at a higher rod angle than when swinging a subsurface fly. The higher angle removes line from the service and allows for acute line control. Finding the right amount of tension on the fly is the key to maintaining an enticing presentation. Too little tension and the fly fails to wake. Too much and it plows underneath. Typically, the rod slightly leads the fly to maintain side pressure and keep it at the surface. When fishing highly buoyant mouse or baitfish patterns, moving the rod tip from side to side gives the impression of a swimming action or the illusion of a struggle at the surface.

Floating Line Subsurface

To fish the fly just below the surface, a floating head or line and long leader is combined with an unhitched wet fly. A heavy wire hook or adding a slight amount of weight to the fly assists in sinking it slightly. This approach works well in clear water for fish that are looking up and tend to move up the water column to intercept a fly.

Another approach for a floating line or head and a long leader is to combine with a fully weighted fly to make a presentation down in the water column. This rigging allows for a stealthier approach than using a sink-tip when fishing low clear water conditions. This rigging also has an advantage of a slower swing particularly when covering a soft inside seam. The lower diameter of the monofilament or fluorocarbon leader has less surface area for the current to push upon than a sink tip. The slower swing is effective for cold water and fish with a lower metabolism. Too much weight on the fly though can make casting with a Scandi or mid-range floating head quite cumbersome.

Sink Tips

To consistently fish the fly down in the water column, sinking leaders or sink tips looped to the front of the head with a leader/tippet of generally three to four feet is the most efficient rig. For smaller waters or for fishing the fly down a few feet, tapered sinking leaders represent an easy to cast option. Lighter sinking leaders can be looped to the front end of a Scandi or mid-range head and cast with a similar feel as a monofilament leader. This rigging can be combined with a lightly weighted fly.

Exchangeable tip lines represent an option for working various levels of the column. Exchanging a floating tip with a loop-to-loop connection for one that sinks effectively creates a sink tip line. Exchangeable tip lines commonly have a 15-foot tip section and a taper of a mid-belly line. This style of line typically includes tips with various sink rates and provides an ability to change the depth profile of the presentation without signifi-

DEVELOPING A SYSTEM TO ADJUST AND MEET VARIOUS CONDITIONS AND CHALLENGES IS PART OF THE ENJOYMENT OF THIS SPORT AND THE KEY FOR EFFECTIVE SPEY FISHING.

cantly changing the overall feel of the line or cast.

For the most versatility and working the fly down in the water column, a Skagit head represents the best delivery system. A Skagit head effectively handles the full range of sinking leaders and sink tips, including heavy tips with very fast sink rates. This rigging can also easily handle a weighted fly for extra depth or for the fly to drop at the same speed as the tip.

Due to the overall mass of a Skagit head, sink tips with a taper are not necessary. Level T-material heads cut to various lengths are commonly combined with a Skagit head. T-material is tungsten-impregnated line of various weights with a number designation that indicates the grains per foot. For example, T-8 weighs eight grains per foot and T-11 weighs 11 grains per foot and so on. The greater the weight the greater the sink rate. Tips constructed of T-17 or even T-20 can reach significant depths. T-material tips can easily be constructed at home by simply adding loops to each end. T-material tips are typically made from seven to 15 feet in length. Both weight and length of the tip impacts how deep it can fish. A longer tip can reach a greater depth than a shorter tip of the same grains per foot.

Density compensated tapered sink tips of ten to 15 feet can add some smoothness to casting modern Skagit tapers and represent an alternative to level T-material tips. The density compensation allows for a uniform sink rate due to the taper. Another option is the multi-density tip. Multi-density refers to various sink rates within the same tip. For example, a typical multi-density may start with an intermediate material looped to the head of the line and then two sink rates of sinking with the fastest sink rate at the end attached to the tippet/leader. This style of tip can allow for more acute depth control.

A multi-density head, either a Skagit or Scandi combined with a sink tip can place the fly even deeper and allow it to maintain depth throughout the entire swing path right into the hangdown. Heads with a section that sinks are difficult or even impossible to mend so that controlling the swing speed can be problematic. But if greater depth is the main objective over swing speed, then the multi-density head with one or more sink rates can be a useful tool.

Presentation Adjustments

When attempting to place the fly at the desired depth, I start by estimating how deep the fly should be fished and then rigging toward that objective. Many factors play into the decision including depth of the water, the species being pursued, water temperature, and the overall nature or aggressiveness of the fish. And of course, personal preference in catching fish on your own terms is always an option.

Unless I expect that the species I am pursuing to rise to intercept the fly, I typically think of fishing the fly in the lower third of the water column. Rarely do I want the fly scraping bottom, but placed in a position that is accessible to the fish and enticing as it swings away. My rig is selected by estimating depth while considering the speed of the flow. Past experience on a particular piece of water can be an important factor in rigging up.

For ease in casting, I prefer to fish an unweighted or lightly weighted fly when casting a sinking leader or sink tip. However, adding a weight in the form of dumbbell eyes, cone, or bead can provide a tactical advantage. Weight on the fly assists with breaking through heavy surface currents and can be the key for getting down quickly to cover troughs, ledges, steep drop offs and pocket water. There are times when I'll rig with a heavy fly and sink tip in combination with a six to eight-foot leader/tippet. This allows the fly to sink faster than the tip and is effective for covering pockets and deep, fast slot water.

When fishing through a pool or run, a rig is selected that should match the entire piece of water. I prefer to fish too light rather than too heavy. Hanging up on the bottom negatively impacts rhythm. If rigged too heavy, a quick tip change is made to lighten it up. It's quite common while working through a pool or run to encounter changes in depth or current speed that impact how deep the fly is fishing relative to the bottom. In some situations where there is a dramatic variation, a tip change is required. However, most variations in depth and current speed can be addressed through other tactics.

Adding or removing a weighted fly is a simple change that can be made to adjust overall fishing depth when working through a pool or run. Carrying a range of flies tied with various weight and bulk has its advantages when fine tuning fishing depth. It is much easier to make a quick fly change than making a full tip change.

My typical cast is made somewhere between 80 to 90 degrees to the casting position. Simply changing the angle of the cast through body rotation and lining up the anchor toward the target allows for casts that can be delivered in a wide directional range. A cast made to 90 degrees or slightly higher gives the fly more time to sink. Casts made to 80 degrees or less maintain the fly higher in the water column and a good tactic as the water becomes more shallow. But a more downstream casting angle tends to increase swing speed changing the overall presentation. Pointing the rod toward the opposite bank can assist in neutralizing the speed increase.

Mending may be the most common approach to depth control. Adding a big upstream mend as the fly hits the water after the cast allows the sink tip and fly to free fall until the line is under tension. Using a mend versus not mending typically has a significant impact on the depth of the fly. Slack and depth can also be obtained by overcasting the target and pulling back on the line by raising the rod tip.

For maximum depth I make a slightly angled upstream cast combined with an upstream mend. The mend is completed with the rod angled high. As the tip and fly begin to drift down the rod is slowly lowered, maintaining slack during the setup and allowing the fly to dig deeper. As the fly approaches 55 to 45 degrees, it comes under tension and begins to swim. A multi-density head allows the fly to stay deep throughout the swing.

Subtle mends and adjustments can be added throughout the swing. I mostly mend during the swing to control speed but adjustments to the line during the presentation also impact depth. A downstream belly increases speed and also has a tendency to pull the fly up. Subtle upstream mends reduce the belly without impacting the swing path of the fly.

There are unlimited combinations of rigging and tactical approaches to impact fishing the fly at any point in the water column. Developing a system to adjust and meet various conditions and challenges is part of the enjoyment of this sport and the key for effective spey fishing.

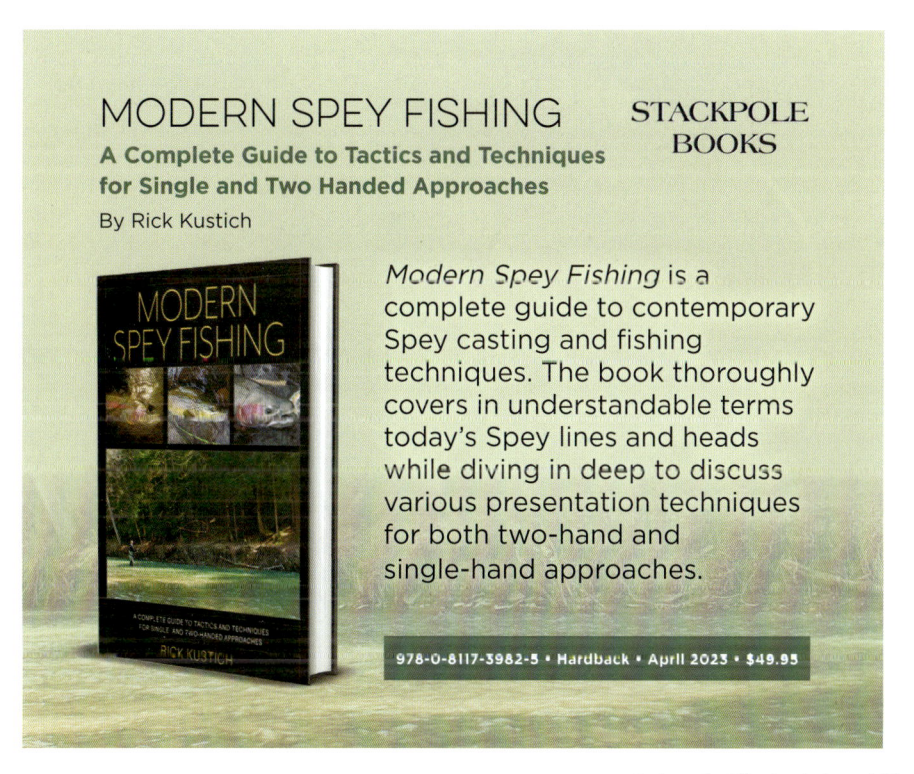

MODERN SPEY FISHING

A Complete Guide to Tactics and Techniques for Single and Two Handed Approaches

By Rick Kustich

STACKPOLE BOOKS

Modern Spey Fishing is a complete guide to contemporary Spey casting and fishing techniques. The book thoroughly covers in understandable terms today's Spey lines and heads while diving in deep to discuss various presentation techniques for both two-hand and single-hand approaches.

978-0-8117-3982-5 • Hardback • April 2023 • $49.95

Swing the Fly Anthology 2023

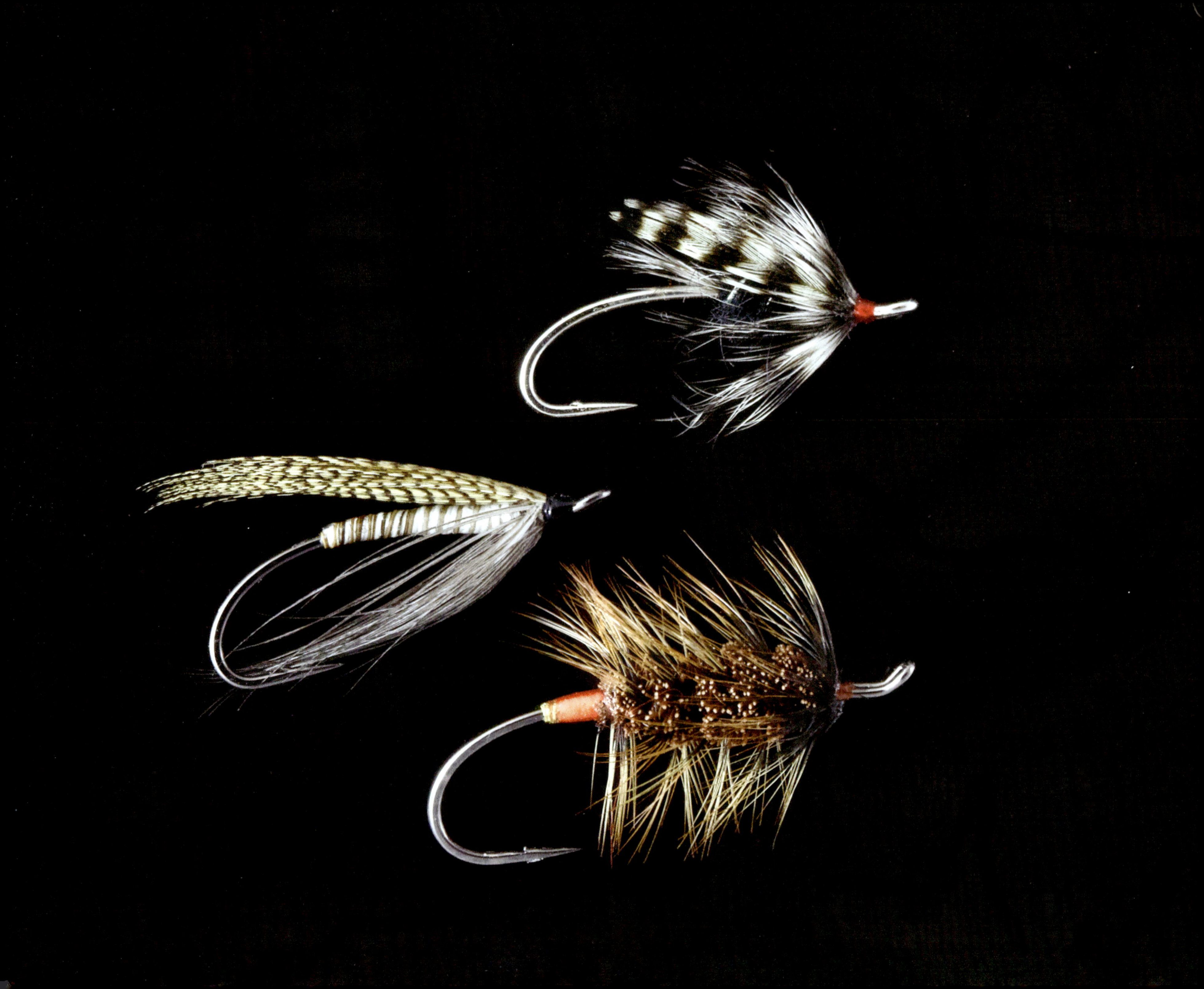

ADAPTABILITY REQUIRED

John Alevras

"Find a favorite rock, and don't leave it. The armada of rafts will start arriving late morning, will continue for the rest of the day and will likely number in the twenties." Our host Dave Larson confirmed what our group of old friends had expected — heavy fishing pressure. Now all we had to decide was who gets which rock.

We would all choose to fish our favorite runs and pools, especially when conditions such as sunlight and shade are most favorable, but the reality on a river such as the Kispiox is that angling pressure inhibits preferred choices and necessitates adaptability. I am fortunate to have fished the river for many years and have learned the locations anglers flock to, often well before sunrise, and when and where the fleet of rafts will overwhelm sections of the river. My choice of where to fish is based on knowing where I will have an excellent opportunity to fish in solitude for three or four hours before the flotilla arrives.

My chosen run is 50 or so yards long and offers steelhead sanctuary along the right bank, where it is deep enough to hold fish from its turbulent head all the way through the tailout, even in low water. It is a challenging stretch of water to fish, which is why I am comfortable making four or five passes and spending a full day there without getting bored. My hope is that courteous floaters will allow that to happen.

The river is low and clear so the plan is to focus the morning on the top half of the run where there is strong, streamy water, depth and no sun until early afternoon. I love to fish the bottom half of the run, but it is bathed in sunlight until mid-afternoon. With such low, clear conditions, I will wait until it is in shade, if boat traffic allows.

My strategy will be strongly influenced by a belief that steelhead have memories that go beyond recent events such as boats and rafts, wading anglers, the repetitive swing of large flashy fly patterns, and being caught. When steelhead return to their natal rivers, I believe they remember their life as juveniles when they aggressively fed upon just about any available food items from miniscule insects to caddis, stoneflies and terrestrials.

The steelhead I will be fishing for have traveled more than 200 miles from the ocean and, depending on river conditions, have been in fresh water for one or two months. My approach will reflect the low, clear water and cloudless sky, my desire to fish very different tactics and flies than other anglers and the theory that the use of fly patterns suggestive of life forms that juvenile steelhead feed upon will be effective.

I start fishing high in the turbulent water at the head of the run where steelhead will likely feel secure. I am using Bob Clay's 11-foot bamboo rod, a floating line with a 12-foot leader tapered to a soft 1x (.010) tippet and a fiery brown Buck Bug.

I am confident one or more fish are lying in the sheltered, comfortable confines of this water and spend considerable time fishing it. When I reach the slower water, I am surprised I have not moved a fish and return to the top of the run. I replace the leader and fly with an intermediate poly-leader and a #8 low-water Blue Quill wet-fly, a famous trout pattern that is suggestive of aquatic life forms. As Bob

Photo: Zack Williams

> THE INTENSITY OF THEIR ROWING SUGGESTS THEY ARE TRYING TO ESCAPE THE SCENE OF A CRIME. THE REST OF THE AFTERNOON IS A CONTINUOUS PARADE OF RAFTS ...

Arnold wrote in *Steelhead & the Floating Line* about his Spade pattern, "They look like nothing in particular and everything in general." I have similar feelings about the Blue Quill and other natural subdued patterns such as the Spade.

Fly selection is more than a lottery pick from a box of colorful flies. The intermediate leader is not intended to fish the fly deep. I want it to swim high in the water column, only several inches below where the Buck Bug swam. Midway through the restless water the tug comes. It is a buck of eight or nine pounds that shows its mettle before being brought to the shallows and released. The rest of the broken water offers no further action.

At the point where the river transitions to a slower, flat surface, I switch back to the mono leader and Buck Bug. Within 15 minutes a subtle bulge in the surface and slow tightening of the line signals a fish. Because the fly is small and sparse and almost on the dangle close to the bank, the rod tip is lowered to give line, and the strike is delayed until the fish begins to move toward the center of the river. A wonderful 15 minutes of mayhem follows before a lovely lady of 13 or 14 pounds is landed, admired and released.

It is almost 11 a.m., and I am very close to sun-drenched water, so I decide to return to the head of the run while it is still in shade. I have no hesitation to make a third pass through the broken water because it is not the same water it was several hours ago when light patterns were different than they are now.

Before resuming fishing, lunch is pulled from the dry bag for a restful 20 or so minutes. While enjoying the relaxation, I see the first of the anticipated flotilla enter an inviting pool several hundred yards above me. As expected, the angler parks his pontoon raft and fishes a small productive corner pool that every angler that follows will fish, if it is available.

I decide to stay with the mono leader and Blue Quill even though I was using an intermediate leader when I caught the first fish. On this pass, the plan is to slow the swing and hold the fly on the dangle where the vigorous current will buffet the fly. A firm grab comes quickly near the top of the run. There is a showy boil and then, nothing. I continue fishing the location with a change of tactics in the hope of enticing the fish again but do not succeed. I fish the balance of fast water with no success and decide to change the fly to a #10 Silver Hilton to fish the flat, slower water. While changing the fly, the angler from above drifts into the run on the opposite side and begins fishing with a sinking line and large weighted fly. We enjoy a cordial conversation that discloses he has not yet moved a fish and had to pass 11 anglers before he found available water. Ugh!

While we are chatting, a second angler has already parked his raft and is fishing the pool above, a scenario that will be repeated often the balance of the day. The movement of the sun has put more of the run in shade and now behind the fish, a positive change that I expect will increase opportunities. In short order I get a player that plucks the fly on four consecutive casts before an accelerated swing delivers a swirl and firm take from another buck of about 10 pounds that is landed and released. The angler is courteous and hugs the far bank, salutes my good fortune, then asks the expected question, "What fly?"

My response is received with a bewildered look and a, "Geez, that is really small." I nod in agreement.

By the time I resume fishing, a conversation signals two more anglers floating by. I ask how they are doing, receive a thumbs down and no further response. The intensity of their rowing suggests they are trying to escape the scene of a crime.

The rest of the afternoon is a continuous parade of rafts that includes several friends who stop for congenial conversation. Their report reflects the obvious, too many anglers for the low, clear conditions, and not a single steelhead known to have been taken. When asked how I have done, I lie and disclose one small buck, not the three landed, nor the one missed on the take.

By 4 p.m. I am back to the head of the run intending one last pass that will include the tailout, which is now in shade and undisturbed. I have been extremely fortunate that not one angler has chosen to fish my side. Instead, one after another has fished the head on the other side that is very fishy, but unyielding.

As I had hoped, the tailout yields a fourth steelhead. She is another beautiful mid-teen fish and the second to be enticed by the little

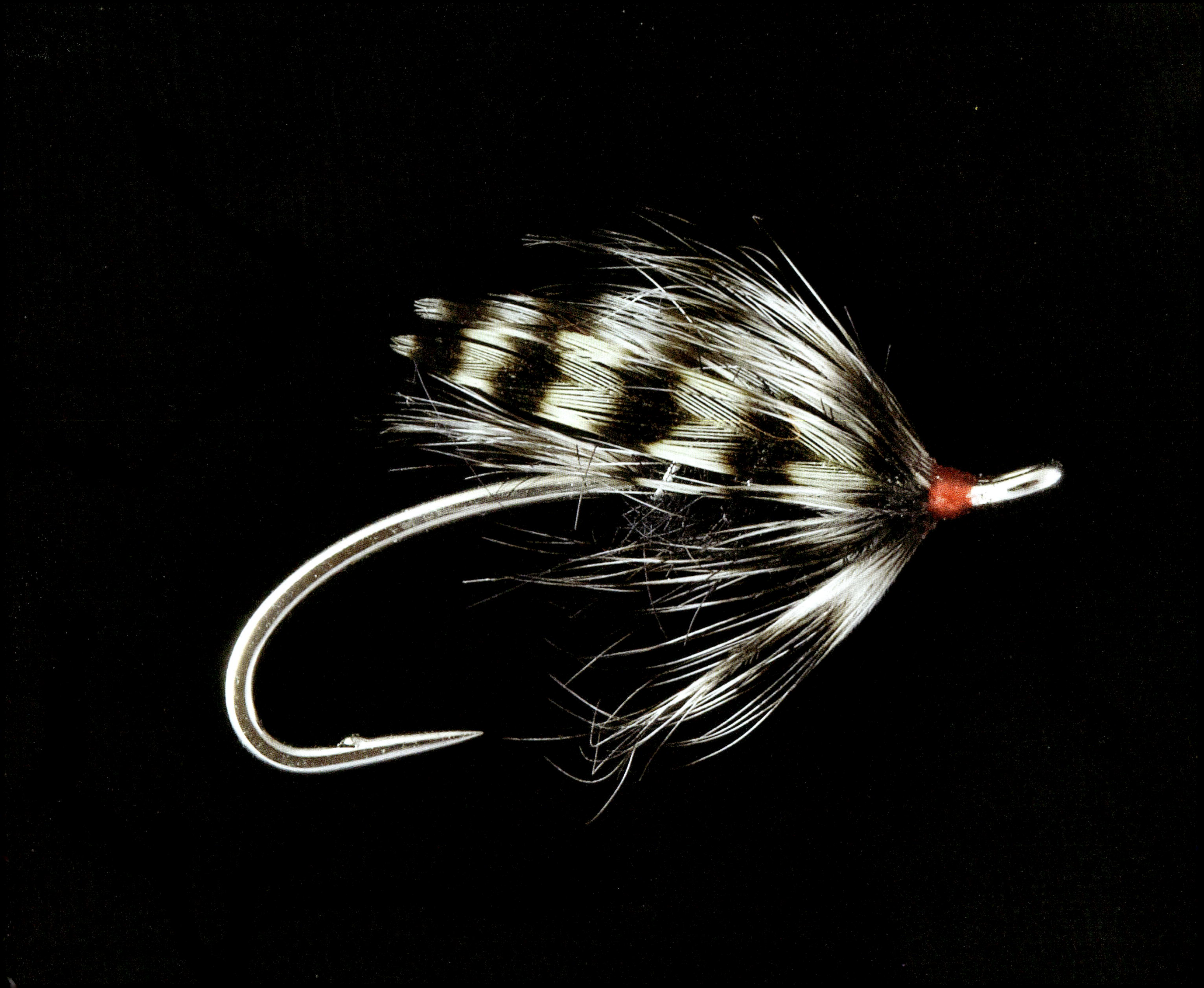

Silver Hilton fished just below the surface. It is almost 6 p.m., a perfect time for a very satisfied angler to call it a day and enjoy the companionship of friends. I hope the rocks they chose were as generous as mine.

It would be easy to argue that this exceptional day was just the result of fishing a productive run with no competition. I would disagree. I believe today's success was reward for understanding how steelhead respond to the challenging environmental conditions and the impact of continuous fishing pressure. Where I fished and the choice of tactics and flies were a response to these conditions.

Fishing pressure is more than boats, rafts and wading anglers that spook and force fish to relocate. The repetitive swing of similar flies, especially large patterns day after day, week after week, turns steelhead off, causing what I reason is a form of dourness that leads anglers to believe there are few fish in the river system. Most likely, that was the reaction of most of the 20-plus anglers who floated by today. Do not get caught-up in what other anglers are doing. Fish different tactics and flies from what steelhead have been encountering.

Today's experience and others that I have described in previous articles are not to suggest small fly tactics be considered a replacement for traditional practices. Rather, they are an important addition that represents a solution to the numerous challenging conditions steelheaders face through the lengthy period summer run fish are present in our river systems.

There will be many more "hopeless" days with low, clear rivers and excessive fishing pressure. Small fly tactics address these common fishing conditions. They also address the long-term memory of steelhead, because in rivers such as the Kispiox, juveniles spend three to four years — which represents 60 to 70% of their life — feeding on small life forms. It is plausible to believe small, simple patterns suggestive of stream life trigger a memory response that translates into the take that can be so elusive.

ANY FOOL CAN MAKE SOMETHING COMPLICATED.
IT TAKES A GENIUS TO MAKE IT SIMPLE.
   -Woody Guthrie

ALO'S PARTRIDGE & PEACOCK

Simply Effective

Armando Quazzo

A conflict of interest can arise between tiers of artificial flies and fishers who buy and fish them. Fly tiers may be tempted to propose unique and complex designs, creating a feeling of inadequacy and uncertainty in those who do not have the indispensable one. History has shown that the real need of fly fishers may simply be a box with a few select and simple flies.

This is a kind of Stockholm Syndrome in the fly tying world. Beginning hundreds of years ago we have numerous examples. The Jock Scott of the Victorian era took about 30 different materials to tie and was indispensable in the world of salmon fishermen. Apart from any consideration on the effectiveness of this fly when compared to others, the commercial message was amazing: salmon fishing is random and only those who can afford complex lures will be successful.

Even today we find similar examples, and we may be inclined to consider complication as the solution, whereas the universal remedy may be simplification.

Keep it Simple

It was the end of season in European rivers descending from the Alps. Water levels were low, and the trout were spooky. Despite these conditions, a dear friend of mine, Allesandro Belluscio — a well known Swiss Italian fly angler and sports photographer — pointed out to me the effectiveness of a very simple fly he had experimented with in the rivers near his home. It was a dry/wet fly to be tied on a wet fly hook with natural grey partridge tail and hackle and a peacock herl body ribbed with a strand of rainbow or pearl Crystal Flash. Nothing more.

My friend recommended using only two peacock herls for the body to keep the fly really "thin and lean". I objected that with the influence of the current, a slender partridge collar would collapse on the body and the fly would almost disappear. He explained to me that the same fly rigged with a slightly more robust body does not attract the attention of the fish so much — the ideal solution being a slender body.

The Litmus Test

I did not believe my friend, so I tied a few flies with my normal 'beefy' body and a pair according to my friend's precise advice: two peacock herls twisted in a loop and ribbed and nothing more. I equipped myself with a long and light rod, a double taper line with a long and thin leader and started fishing with the slender fly my friend had suggested. After a few swings I attracted the attention of a first trout and shortly after, another. Then I exchanged this fly with a similar one with a beefier body and fished the rest of the pool. Useless, no takes. I switched back to the fly with the recommended slender body — and as if by magic, two more trout were convinced and hit the fly; one so big I could not get it into my landing net. I did the same test on several other fishing trips with the same result: the lean version outperformed the competitor by a ratio of 3:1. I was convinced. There was no contest.

To be honest, I could not understand the reason for the effectiveness of this wet fly. It seemed to me impossible that such a small difference could be so decisive. I then remembered a similar phenomenon that had occurred many years ago on the River Po where a highly effective streamer — the Black Nose Dace — had proved to be effective if tied with few bucktail fibers and almost useless if tied with a rich wing.

The Secret of Peacock Herl

Part of the explanation of the effectiveness of this fly could lie in the chromatic characteristics of peacock herl. Two of my friends, both skilled fishermen and excellent tiers — Runar Warhuus in Norway and Wayne Luallen in California — observed that peacock herl significantly changes its coloration when wet, changing from iridescent green when dry to a brownish-bronze colour when wet. This coloration closely matches the bottom of several European rivers (and I imagine also in the United States). In refracted sunlight the tips of the herl barbules will shine in a lively brownish lustre becoming a nature's own sparkle material. This may help explain why peacock herl has been a proven and widely used material in fishing flies since the early Middle Ages.

Coincidentally, the green-grey and brown-bronze colours are the most recurring in all the rivers of the world, except for rivers that flow in volcanic areas such as those in Iceland. So, this chromatic change in the fly — from dry to wet — makes the body of the fly more like the color of the bottom of many watercourses. This could be one of the keys to understanding its effectiveness. This is one of the many mysteries of fly fishing that makes it particularly fascinating.

In summary, the APP (Alo's Partridge & Peacock) appears to fish as a very slender body and of a colour certainly similar to the bottom, surrounded by partridge barbs, which have a strong light-dark contrast. The barbs are very mobile, like the legs of an insect worth eating.

Dressing

Hook: wet fly size 10 or 8
Tying thread: 8/0 pre-waxed black
Tail: natural grey partridge feather barbs
Body: two peacock herls twisted in a loop and wound
Ribbing: a strand of Krystal Flash rainbow or pearl, alternatively fine Mirage Tinsel
Hackle: natural grey partridge feather

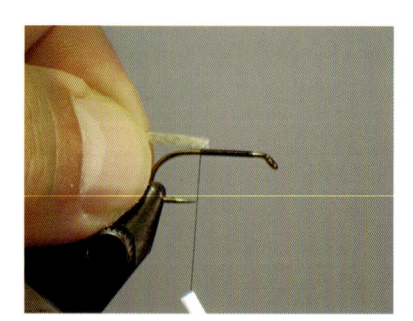

Step 1. Cover the hook shank with your tying thread and tie in the barbs for the tail.

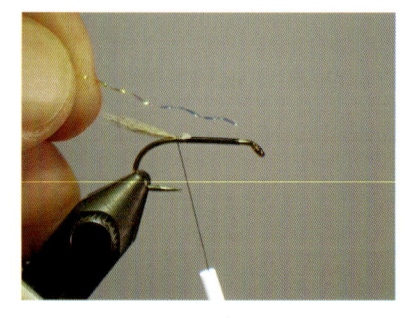

Step 2. Tie in the ribbing.

90

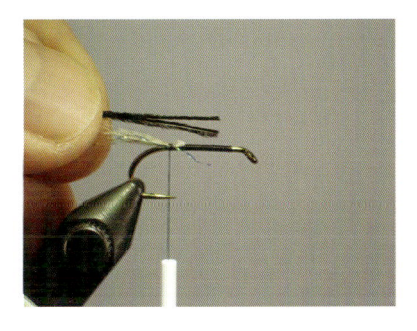

Step 3. Tie in two peacock herls together and wind them forward along the hook shank.

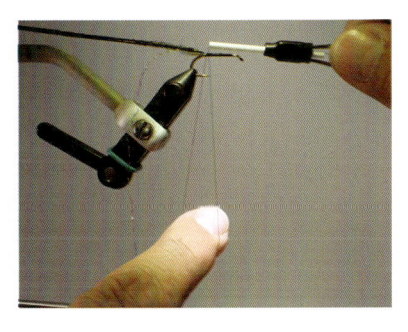

Step 4. Form a loop with the tying thread.

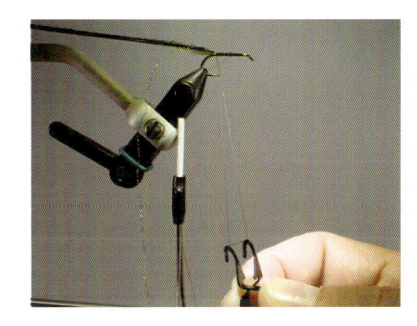

Step 5. Insert the peacock herls into the loop.

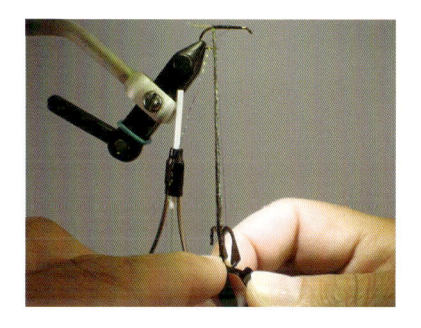

Step 6. After twisting a robust peacock chenille is formed.

Step 7. Wind the fly body towards the eye.

Step 8. Wind the body ribbing.

Step 9. Tie in the partridge hackle by the tip.

Step 10. Fold the feather barbs using the back of your scissors.

Step 11. Wind the hackle while stroking the barbs backwards.

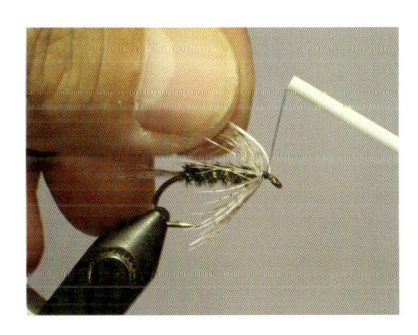

Step 12. Lock and turn the feather stem over and tie down for added strength. Clip off the excess.

Step 13. Whip finish and varnish the fly head.

Step 14. Alo's Partridge & Peacock is ready to fish.

Swing the Fly Anthology 2023   91

"Rogue in Winter II," by Richard C. Harrington

Grand Venues

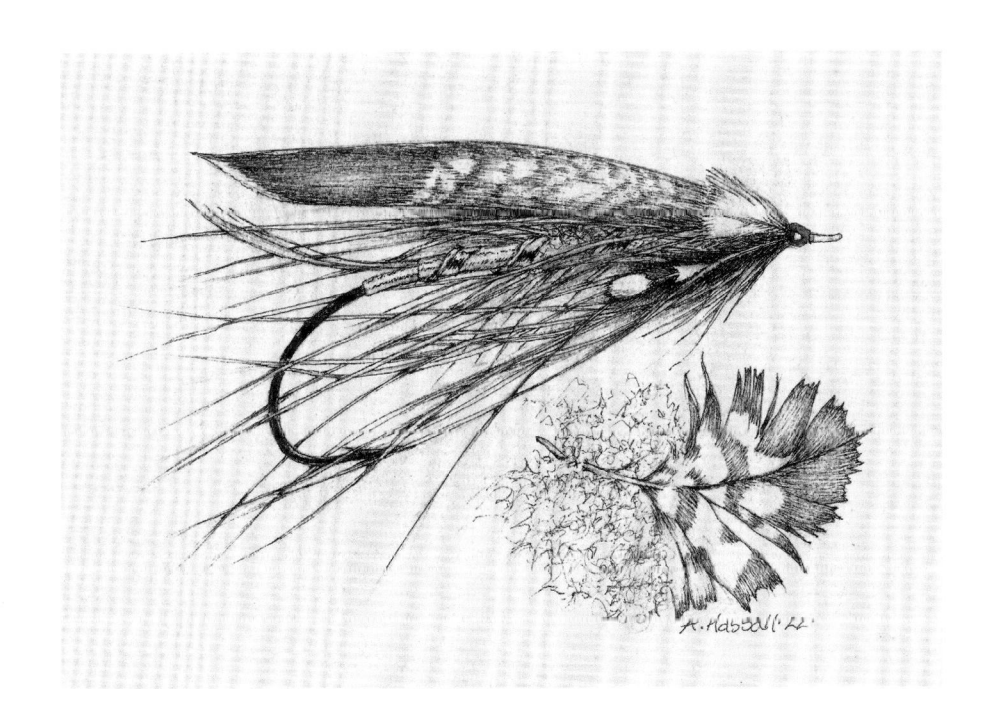

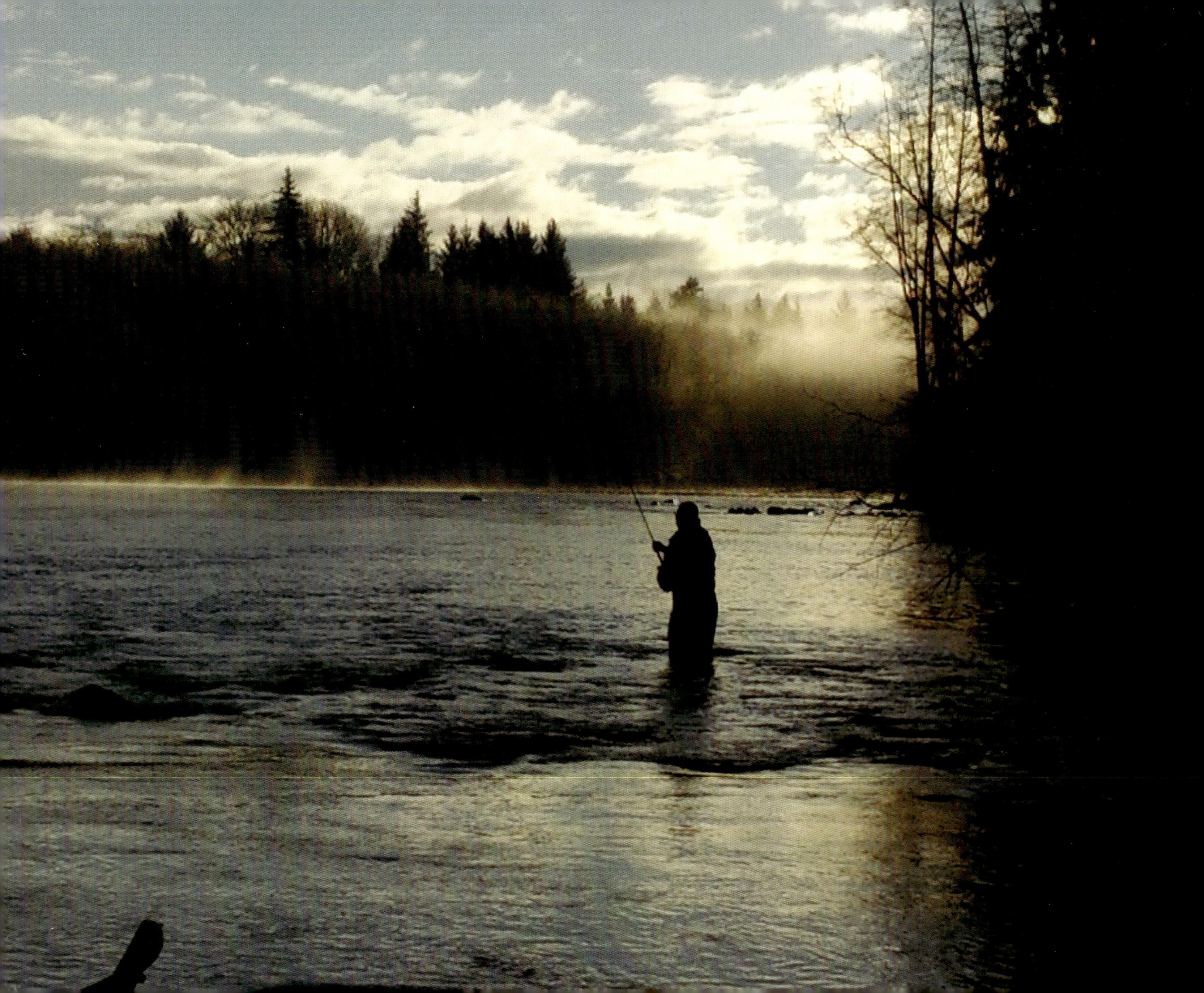

RESOLVE

Jim Ray

I never thought it'd be this way, this coming of old age.
Somehow I thought it'd pass me by and I'd be young until I die.
My joints began to creak and groan a dozen years ago:
I need ever stronger glasses now when tying fishing flies.

Now here I am, with rod in hand, upon these rounded river rocks.
Where once the bank was not a thought, I pause to plan my course.
Familiar ground's less certain now as age has changed my gait.
The path looks steeper than recalled, the river has more pace.

Was the water somewhat lower when I fished here in the past?
Can I once again wade boldly to that hidden mid-stream bar?
The fish are there, I'm certain now; somehow the run seems not so deep.
With confidence I use my staff; my creaky joints at work at last,
And that long-remembered run grows closer with each step.

My pace is slower now for sure, but I will not concede.
The river's cold has warmed my soul in ways I can't express.
Two steps down I make my cast; the river swings it tight.
I feel the tug at last, and smiling now, resolve to not regress.
There are so many memories to make, before the final cast.

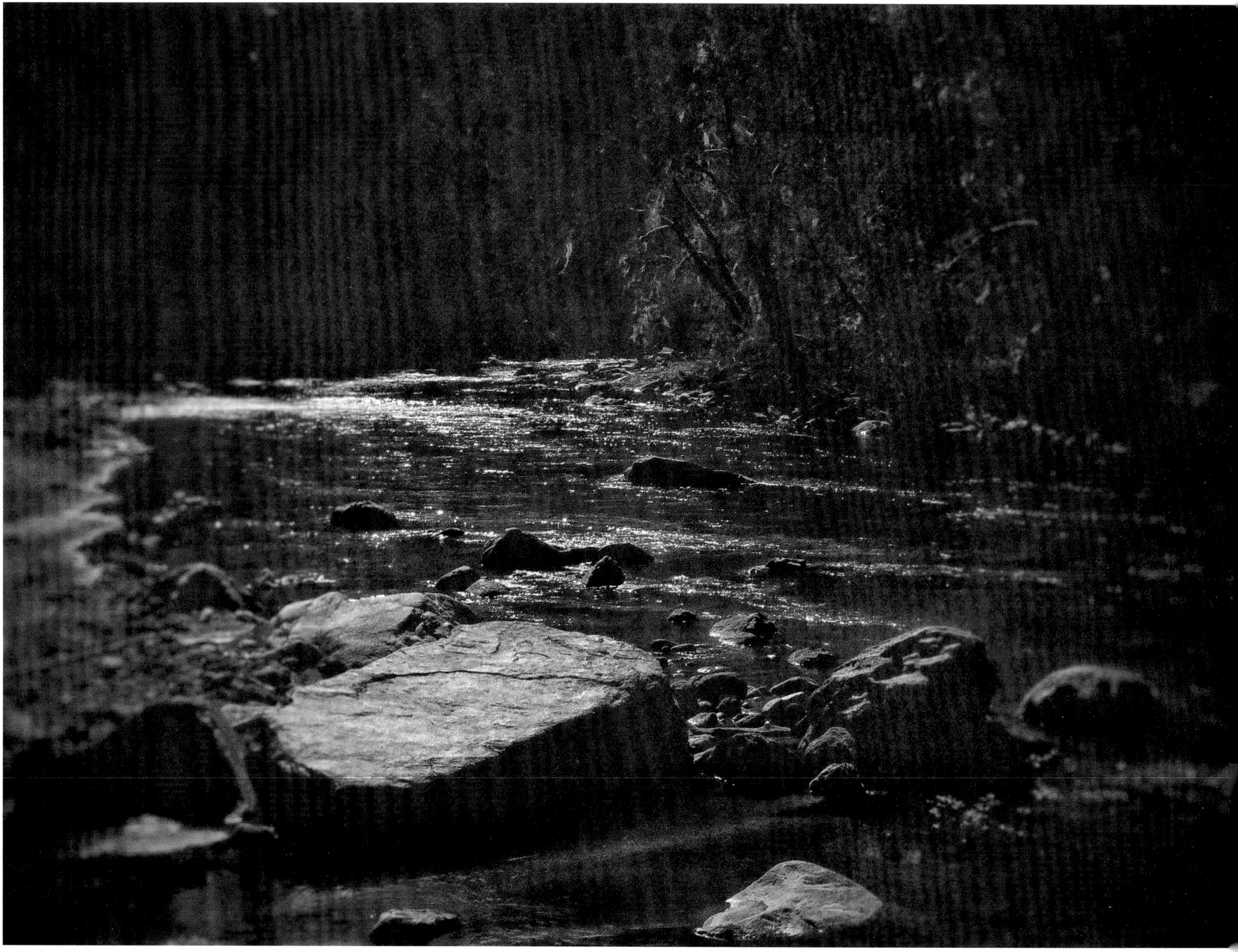

RIVERS

Joseph Rossano

W*hat is a river?* The question does not seek a literal answer. In the nearly 40 years since my moving to the Pacific Northwest, understanding the rivers of my home and the life which they support has been an all-consuming endeavor. This obsessive curiosity has permeated my artwork, my free time, and my understanding of life in general.

For at least 12 months leading up to this writing, I had been wrestling with the question above. Rivers hold something different for each of us — what do they mean to you? I found time to consider my question more closely as 2023 saw a return to the past. For five days each week from March 26 through April 30, my home rivers again played host to a catch-and-release fishery. During those 30 days, I was able to reconnect with my backyard. It was glorious. Time focused on these rivers offered an opportunity to reflect on what it was that drew me here — and to reflect on what it is about rivers that draws others to them, too. I found that, for me, it's only marginally about the fish. Yet, after those 30 days immersed in my backyard, I came away with many more questions than answers — what follows are some of both.

Identity

Most know that a river is a pathway for water moving downhill, seeking its way to the sea — all the while meandering through the countryside, cutting through steep mountains, reshaping landscapes — constantly changing, constantly moving. Rivers are arteries bringing life, bringing nutrients to the land — the water that forms them the blood of an ecosystem. They are highways for migration, for birds, fish, seeds, people and soil. Rivers are the liquid of life — the protoplasm that takes on the hue of the sky and trees — not to mention the many species of fish, insects, and organic matter that are borne by, or swim in, their depths.

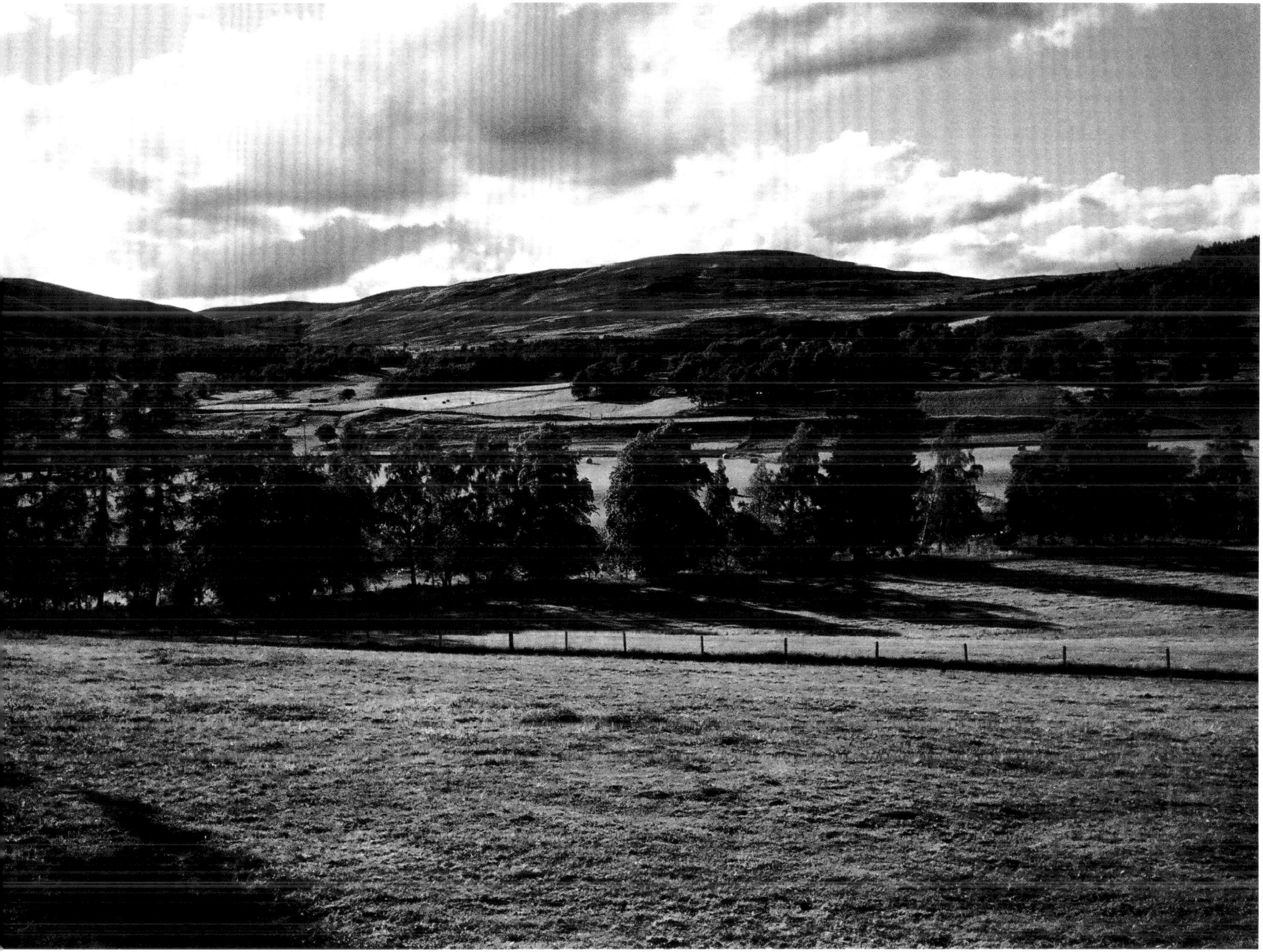

People

Are rivers the people with whom we share them — the relationships we develop while streamside — the locals who put up with our fanaticism — those with whom we later relate our experiences in the comfort of our own home, or around the campfire? Those to whom we impart a river's truth — revealed through a solitary experience — now, too, part of how we remember the river.

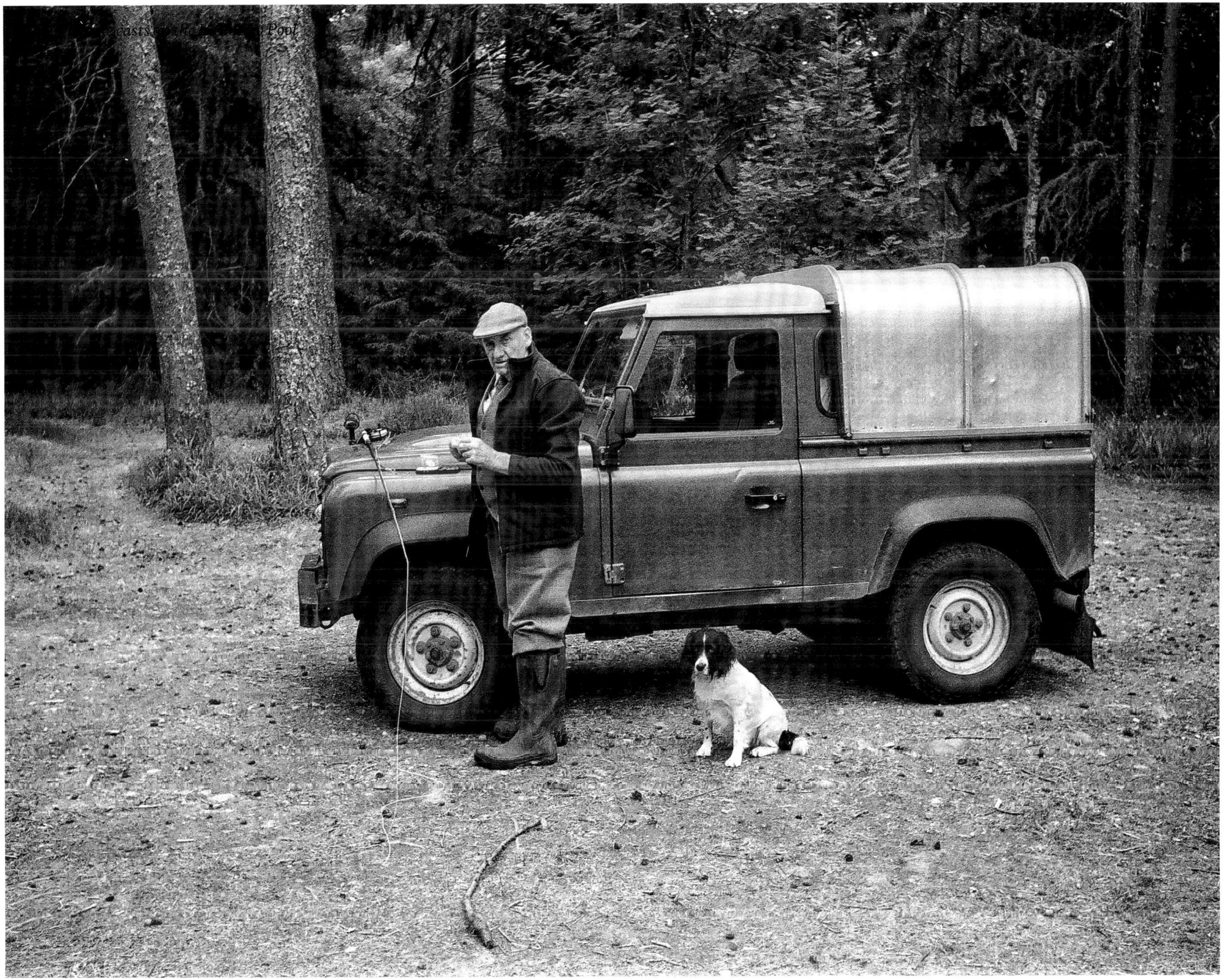

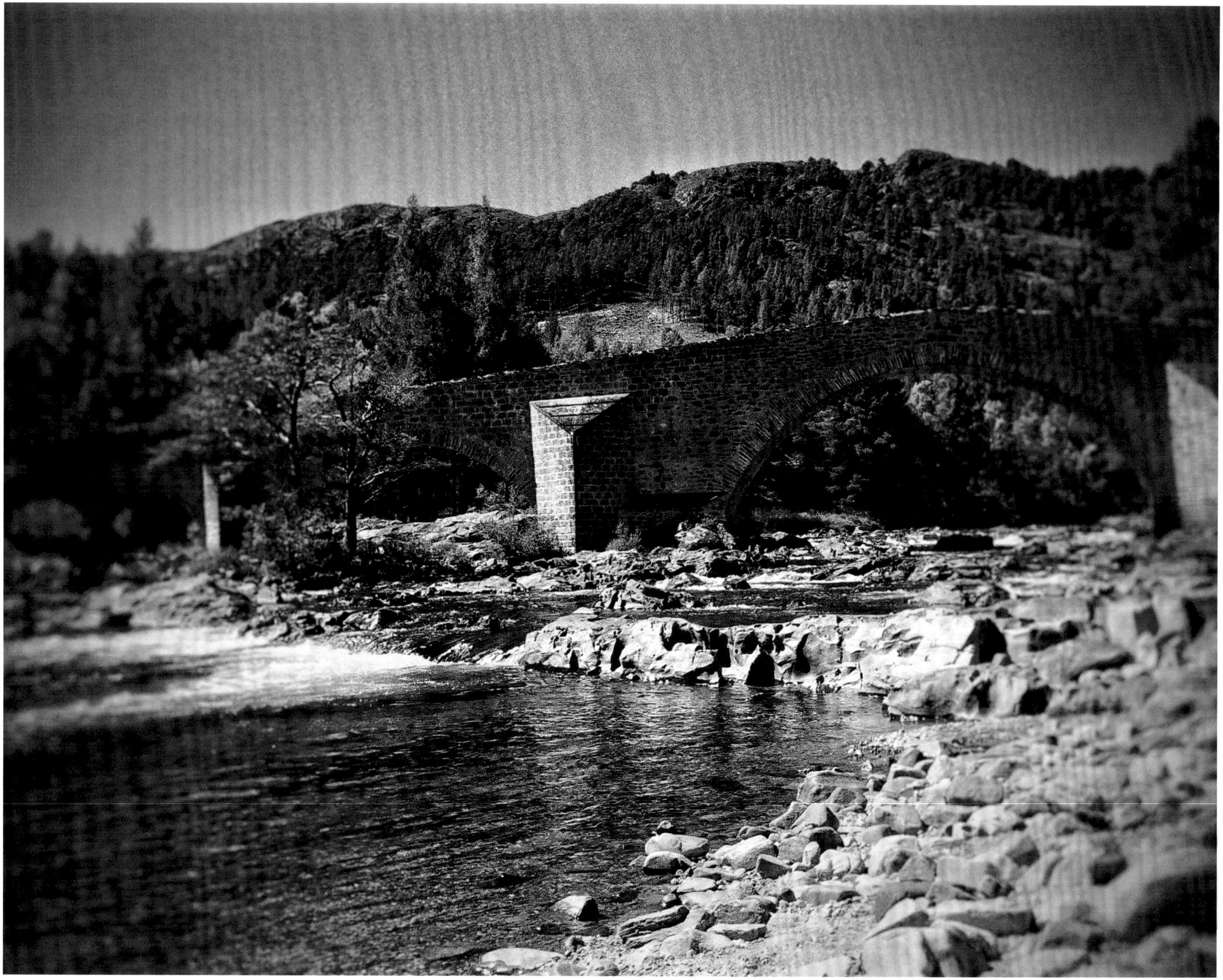

Moods

To understand rivers, do we have to understand their moods — do rivers even have moods, or are moods how we ascribe our logic to these living geologic phenomena? In late autumn, when approaching flood stage, swollen and filled with the detritus of the land — are they angry — or is this what a baptism looks like, both nutrients and waste washed to the sea? At the peak of summer, in near drought conditions, are they suffocating — are they choking, or — have they become subterranean, living an air-conditioned life? In the darkest days of winter, when the pancake ice has become one solid mass from bank to bank — is the river sleeping, or — is it birthing a new generation?

Associations

For us to see rivers, to understand them, we create associations — observing characteristics, defining the rivers — defining our memories of them. The trees, giant cedars or maples, through which their waters course — the fish hiding, resting in the cover their shadows provide — and we, too, taking comfort in their shade. Rivers are their boulders — giant stones, boulders of basalt, round and black — or flowing over metamorphic rock, jagged, in hues of pink and red — or meandering, serpent-like, through a sand-filled landscape. We anticipate every visit streamside — finding the places that quicken our heartbeats, that bring us calm — some call this inner peace.

To some, a river is springtime — the smell of cottonwood and alder sprouts — that sweet syrupy fragrance — or the tracks of an otter, tail slithering between its footprints in the sand — or morels poking up through the previous year's decaying leaves. Children sharing a pool with king salmon on hot summer days. A fall afternoon — watching as two minks chase each other. Many log their hope in the time they spend on a river — those extra minutes streamside in July counteracting the hard frost of a northeastern winter's night. Returning to the river in our old age — a return to our youth — a return of life. We are made whole by rivers.

Life

In your heart, your soul, your mind, your dreams, your waking visions, your senses of smell and touch — and a host of other things unique to each and every one of you — what is a river? Maybe it is simple — maybe rivers are life? How we think about them, and what they hold for each of us, is precious. And protecting those memories, and the places from which they are born, will ensure that others will also have these experiences — will also appreciate these places that are so precious.

How do we return life to our rivers? In those moments between casts, or walking a familiar path through the forest while headed to a favorite pool, or paddling between runs, or driving a mist-filled canyon, or leaning upstream against the river's push — in those moments, we become immersed in our surroundings. In those moments — moments when we truly become connected to a river — we are filled with calm. And at those moments, it's not about the fish. We are caught up in something much bigger than the fish, bigger than us. Maybe, it's at these moments — when we are truly connected — that we give a little of our life back to the rivers that have given us so much of theirs.

Memories

Yet, do rivers see us — are rivers in some way sentient — sapient — do they know we have been here, do they remember us — do they remember those who revere them so? Do the trees that have stood still against time, flood, and fire, silent witnesses to our passing — do they hold a memory of us? The land through which these arteries pulse life — does it record our interaction?

Do rivers remember washing us clean — baptizing us, returning life — and hope? Can we love a river — and how does it love us back? How a river returns our love is different for each of us. The transaction between rivers and humans — life — we are swept into. We become part of the flow. All the water contained on this planet has been here since the moment our blue spot began spinning. The dinosaurs are long gone, any evidence of their existence nearly wiped clean — but water is still here. And it flows to the sea.

(Also on the cover) The big falls at the Big Laxa in Iceland. What a playground to present your flies. I even tried to swing a big Sunray Shadow from the high wall at the other side of the falls but cannot deny that I was glad when those 10 minutes so close to that falls were over, and we changed from the high bank into lower ground and wading in the river.

A BAVARIAN TRAVELING MAN

Thomas Wöelfle

Traveling these days always is paired with a big question mark, especially if you see it from the green side. I don't want to make a big drama out of it, but if you fly and use the plane you are a potential environmental bad guy, at least from the side of all the green politicians and those who think they are.

I drive an electric car — and rode an e-bike for exactly two weeks until it was stolen — to compensate for my travels but have the feeling that driving with e-power does not make it better. I accept it, live with it, try my best, but I don't want to give up my fishing on salmon, trout and steelhead rivers around the globe. It is selfish, but I benefited so much from traveling that even with all the negative aspects to the world's climate I also see the importance of getting together, especially in times like we have now.

Here in Germany we are not too far away from war [Ukraine]. My biggest fear is losing our greatest value: freedom. Being free in my thoughts, my point of view is elementary in my life.

I grew up in times when the world opened, the wall fell, Germany was reunited, and people were eager to travel, explore and get to know each other. Lots of discussions, hefty ones, good ones and bad ones followed on many banks of different rivers with one thing in common — learning from each other and accepting each other. Live and let live.

My first big step over the Atlantic was in 1989. I booked a flight to Salt Lake City, hired a car, drove north, slept in a tent beside the car and just fished all the great rivers in Montana, Wyoming and Utah for five weeks.

In those days I had no kids. Relationships simply ended whenever I booked a flight to fish somewhere in the States or elsewhere.

Those were great times where pressure on rivers was low, and I learned so much from all the fishermen there. I think they also learned a little from me.

Looking at life from different angles is important. That also helps in fishing. I got so much input, shared great experiences along the river banks, sometimes small things, sometimes big things, sometimes rewarded with a big, bright salmon or trout in my hands. When I put it together I definitely can say that traveling made me wiser, kept me open and prevented me from getting blind. No matter where and in which country I swung my flies, the people I met — with a few exceptions — just wanted to have a good and peaceful time together.

So you see there still are good reasons to pack your stuff together, take the plane and explore. But in all the traveling I did, the fishing was and is my motor. I try to keep it going and as long as I fill it with days on the water, the rivers and lakes, it runs smoothly, relaxed, unstressed and steady. This is my approach to an open-minded life.

Fishing was and is my way to connect to different people from different nations, to share point of views and go through the world with open eyes without forgetting my roots. That's why I cannot let you go without a parting picture from the River Isar — my river, my home ... my life.

Bears that are so abundant at times that you really get used to it, although with a slight queasy feeling like this situation at the Ayakulik River on Kodiak Island. Big Mama and her two cubs came by every day to have a quick look of what we do, what we catch and probably what we leave behind. Or was it the tree that gained great popularity among bears and eagles?

For me ... this is a picture that, beside the steelhead itself, shows the reason why I jump in the plane to cross the Atlantic. The scenery where you or I can swing the fly is outstanding. This was an early morning that gave me just two minutes to "shoot." Two minutes where the clouds opened up to give the sun the space to light Hudson Bay Mountain along the Bulkley River.

Swing the Fly Anthology 2023

This lake in Italy I can reach by car in about four hours from Munich. It is a lake in Trentino. I love Italy, South Tyrol and Trentino, where you can catch trout in overwhelming scenery and get a perfect espresso even in the smallest hut. Here Romano is getting a gentle take on a soft hackle at Lago Malghette, near Madonna di Campiglio. At this place, a small river runs into the lake and gives you just the right speed to do a loooong and slooooow swing.

Rain ... a magic word in the life of a salmon and steelhead fisherman. It can make your day or ruin your day. Here my friend Michael is swinging his fly for Atlantic salmon at Renna Pool at the Gaula River in Norway. Believe it or not, I had one of my best days right there in pouring rain and rising water. Three bright Atlantics in four hours, none below 20 pounds ... feels good to talk about that, but it was quite a while ago.

The de Havilland Beaver planes of Alaska are legendary and well restored and looked after. This one one from Garry Butch King from Wildman Lodge is an eye catcher. I suggested a short break on the dark sand at sea in front of the plane to get my picture.

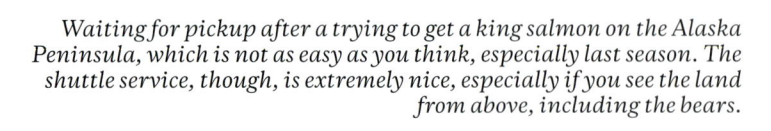

Waiting for pickup after a trying to get a king salmon on the Alaska Peninsula, which is not as easy as you think, especially last season. The shuttle service, though, is extremely nice, especially if you see the land from above, including the bears.

My home; my river. Here ist is a portrait of myself in front of the Wittelsbacher Bridge at the River Isar in downtown Munich. That morning I crossed the river to an island placed my tripod with camera to get and shoot myself in the river with the full moon in the background. After that I waded downstream and finished the morning with two perfect rainbows on the swing.

Photo: Patrick Parry

Conservation Corner

MY DAUGHTER'S NORTH UMPQUA

Kirk Blaine, Native Fish Society

Sitting here writing next to my three-day-old daughter, I am already thinking about spending countless hours on the river with her watching the birds, looking for holding fish, and hiking the banks of my favorite river. If my passion rubs off, it won't be long before she is knee deep wet wading next to me, swinging a scraggly Muddler looking for her first North Umpqua summer steelhead. I can hardly wait.

Six years ago, I moved to southern Oregon from Colorado. I knew little to nothing about the North Umpqua River, let alone steelhead fishing. Fast-forward to now, I'm hooked — obsessed — with the commitment of swinging flies for these iconic fish, not to mention neck deep in conservation, working to protect this magical watershed and the fish that call it home. As a passionate angler, I feel privileged to live only a short distance from the prized North Umpqua fly water and spend countless hours and days fishing for that single pull or explosion on my fly. It hardens my heart to think about the future of this river and these fish.

As many know, the North Umpqua River's angling history runs deep. Parallel to angling runs an ethic and commitment to conservation. It started with anglers such as Zane Grey back in the 1930s advocating for fewer salmon traps causing unintended harm to summer steelhead.

During this timeframe, the 33 miles of the upper North Umpqua were designated fly fishing only. Frank and Jeanne Moore moved to the watershed shortly after Frank returned from World War II — idols whose sincere grace and loving personalities have improved the North Umpqua and life on earth. In early January of 2021, the legendary Frank Moore left the banks of the North Umpqua River after 98 years. He spent a number of those working to protect and conserve this steelhead Shangri-La.

Despite hard work, dedication and persistence, we have fewer fish than ever before. The beloved North Umpqua steelhead, both summer and winter, continue to decline before our very eyes.

Exactly 1,349 wild summer steelhead returned to the North Umpqua in 2022. One of the lowest returns ever on record. This followed the catastrophic return of 2021, where only 450 wild summer steelhead returned. Historically, the 20-year average is close to 3,000 wild fish. The last five years, returns have averaged 1,412 wild summer steelhead. To say runs are declining would be an understatement. To say things are cyclical would be wrong.

The North Umpqua River continues to die a tragic death — large-scale logging, dilapidated old dams, excessive hatchery fish spawning in the wild, and catastrophic wildfires. Death by a thousand cuts.

To their credit, in 2022, the Oregon Department of Fish and Wildlife Commission recognized how these fish could thrive — not through human alteration or production of artificial fish, but through natural selection of the wild that are determined to survive. The Commission halted the production of hatchery summer steelhead to eliminate the competition and introgression on wild fish. This management change will increase productivity of wild fish for generations to come. These are the fish that will help ensure summer steelhead will persist. A step in the right direction to further heal this wounded river.

The Native Fish Society and other local conservation organizations are working together to bring positive change to the North Umpqua. Last spring, advocates gathered to plant trees on decommissioned roads. Land managers are completing massive floodplain reconnection work, replanting riparian areas post fire, and developing plans to replace culverts inhibiting fish passage. Amazing work that will improve the long-term sustainability of this magical river.

Yet, a quite literal block stands, impeding progress of our work. Below the upper stretches of the North Umpqua River near the town of Roseburg sits Winchester Dam. The dam is a 140-year-old timber crib dam that was primarily designed for water collection and hydropower and sits 118 miles upriver from the Pacific Ocean. Hydropower was removed from the dam in the 1980s and the City of Roseburg's water intake was moved downstream. Ownership of the dam changed to the Winchester Water Control District, a group of wealthy homeowners that live on the reservoir pool above the dam. Its main purpose? Provide private recreation to a few hundred homeowners living above the dam. A hoity-toity private water ski lake on a public waterway causing delay, harm and death to salmon, steelhead and lamprey, that depend on the river's moving water.

The major 'why' the Winchester Dam is one of the largest fish-killing dams in the Pacific Northwest surrounds the fish ladder, ladder placement and complete neglect to maintain the dam. The ladder was built in the early 1940s to provide fish passage and

Photo: Chris Corbin

Photo: Chris Corbin

has had little to no updates. Since then, there has been no substantial maintenance, no ladder updates to better pass salmon and steelhead. It remains as is, a 1940s style fish ladder falling apart, harming and killing fish. Winchester dam fails to pass state or federal fish passage regulations. Removing this neglected dam would open 160 miles of prime spawning and rearing habitat for fish to thrive.

To top it all off, despite a confusing design that is outdated and dilapidated, the ladder sits in the wrong spot to provide uninterrupted fish passage. It sits on the shallowest portion of the river. Fish traveling upstream must move from the south side of the dam, banging their heads against the dam face to the north side of the dam before finally reaching the entrance to the fish ladder. While making this journey, fish encounter hundreds of false attraction holes (holes in the dam that look like a possible passage for fish).

In 2018 the owners "repaired" Winchester Dam on the North Umpqua River, obtaining emergency repair permits from regulators and pouring green concrete into the river, killing hundreds of fish. The Oregon Department of Fish and Wildlife (ODFW) clearly documented these abusive and neglectful actions to the river. Conservation groups notified DEQ, who pressed charges. The homeowners, Winchester Water Control District, fought the charges in court, claiming they were not guilty, ultimately losing and were fined a mere $56,000.

As of the writing of this article, the Winchester Water Control District intends to repair false attraction holes in August 2023. The owners are requesting to shut down the ladder function and fish passage for three weeks or 21 days while these repairs occur during the tail end of peak summer steelhead migration. According to historic dam counts 10 percent of the summer steelhead migration occurs during this time. However, repairs don't require the owners to shut down fish ladder function, engineers and project managers could easily propose building coffer dams (earthen dams that isolate the dam face) instead of dewatering the dam. ODFW has authorized these plans and is not requiring homeowners to build coffer dams — a clear disregard to protecting our public resources.

Dewatering the dam will strand fish migrating at that time, cooking them in the danger-

Swing the Fly Anthology 2023   117

Photo: Chris Corbin

ously hot waters downstream. A true summer steelhead massacre is currently brewing in the planning and approval by ODFW and dc. In 2015 conservation groups managed and funded the removal of Gold Ray Dam on the famous Rogue River of southern Oregon — a project that was designed to overwhelmingly support restoring salmon and steelhead. When completing this project ODFW did not allow for one minute of uninterrupted fish passage, while allowing Winchester Water Control District to block fish passage for three weeks.

The plans to repair the dam this August will not solve the long-term issues or problems with the dam or ladder. Plans will simply fill holes that have been created from decades of neglect by using polyurethane plastic foam — another way the owners are pinching pennies to make repairs — putting harmful plastics in our rivers, affecting drinking water and our fish. Instead of using plastic, owners could easily use cobble, as they have in prior repairs. Included in the plans for repair is fixing the hole on the south side of the dam that was attempted to be repaired in 2018 by pouring green concrete into the river. The repair in 2018 lasted less than four years.

Winchester Water Control District continues to avoid the rule of law when it comes to maintaining their private dam. They have disregarded maintenance for the past 30 years and continue to pinch pennies at the cost of our river and our fish. A coalition of 17 conservation organizations offered to remove the dam for free, with no cost to homeowners. That offer was ignored and disregarded as though that would never happen.

Every cut continues to cause pain to the North Umpqua and its steelhead. The worst is those we can control — ways we can prevent these massive gouges in a river we all enjoy. Winchester Dam is one of those massive gouges that we can control.

As an angler and conservationist, I reflect on the history of the North Umpqua River — on Frank Moore and Zane Grey. I think about heroes of my past, pondering what I can do to make an impact. What can we as a community do to help save the North Umpqua River?

As anglers and advocates, it is our job to apply constant social and political pressure pushing Winchester Water Control District to make the right decision in removing this deadbeat dam. We need advocates across the region, nation and world to speak up for this river and these fish. Call folks locally and share why the North Umpqua is important to you. Tell Douglas County and Roseburg political leadership this dam must be removed or rebuilt to state and federal regulations. Write an opinion piece in your local paper or the Roseburg News Review sharing why you come to these iconic waters. Talk with your colleagues at work. Inform your neighbors who might gear fish rather than swing flies. Now is the time we build an overwhelming groundswell of advocates demanding Winchester Dam follow the rule of law!

As for my daughter's future here on the North Umpqua, I hope she gets the opportunity to experience these amazing waters. Swing a fly for summer steelhead. Spend a cold rainy day out searching for unicorns in March. It's those thoughts that empower my work for the North Umpqua — to give her the same opportunities. I want these fish around for her. In the words of my wife, "Our hope is one day she will be able to enjoy the natural world as much as we have — that it will foster her sense of adventure, bring her peace, and give her a place to always belong."

To experience the opportunity to swing a fly for a bright summer steelhead on the North Umpqua River.

YES. HE NAMED THE WRONG RIVER.

Conservation Corner

THREE-EYE SEEING

Daniel Ritz

Developments in the Campaign to Save Upper Columbia and Snake River Steelhead and Salmon

It's late March, and the most recent volley of political outrage and partisan legislation is all over the news. Speaking at a conservation summit at the interior department, President Joe Biden recently said he was re-committing to working with tribal leaders, Idaho Republican Rep. Mike Simpson and Washington's Democratic Sens. Patty Murray and Maria Cantwell, "to bring healthy and abundant salmon runs back to the Colorado River system."

Yes. He named the wrong river. Goes to show how committed they are.

Only days later, this commitment to the fish was countered with the presentation of the Northwest Energy Security Act by Rep. Dan Newhouse (R-WA), Rep. Cathy McMorris Rogers (R-WA), Sen. Jim Risch (R-ID) and Sen. Steve Daines (R-MT) to save the lower Snake River dams (LSRDs.)

"The four LSRDs are integral to flood control, navigation, irrigation, agriculture, and recreation in Central Washington and throughout the Pacific Northwest (PNW) — to put it simply, we cannot afford to lose them," Newhouse claimed.

Insert a communal chorus of sighs. The LSRDs were designed to provide exactly zero flood control.

"It's time to recognize that salmon runs are improving at record rates ..." chimed in Rodgers. This year (2023), National Oceanic and Atmospheric Administration (NOAA) fish return forecasts show the Tucannon — which, worth noting, is in Rodgers' own district and once produced tens of thousands of salmon annually — is expected to have as few as 50 spawning spring Chinook hit the gravel. Currently the Tucannon supports the only remaining population of spring Chinook in the lower Snake River, as well as summer steelhead, fall Chinook and bull trout.

Dismal forecasts from NOAA include summer run Snake River steelhead returns, which in 2023 are expected to be the lowest of all time. Rampant finger pointing between environmentalists and free-market zealots suggest this year will be a year not unlike the decades of others before it. That devilish shifting baseline syndrome has some celebrating anything better than the worst of all time. However, the real truth is that the saga of saving Columbia and Snake River salmon and steelhead has turned a monumental corner.

A New Chapter

For decades, anglers throughout the PNW have been focused on discovering what is causing and what can be done to salvage the scraps of North America's historically largest anadromous fish populations.

This last year was a crucial transition, even while the public-facing political and social

WHILE PROGRESS APPEARS TO HAVE BEEN MADE TO RIGHT THE SHIP IN WHAT WILL GO DOWN AS THE MOST EXPENSIVE FAILED RESTORATION EFFORT IN THE HISTORY OF THE PLANET ($24-BILLION SINCE 1980, AFTER INFLATION), SALMON AND STEELHEAD, AS THE SAYING GOES, SUFFER THE DEATH OF A THOUSAND CUTS.

pissing matches remain fixated on scientific consensus as to the cause and solution to these cataclysmic declines. At the highest levels, this campaign has shifted from "why is this happening" and "what is responsible" to "how exactly are we going to fix the problem?"

In July of 2022, in an unprecedented level of clarity, NOAA came out with its Rebuilding Interior Columbia River Salmon and Steelhead report. The report, in no uncertain terms, states: "For Snake River stocks, the centerpiece action is restoring the lower Snake River via dam breaching. Restoring more normalized reach-scale hydrology and hydraulics, and thus river conditions and function in the lower Snake River, requires dam breaching. Breaching can address the hydrosystem threat by decreasing travel time for water and juvenile fish, reducing powerhouse encounters, reducing stress on juvenile fish associated with their hydrosystem experience that may contribute to delayed mortality after reaching the ocean, and providing additional rearing and spawning habitat."

To be clear, in order of importance, certainty of need and confidence in action consequences, NOAA laid out the following:

1. Snake River spring/summer Chinook salmon and Snake River steelhead are listed along with upper Columbia River fall Chinook, upper Columbia spring Chinook and upper Columbia steelhead as the highest priority for protection and rebuilding.
2. The largest threats and limiting factors to be impacts from the hydrosystem, including direct and indirect mortality, where delayed effects from transitioning the hydrosystem occur the first year of ocean residence. Hydrosystem (direct and indirect) was listed as the highest magnitude of impact for ALL Snake River anadromous species.
3. A comprehensive suite of actions is essential to fully restore the basin's salmon and steelhead, but there are several centerpiece actions that are paramount for specific stocks. This includes Snake River stocks, where they describe the need to restore normative river conditions and function in the lower Snake River through dam breach as essential to population recovery.
4. Achieving the Columbia Basin Partnership (CBP) mid-range goals by 2050 requires urgent action. The analysis states that while 2021 offered a welcome respite, that is NOT expected to reverse the overwhelming decline in stocks (i.e., the increased frequency, magnitude, duration and scope of environmental downturn.)
5. Salmon life-cycle models predict that breaching the LSRDs — in combination with other fish protection measures (e.g., enhanced spill at the four lower Columbia River dams and freshwater habitat restoration) will likely achieve regional survival targets for Snake River Chinook salmon and steelhead.

Not only did NOAA finally decide to confirm what scientists have been screaming since at least the 1980s, the owners of the four LSRDs themselves, the Bonneville Power Administration (BPA), showed in a report — commissioned by BPA and conducted by the private consulting firm Energy and Environmental Economics (E3) — the cost of replacing energy from the LSRDs is within existing estimates and could potentially drop power bills for ratepayers.

This study, also published in July 2022, on potential power portfolios is unique as it presents a range of power production scenarios and costs associated with replacing the electrical power from four federal dams on the Lower Snake River in the event Congress were to authorize breaching or removing the dams.

That same week in July 2022, Gov. Inslee and Sen. Murray completed and released their final recommendations based on the joint federal-state LSRDs: Benefit Replacement Report to evaluate the future of the four LSRDs. In it, the Washington leaders clearly state "status quo is not a responsible option; extinction of salmon and steelhead is categorically unacceptable," and "action is needed to make breaching a viable option."

The joint federal-state process makes clear that — with adequate investment and coordination — it is possible to replace the services and benefits provided by the Dams in the event of breach and to mitigate the loss of others. It makes it clear that key infrastructure, energy, and other investments are needed to responsibly breach. "We are adamant that in any circumstance where the LSRDs would be breached, the replacement and mitigation of their benefits must be pursued before decommissioning and breaching" the recommendations state.

That brings us to April 2023, when multiple budget items are being debated in various committees of the Washington state legislature in Olympia. These three budget items could fund a robust energy study, an intensive irrigation analysis, and provide crucial details as to transportation needs specific to LSRD service replacement.

While the ultimate course to action, an act of Congress, remains painfully unclear, when the time comes, advocates may be able to make their requests in earnest, for not only has the "why," and the "what" been identified, we will truly be equipped with the "how."

The Third Eye

While progress appears to have been made to right the ship in what will go down as the most expensive failed restoration effort in the history of the planet ($24-billion since 1980, after inflation), salmon and steelhead, as the saying goes, suffer the death of a thousand cuts.

No one action, even one intended to fix the highest priority populations, is likely to be a cure-all.

Jim Lichatowich, author of *Salmon without Rivers: A History of the Pacific Salmon Crisis* and *Salmon, People, Place: A Biologists Search*

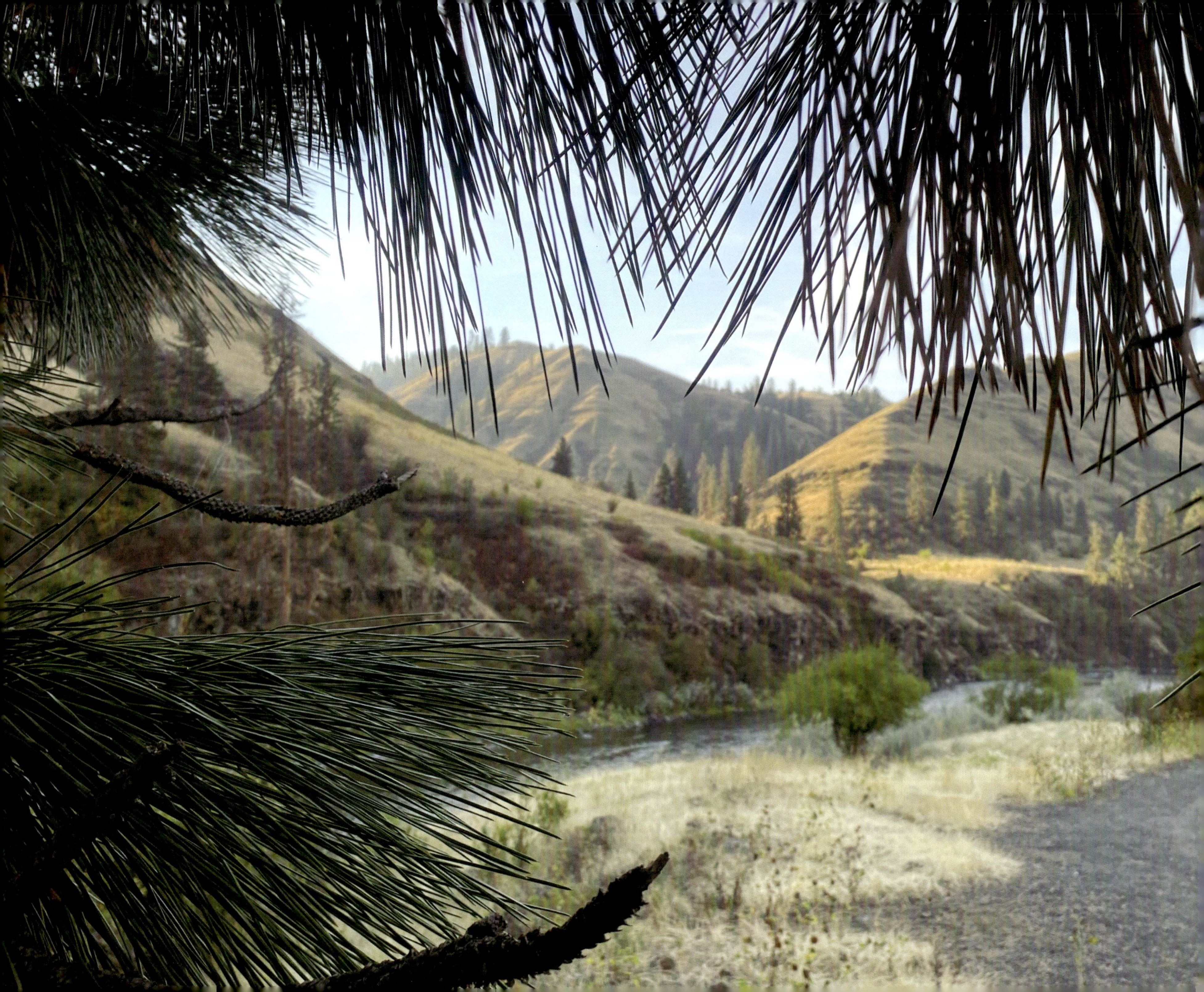

> IT [TWO-EYED SEEING] BRINGS TOGETHER TWO WAYS OF KNOWING TO ALLOW A DIVERSE GROUP OF PEOPLE TO USE ALL UNDERSTANDINGS TO IMPROVE THE WORLD."

for Salmon Recovery and Rick Williams, Research Associate in the Department of Biology at The College of Idaho, a third generation Idahoan and the author of ***Return To The River: Restoring Salmon Back to the Columbia River***, are recommending a new approach to exactly that dilemma in a new book.

These lions of science-based regional conservation are writing a new book — not yet titled but expected some time in late 2023 — explaining how the key to restoration of the Columbia River and all northwest anadromous fish stocks could be local, and best viewed through the eye of the fish itself. Williams shared that he and Lichatowich believe the answer lies in what he described as an extension of a key indigenous perspective.

The BC Medical Journal describes Two-Eyed Seeing as "developed from the teachings of Chief Charles Labrador of Acadia First Nation, but Mi'kmaw Elder Albert Marshall of the Eskasoni First Nation was the first to apply the concept of Two-Eyed Seeing in a Western setting. Specifically, Two-Eyed Seeing "refers to learning to see from one eye with the strengths of Indigenous knowledges and ways of knowing, and from the other eye with the strengths of Western knowledges and ways of knowing, and to use both of these eyes together for the benefit of all." Elder Albert Marshall emphasizes that Two-Eyed Seeing requires groups to weave between each respective way of knowing, as Indigenous knowledge may be more applicable than Western in certain situations, and vice versa. It brings together two ways of knowing to allow a diverse group of people to use all understandings to improve the world."

Williams and Lichatowich are building on that framework.

"Part 5, the last chapter, jumps into the more existential concepts," Williams says. "It ends saying there needs to be a new paradigm, and it needs to be salmon-centric. We're suggesting three paradigms: Western science, traditional ecological knowledge, and then there is a third, what we're calling Salmon Ecological Knowledge (SEJ).

"There will be five parts to the new book. The final chapter, which we're working on completing now, reveals a new conceptual foundation which is really giving them habitat, making sure they have access and get out of the way," Williams said.

"We're so focused on the big rivers that we've kind of forgotten about the success of the work of all these coastal watersheds," Williams says, sharing how across coastal Oregon, Washington and California, "movements for restoration and rebuilding are being born from local stakeholders." He described these movements, like the Smith River Alliance and the successful work being done by the Oregon Coast Coho Partnership, as "often very small in scale but intensely collaborative and very often include — if they aren't centered around — tribal perspectives."

"Many First People's perspectives viewed themselves as a part of the ecological community, with all other living things, and that many of those other living things provided food and resources for what they needed to live," Williams said. "They considered it a gift, and that gift created responsibility of stewardship and reciprocity so that you would treat that resource with respect."

So, in the fall of 2023, what can we take away from these undermentioned success stories and how do we apply them across cultures, states, management agencies and fishing communities?

Shannon Wheeler, Vice Chairperson of the Nez Perce Tribal Executive Committee, may have summarized it best when he told Eric Barker of the Lewiston Tribune, the tribe is ready to work with anyone to not only save salmon but also build a stronger future for the region. "We have come to the table and want to talk about what the energy system looks like,

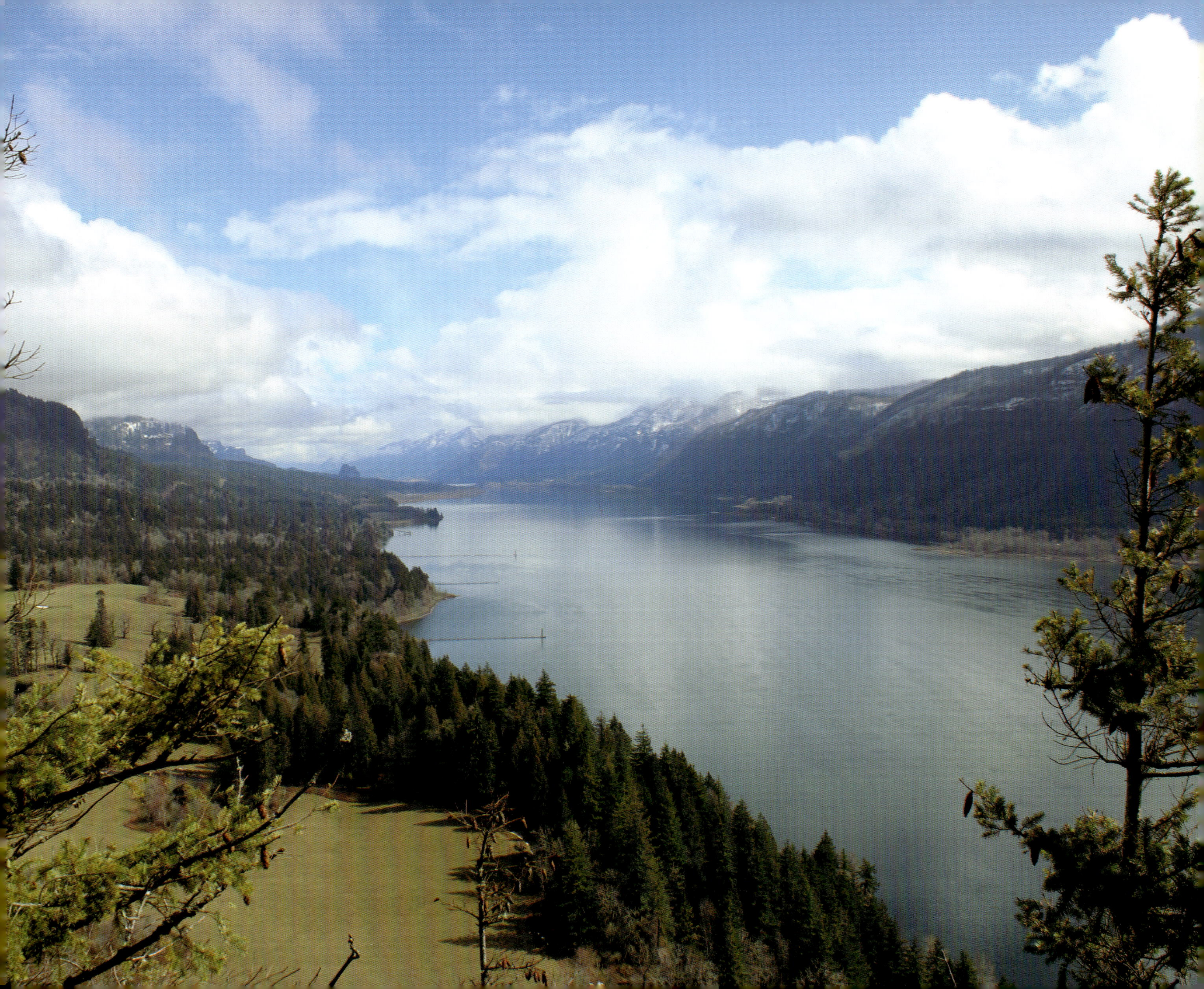

what the transportation system looks like and what we want the PNW to look like. We want it to grow and prosper and for salmon to grow and prosper," Wheeler said.

To Be Neighborly

So, what does all of this political boxing and paradigm shifting hyperbole mean for the Columbia and Snake River salmon and steelhead spey community? It shows us the key to truly sustainable restoration lies in our ability to extend our niche subculture into the greater fabric of our communities. The key to restoring the fish stocks we hold near and dear occurs by expanding our focus to far beyond our self-serving interests. The key may be in being neighborly and tackling the largest regional issues hammer and tong with the same approach that has shown success in these small, collaborative campaigns on coastal rivers.

True change, generational change, can happen when fishermen recognize that there are steps that can be taken that can increase fish returns, enable agriculture, and ensure energy for a growing PNW. Farmers, energy co-ops, and businessmen may then realize that conservationists and tribal voices are willing to cross historically impassable political, social and geographically barriers to get the Columbia and Snake Rivers somewhat closer to being connected.

There is a unique opportunity in front of us. There is a chance to reach across aisles, to break bread as a member of a disproportionately impacted community, and remember a rising tide raises all ships, as the kids say.

There will come a day, sooner than ever before, when those leading our communities into the future will have to be held accountable to us as constituents, as economic drivers, to ensure that common-sense action is taken responsibly to ensure that our children's future contains abundant salmon and steelhead.

If this past year showed us nothing, it showed us the changes needed for the fish are necessary and possible and could be a net benefit for all people.

Something we could venture to say — at risk of anthropomorphizing a Snake River steelhead's perspective — the fish have been able to "see" for time millennia.

Swing the Fly Anthology 2023

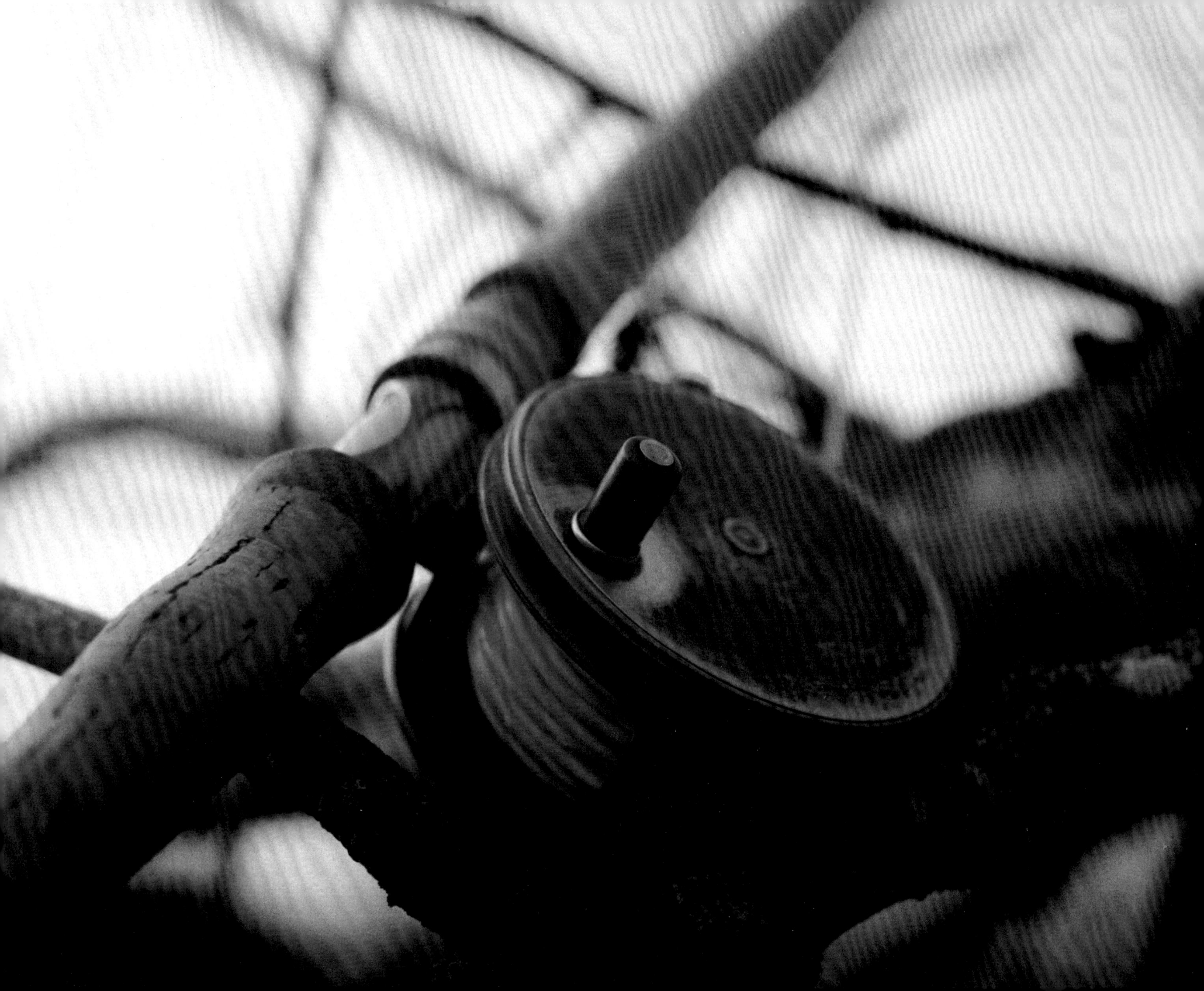

FILM IS NOT DEAD

Aaron Goodis

Shooting film and steelhead fly fishing are a lot alike. There is no room for instant gratification. You must truly enjoy the process, not knowing what the result may be.

Here in the Pacific Northwest I fly fish for winter steelhead, a fish of 10,000 casts. During my career as a fly fishing photographer, I have shot primarily digital images. The joke I often say is that at least when I'm shooting photos I can see the result and I know I've got something — basically I never get skunked!

When documenting a day or a season, I look for all the other reasons why we do this. It's the aesthetic of the sport, the spey casting, the camaraderie, the beautiful nature and rivers. And of course, the anticipation of catching one, or in my case, getting that perfect shot. I also love the equipment, old Hardy reels, double-handed spey rods and eye catching flies.

This season I wanted to try something different. I thought by documenting my days out with a film camera and a few rolls of black-and-white HP 5 film I would create the same feeling as I get when swinging through a likely steelhead run. No instant gratification. No way to see the finished results of the photos. I would have to wait and at the end of the season I would develop the rolls of film and hope for the best. I would hope that I would have enough photos to create this photo essay!

The anticipation is crazy, much like steelheading. I would have the lab develop the film then I would take the negatives into my studio and scan them. Once the images are scanned, I import them into the computer and use the software to convert the negatives into positives. Now I can see the finished results and like all rolls of film I have shot in the past, they never turn out exactly as I hoped! But that's the beauty of film photography, to be truly caught up in the moment when shooting with no way of knowing what the outcome will be.

In my mind, this is a direct comparison to fly fishing for steelhead — not knowing that the outcome and likely that we don't catch one — but the process is so enjoyable that it doesn't matter!

This season I fished primarily with my father and/or by myself. Fishing alone also made for an interesting challenge when trying to document the season with a film camera. And like most seasons, we did not catch a steelhead! I truly enjoyed the process and immersion that goes into shooting film with a manual SLR camera, fishing with my dad and of course swinging some flies! I hope you enjoy this photo essay and maybe you too will pick up a few rolls of film yourself! Film is definitely not dead yet! Cheers!

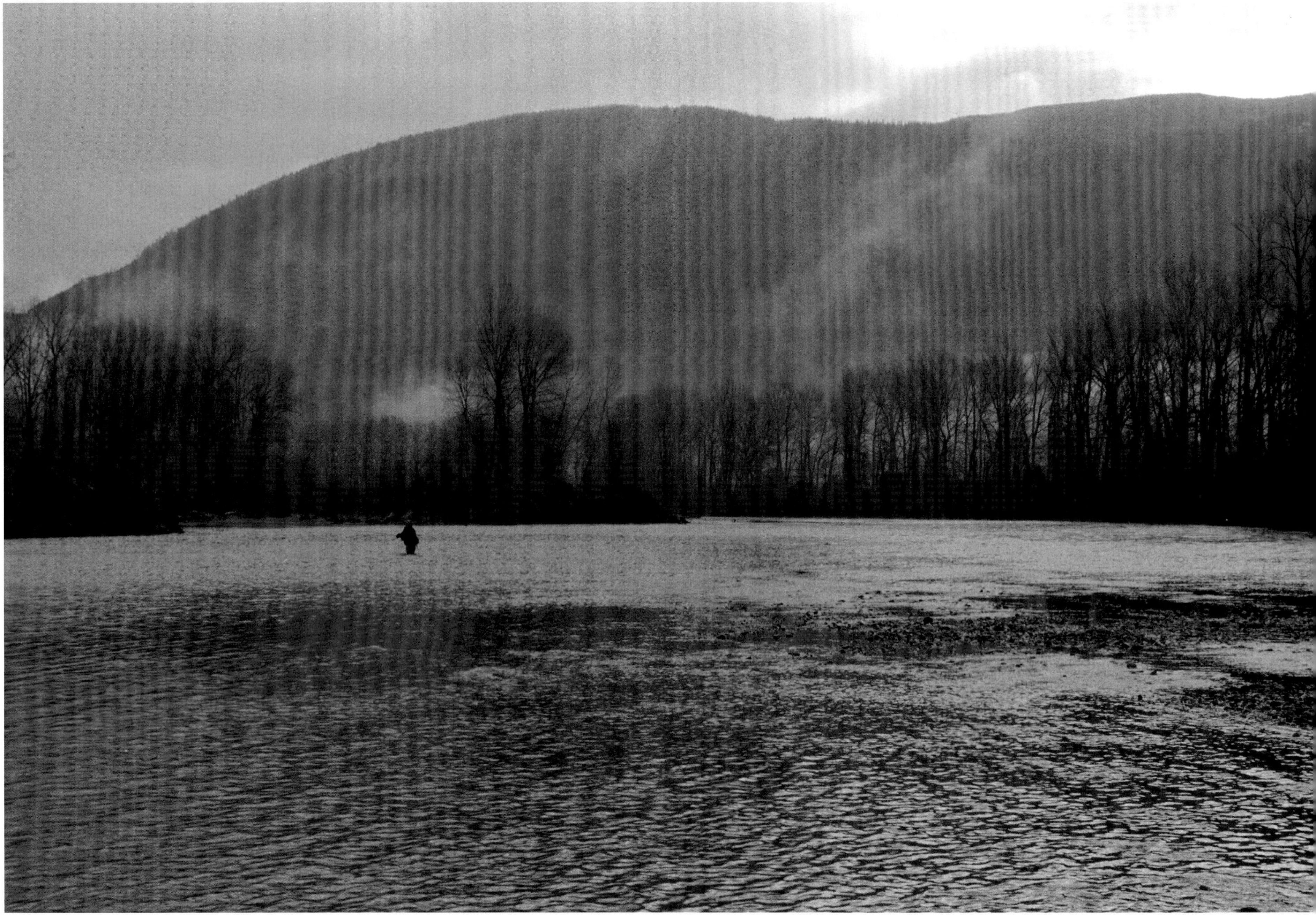

Swing the Fly Anthology 2023   131

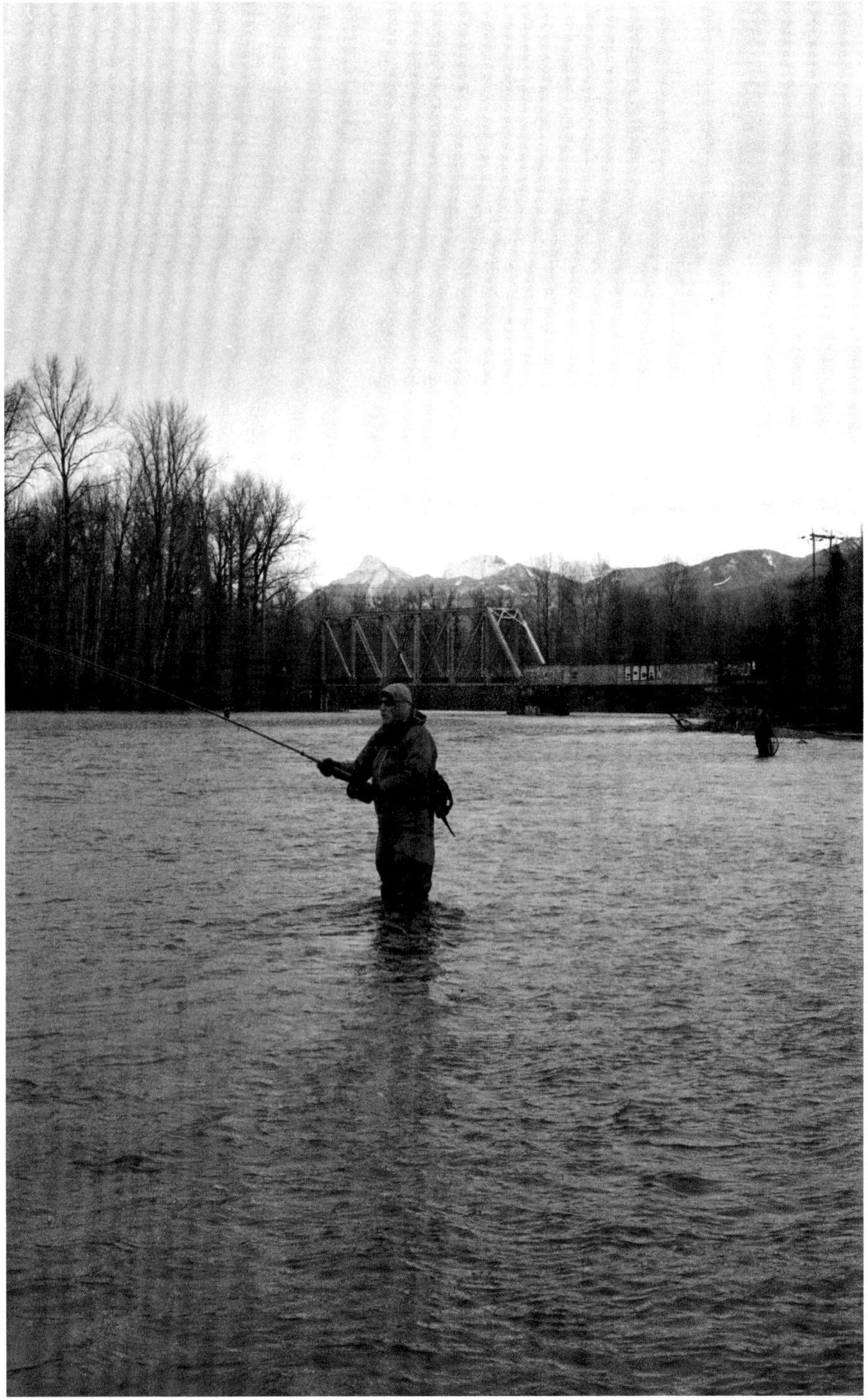

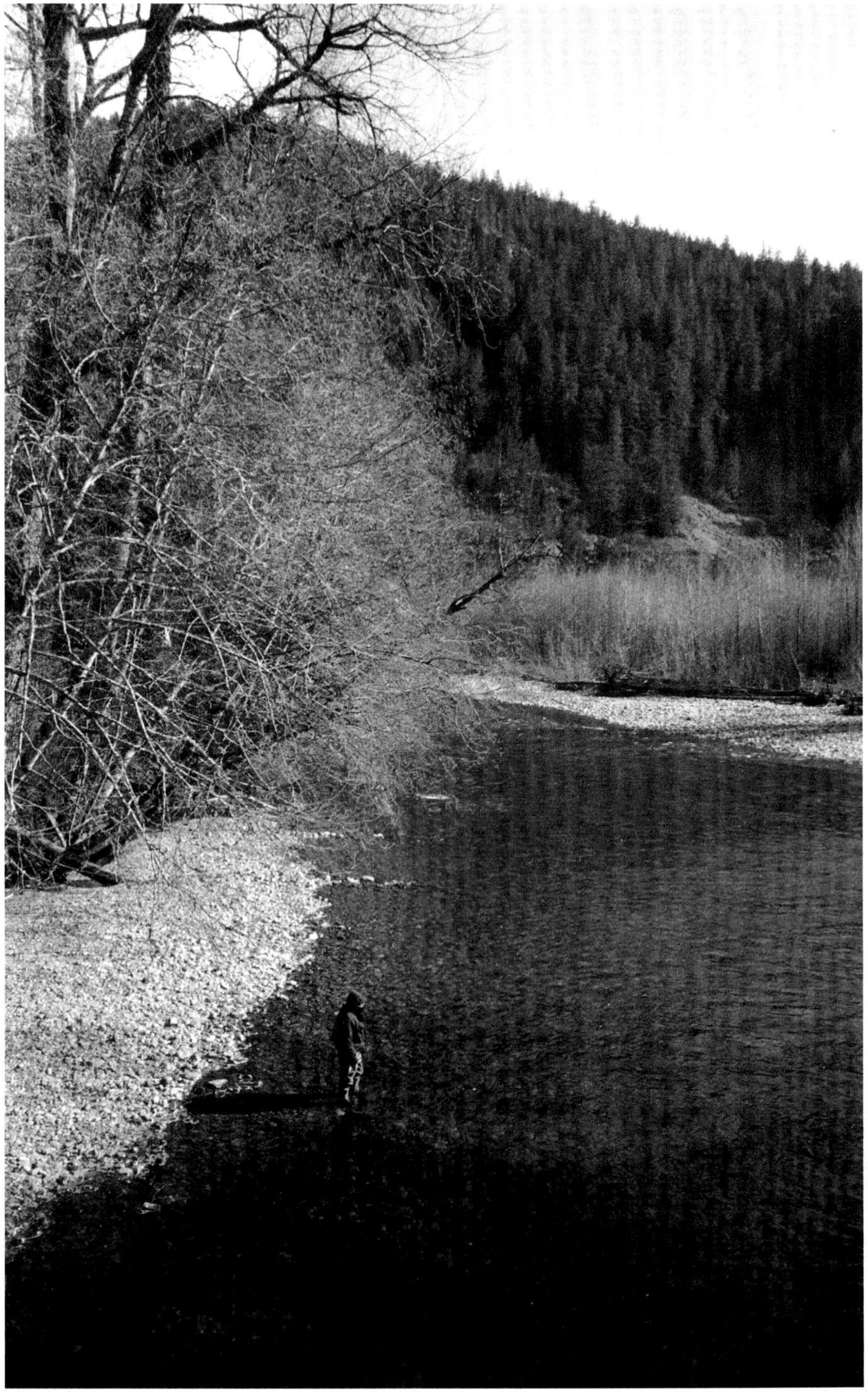

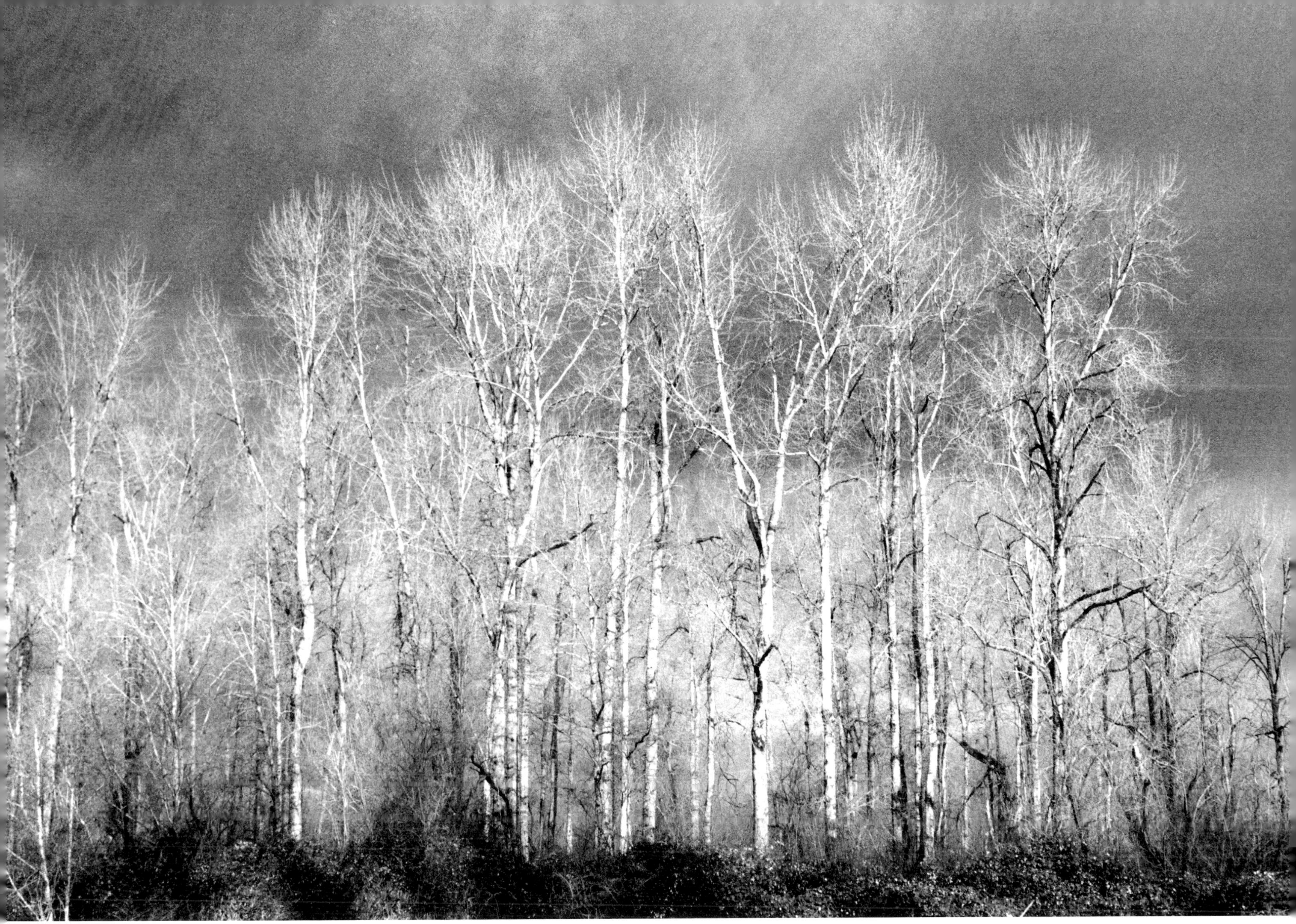

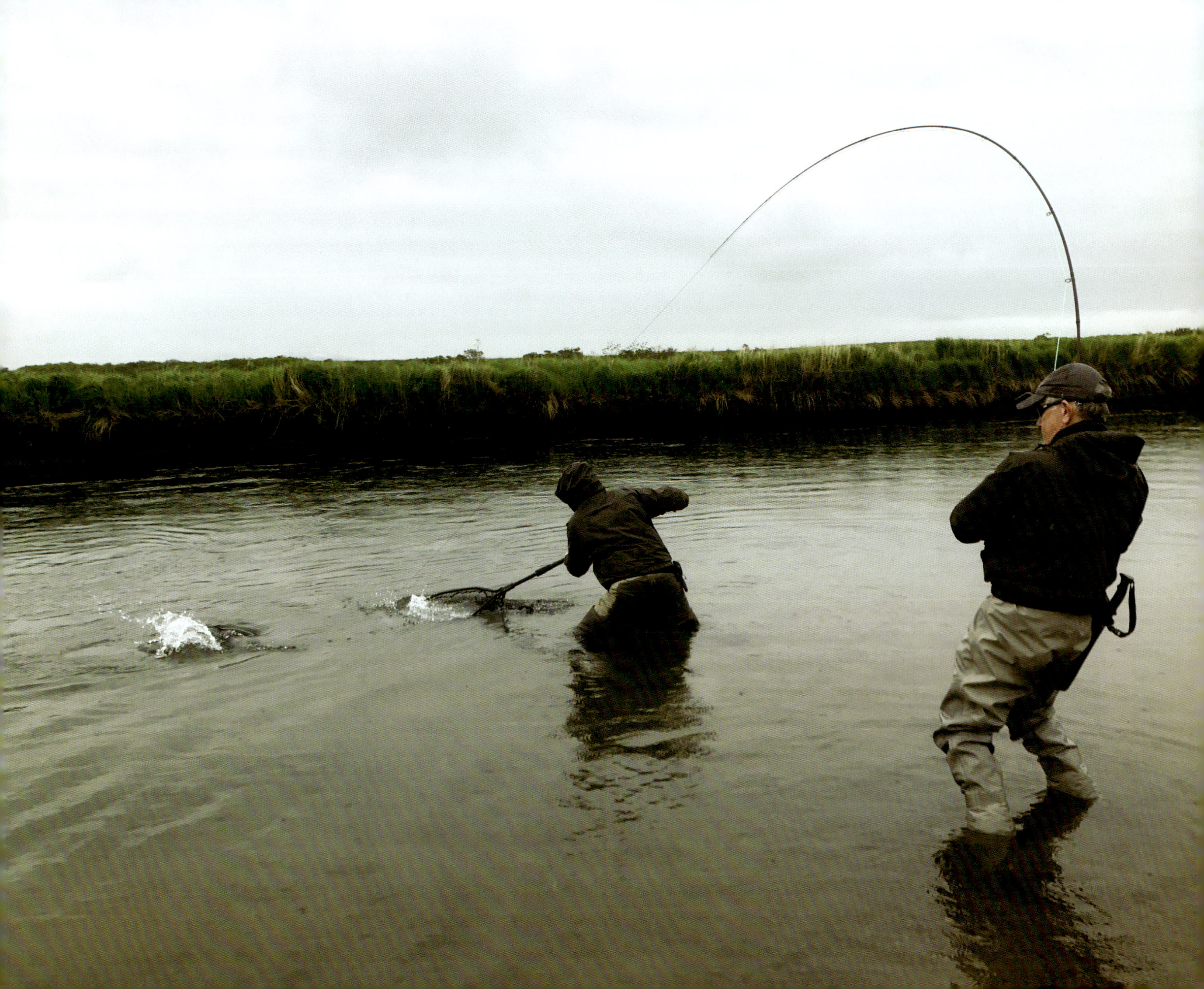

CHINOOK ON THE DECLINE

A review of the current state of Alaska's Chinook

Glenn K. Chen

The Chinook or king salmon (*Oncorhynchus tschawytscha*) is the largest member of the Pacific salmon clan. It is Alaska's state fish and is one of our most sought-after species, avidly pursued by both resident and visiting sport anglers who wet a line here in the Last Frontier.

As many Chinook salmon devotees will concur, populations of these fish here in Alaska have continued to decline significantly during recent years. Such downturns have occurred across the entire state, with numbers in major rivers such as the Yukon and Kuskokwim being so low that these systems have been closed to all king salmon fishing. Returns of early- and late-run Chinook to the Kenai River have not achieved escapement goals during half of the last 12 years, and counts for the Nushagak River have missed their objectives in five of the previous six seasons. Fishing restrictions continue to be placed on most systems, and while the Alaska Peninsula has remained open for catch and release, anglers there report reduced success in the Sandy River and Sapsuk River, with both the numbers and sizes of Chinook landed during the 2021 and 2022 seasons down substantially.

The ongoing reductions in Alaska's king salmon populations are very worrisome to the subsistence, sport and commercial fishermen who have long relied on these fish to meet dietary, economic and recreational needs. As a fisheries biologist who has lived and worked here for more than two decades, I've paid close attention to the efforts conducted by state, federal and Tribal researchers to discern the reasons behind these patterns. Results from their studies indicate that a number of natural and human-caused factors may be contributing to our Alaska Chinook declines. In the following sections I'll highlight these findings to provide an understanding of what's affecting this iconic species. I will also provide some personal perspectives regarding our current and future swing fishing endeavors for these prized fish.

Chinook Salmon Life History

Like other Pacific Coast salmon, Chinook hatch in freshwater, spend part of their early life in rivers, and then migrate out to sea before returning to spawn in natal systems. Scientists believe that this anadromous life history evolved because inland habitats have fewer sources of mortality — which favors survival for the more vulnerable juvenile fish — while migration to the ocean at a larger size enables them to access the more abundant food supplies in marine ecosystems, fostering the rapid growth necessary for reproductive maturity.

Each phase of an Alaska king salmon's life is beset with environmental and biological hazards. Fall floods can upturn spawning redds, and severe winters create ice flows that scour riverbeds, killing young salmon and the food that they rely upon. Freshwater predators include other salmonids and fishes, plus birds and mammals. These piscivores will congregate during the Chinook's trek to the sea, staging at locations along their migration routes to intercept the out-migrating smolts.

Upon entering the marine environment, more hungry mouths await these juveniles. Predation mortality increases significantly. Timing of ocean entry is also extremely important, as salmon have evolved to take advantage of the plankton abundance usually associated with spring and early summer upwelling of currents. This process brings nutrient rich water from the depths up into the shallow coastal areas, spurring blooms of algae phytoplankton and kick starting the food chain necessary for their survival. Should this occur out of sync with their arrival by as little as a few weeks, many juvenile Chinook will starve.

During their time at sea, kings feed on marine crustaceans (such as krill), small fish including capelin, sand lance, and herring and squid. They swim vast distances across the North Pacific in pursuit of their prey, for which distributions and abundance are influenced by an array of complex physical and biological factors that include temperature, nutrient availability and competition from a multitude of other species. This wide-ranging oceanic foraging also exposes the salmon themselves to a host of predators (including commercial and sport fishers). During spawning runs back to their rivers of origin, Chinook face additional hazards from orca and beluga whales, harbor seals, Steller sea lions, and more human harvesters, plus those associated with our resource development activities (e.g. chemical pollution from mines, hydropower migration barriers, etc.). It is indeed a testament to the indomitable will of kings that they can survive these obstacles and dangers in order to return to spawn and successfully perpetuate their populations generation after generation.

Possible Factors Contributing to Declines of Alaska Chinook

Scientists do not think that there is a single reason causing the current declines in the numbers of Alaska king salmon. Rather, it is likely that a combination of natural and human-caused issues are involved, which include the following:

- Changes in the marine environment that are reducing ocean survival
- High mortality of smolts upon ocean entry
- Younger age of returning spawners and reduced fecundity
- Oceanic competition from hatchery-origin pink and chum salmon
- Elevated river temperatures and increases in diseases/mortality
- Marine by-catch mortality from other commercial fisheries
- Selective predation by marine mammals

Marine Ecosystem Changes

The recent, unprecedented warming of the North Pacific has had profound effects on all aspects of this ecosystem, causing changes to the productivity and distribution of many marine species — which has likely influenced populations of Alaska's Chinook salmon.

An international effort led by the International Year of the Salmon (IYS) to study the winter marine survival of salmon throughout the North Pacific was conducted in 2022 (adding to ongoing IYS studies in this region since 2018). Vast areas were systematically sampled for all species of salmon beginning in early February, accompanied by the collection of associated chemical/physical/biological data that will be important to evaluate these results. Initial findings showed that the captured juvenile salmon were in poor condition (i.e. undernourished), suggesting that their prey was not abundant. This would be consistent with other concurrent data documenting the lack of food for other species such as seabirds, for which large-scale die-offs and multiple nesting failures have occurred. Further information about this research can be found at yearofthesalmon.org (with a synthesis of the 2022 work available on this website).

Not all kinds of marine plankton are beneficial to salmon: in recent years, there have been huge blooms of coccolithophores — a microscopic plant that isn't consumed by many oceanic fauna — across large areas of the North Pacific. The high concentrations of these inedible species reduce the amount of nutrients available for other types of plankton. These events coincide with periods of elevated surface water temperatures, and have been linked to lower survival of many marine animals (including Pacific salmon). Scientists from the National Oceanographic and Atmospheric Administration (NOAA) documented another such bloom in the Bering Sea during their 2022 surveys.

Results from the annual NOAA ecosystem research programs in the Bering Sea, Aleutian Islands and Gulf of Alaska are available at fisheries.noaa.gov/alaska/ecosystems/ecosystem-status-reports-gulf-alaska-bering-sea-and-aleutian-islands.

High Mortality Upon Ocean Entry

As mentioned previously, timing of ocean entry by smolts is critical to their survival. The nearshore waters of the Bering Sea and the Gulf of Alaska must be productive when the young salmon exit the rivers. Onshore winds are needed to bring nutrient-rich water from the ocean depths up towards the surface, where plankton can utilize the long daylight hours to bloom. The juvenile fish rely on the copepods and other zooplankton that graze upon these microscopic plants, until they grow enough to feed on larger prey.

Studies began in 2014 to assess the survival of Chinook salmon smolts upon their initial entry into the Bering Sea from western Alaska rivers. During some years, researchers found that more than 30% of these young salmon may have died during their first month in the ocean — a result that has greatly concerned managers, as such losses could have substantial implications on the number of adults returning to spawn. Ongoing efforts by NOAA, the Alaska Department of Fish and Game (ADF&G), and the Yukon River Fisheries Development Association (YRFDA) have continued to determine if such trends in early marine mortality will further affect Alaska king populations.

Life History Changes

For Chinook, the early freshwater residency period can be from 18 months to over two years in duration. The subsequent marine phase of their life will last from one to five years, with a preponderance of fish returning to spawn after spending two to four years at sea. Timing of returns is spread out among each year class of fish, which enables every brood to persist should a catastrophe occur that kills most of the fish in a particular year.

Researchers from ADF&G have documented that Alaska Chinook appear to be returning at an increasingly earlier age, with a growing proportion of spawning adult females now comprised of fish that have spent only two years at sea. As a salmon's reproductive capacity is based upon its size, these younger and smaller two-salt hens will produce fewer eggs. This reduced fecundity may already be contributing to the declines of our king salmon populations, and biologists are concerned that such life history shifts could further impact their numbers if they persist into the future.

Competition from Hatchery Salmon

Scientists now estimate that total salmon abundance in the North Pacific are at an all time high — so why are Chinook declining?

The large numbers of salmon are due primarily to the massive output from hatcheries in North America and Asia. Much of this biomass is comprised of pink salmon, which are favored for such culture because of their short freshwater rearing requirements (which enables these facilities to release the juveniles soon after hatching, thereby lowering production costs). Millions of hatchery-origin pinks — plus chums and sockeyes — now compete with Chinook and other wild salmon species in the North Pacific. Several scientists have hypothesized that these additional fish may be out-stripping the food supplies in this ecosystem and thus contributing to the current declines of king stocks. (More information about this can be found in the following publication: Ruggerone, G.T. and R.A. Irvine. [2018]. Numbers and Biomass of Natural- and Hatchery-Origin Pink Salmon, Chum Salmon, and Sockeye Salmon in the North Pacific Ocean, 1925-2015. Marine and Coastal Fisheries 10[2]: 152-168.)

Elevated River Temperatures and Increases in Diseases/Mortality

In recent years, hotter summers across much of Alaska have resulted in elevated stream temperatures, and waters in our northern latitude systems are warming at rates nearly twice as rapid as more temperate areas. This has affected salmon during their time in freshwater environments, leading to physiological stress, changes in migration timing/duration, and large-scale die-offs among juvenile and adult fish.

Higher temperatures reduce the amount of dissolved oxygen in the water, which often forces stream fish to seek out riffles and rapids where the turbulence increases O_2 levels. The faster current in these habitat types, however, subject salmon to greater metabolic demands, depleting their energy reserves and thereby affecting spawning success. At times, the combination of lethal water temperatures and low oxygen levels result in outright fish kills. This was documented during the summer of 2019, when such factors caused the mortality of more than 100,000 adult salmon in several Bristol Bay and Yukon tributaries.

Chinook salmon can be infected by a parasite called Icthyophonus, which is acquired from prey that they consume at sea. Scientists have found this disease among a significant proportion of adult Yukon River kings, noting that high levels of the pathogen results in loss of swimming ability — and they hypothesize that such weakened fish may be unable to survive the rigorous upstream spawning journeys. In addition, Icthyophonus infection severity appears to be correlated with elevated temperatures, so the observed trends of warming rivers here in Alaska have raised much concern about the potential for this parasite to cause further impacts on the already declining king salmon populations.

Bycatch Mortality From Other Commercial Fisheries

In fisheries management, "bycatch" is defined as the unwanted fish and other biota caught during commercial harvests for a different species.

Research has documented that Chinook originating from Alaska rivers are captured in large scale industrial marine fisheries, such as the pollock mid-water trawl fishery operating in the Bering Sea and the Gulf of Alaska. Pollock is an oceanic species that supports high value harvests each year, and is the most common fish that's used in frozen filets, breaded fish sticks, imitation crab, and other popular seafood products.

Chinook and chum salmon are known to aggregate with pollock at sea, and NOAA scientists found that the incidental take of these salmon by the trawl fleet reached a peak of approximately 122,000 Chinook and 700,000 chums during 2007. This triggered the North Pacific Fisheries Management Council (NPFMC) to expand their bycatch reduction measures, which include net modifications that allow some salmon to escape, as well as real-time identification of specific areas with higher salmon encounters so that the fleet can re-position fishing efforts. The Council also adopted salmon bycatch caps for both the Bering Sea and Gulf of Alaska trawl fisheries, whereupon these would be closed if and when the incidental catches exceeded these established limits. (Note: None of the incidentally taken salmon can be sold; while the industry does participate in the Sea Share program — wherein a portion of these fish are processed and then subsequently donated to charities — much of this bycatch is discarded.)

On-board observers, along with electronic surveillance devices placed on vessels and processing facilities, are used to obtain a full count of all salmon that are incidentally taken. Tallies for 2022 documented that a bycatch of 29,931 Chinook salmon occurred in commercial fisheries operating within Alaska's marine waters. These include 6,637 Chinook from the Bering Sea pollock fishery, 8,745 in the Bering Sea non pollock trawl plus other non trawl fisheries, and another 14,549 from the Gulf of Alaska pollock and non-pollock trawl/non-trawl fisheries. According to NOAA, this figure is below the 1991-2019 historical Chinook total bycatch average of 34,589 per year.

Genetic testing from a subsample (10%) of these kings are conducted each year. Recent results available from 2020 indicating that 52% of these fish originated from western Alaska coastal rivers — an increase from the 10-year average of 44% — and 13% were from the North Alaska Peninsula systems (e.g. the Sapsuk, Sandy, and other adjacent watersheds). Due to the length of time needed to process and analyze the samples, genetic-based origin data are available from the National Marine Fisheries Service labs two years after they are collected.

Information about salmon bycatch in Alaska's commercial marine fisheries is available on NOAA's websitenpfmc.org/fisheries-issues/bycatch/salmon-bycatch/

Selective Predation by Marine Mammals

As part of a statewide effort to determine the causes behind recent declines, ADF&G initiated a marine Chinook telemetry study using electronic tags. Researchers noted some odd distribution patterns among the fish they were tracking — and subsequently determined that they had likely been eaten by marine mammals, specifically orca whales. The large percentage of tagged kings consumed by these particular cetaceans suggests that such predation may be selective (similar to the dietary preferences of orcas in Washington's Puget Sound). Additional research is needed to determine if these sources of mortality is occurring at levels that can affect the abundance of Alaska Chinook.

Outlook for Alaska's King Salmon

Chinook are an important Alaska species that support high value fisheries. While there has been a couple of recent years with returns sufficient to provide good angling, overall trends indicate that seasons with continued depressed runs are likely in the near future.

Alaska managers are predicting that king salmon return will be low again this season, and they've already taken action to close a number of both salt and freshwater areas to fishing. This includes Cook Inlet plus the rivers with wild-only Chinook populations on the Kenai Peninsula, the Susitna River drainage north of Anchorage and the entire Kuskokwim River. The Yukon River basin may soon have fishing restrictions and/or closures again as well. (At this time, Kuskokwim Bay systems including the Goodnews and Kanektok rivers are open for king salmon sport anglers.) Potential Chinook salmon management actions on the Nushagak River have been delayed so that a plan for addressing this stock of concern can be developed. The forecast for kings on the Copper River is for a return higher than 2022, which is welcome news as this system was one of the few that achieved its escapement goals last year.

During the late fall 2022 meetings of the NPFMC regarding Alaska groundfish management, the Council heard extensive testimony from many in-river salmon users, tribal representatives, and concerned community members about salmon bycatch in the eastern Bering Sea pollock trawl fishery. They established a special committee to develop recommendations for reducing these incidental harvests. As of March 2023, this group has met twice, and their proposed measures will be discussed during the April 2023 Council meeting. The NPMFC also increased the pollock trawl quota by 17% for 2023, and as of early spring a total pollock trawl bycatch of 8,265 Chinook salmon has been recorded.

NOAA scientists report that the elevated sea temperatures in the North Pacific — which began in 2014 and significantly affected this marine ecosystem — have subsided during 2021-2022. Researchers observed that the abundance of krill — which are an important food source for salmon — was higher in these regions last fall. However, they also noted that both phytoplankton and small-sized zooplankton abundance declined in the Aleutian Islands, and forage fish surveys there found an increased number of Kamchatka (Asian-origin) pink salmon, which have heightened concerns regarding yet more competition with our king and other salmon species. In addition, the data shows that another marine heat wave is already developing in the southern Bering Sea for 2023.

Efforts by tribes to address concerns regarding Chinook here in Alaska have resulted in considerable success. Three organizations - the Kuskokwim River Inter-Tribal Fisheries Commission, the Yukon River Inter-Tribal Fisheries Commission, and the Ahtna Inter-Tribal Resources Commission, representing scores of Federally-recognized Tribes and funded with dollars from Congress — have been working since 2015 with Federal agencies and ADF&G to help address king salmon issues. Through the application of traditional ecological knowledge, collection of run timing and abundance information, plus harvest assessments, these indigenous groups have been able to collaboratively manage an important species that has been a vital subsistence resource for innumerable generations of Native people.

Swinging for Alaska Chinook: Personal Perspectives

I chase anadromous salmonids all across Alaska during our brief season, and consider catching kings to be among my most enjoyable annual experiences. There's little that can compare to the powerful grab of a chrome-sided Chinook as it takes a swing fly, and the ensuing mighty battle will challenge your tackle to the utmost. The odds are heavily in favor of the fish, so landing one requires considerable skill plus a healthy dose of luck as well.

During the upcoming years and with populations still at significantly reduced numbers, it will be important to maintain a suitable perspective with regards to Chinook fishing here in the 49th state. In contrast to angling for more abundant species such as cohos, king swinging success isn't determined by how many grabs you'll have — rather, it's about the unique opportunity to pursue the largest Pacific salmon within pristine wilderness settings little disturbed by humankind.

Alaska has excellent freshwater habitats that will support Chinook salmon rebounds if and when our populations thrive again. If you're fortunate enough to have the opportunity to fish for kings anywhere in the state, take the time to savor every hookup as well as the beautiful wild places where we anglers chase these amazing fish. Use the same patience in awaiting that fierce yank to await future increases in their numbers. Continue to support research and management and be involved with ongoing conservation work. Know that your efforts will be vital to ensure that we and future fishers will be able to catch Alaska Chinook in the years to come.

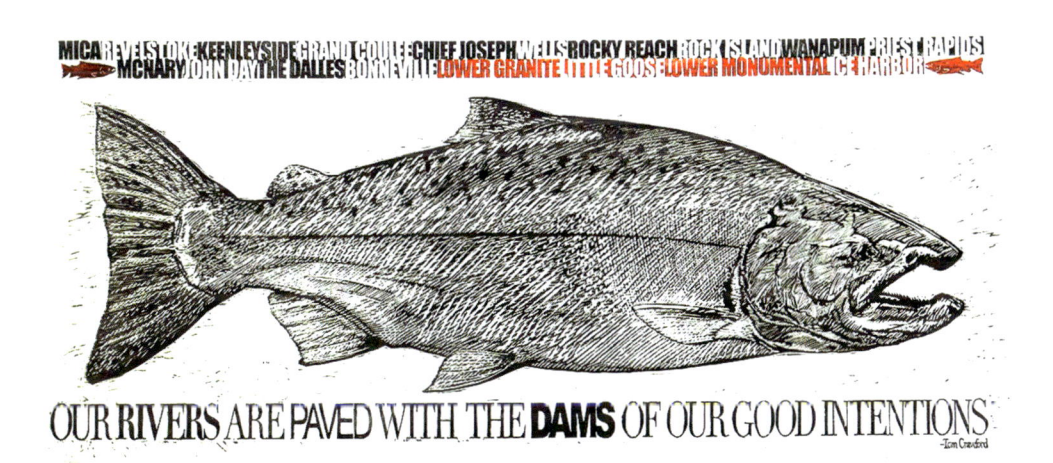

The giant chinook of the Columbia River. The words of poet Tom Crawford. The fish, some of the barriers they face, and the possibility of dam removal on the Snake River. Motivations got ahead of our ability to see all possible impacts. Done with the best of intentions, and that same intention can lead us to solutions. For salmon, for the environment, and for us.

Paper size of 31 x 68 inches.
Image is a hand carved and pulled woodcut print, and is available at:

http://www.richardcharrington.com/store/our-rivers-are-paved-first-painting

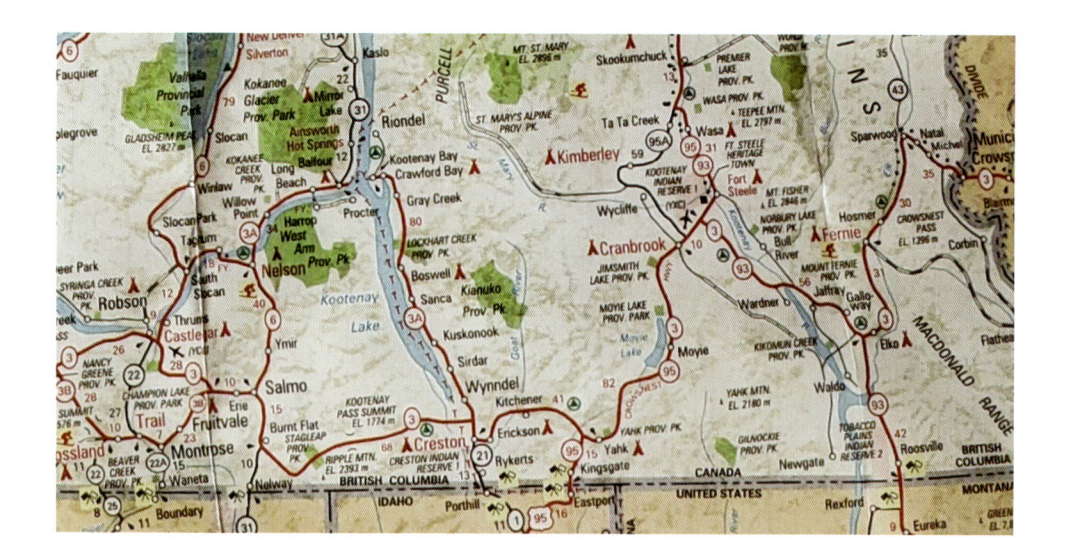

Bruce Kruk admiring Dan Holder's David Reid two-handed bamboo rod.

TRAVELS THROUGH BC

with Bamboo Rods

Art Lingren

This would be a new adventure to waters in a historic part of British Columbia, the southeast, where, now extinct salmon and steelhead were once abundant pre-dams in many of the rivers. I have never fished waters east of Pennask Lake, located between Merritt and Kelowna, near the divide between the Fraser and Columbia watersheds; even though most of my life I spent my fishing days on British Columbia waters in the western parts of the province.

On my bucket list was the desire to fish some rivers tributary to the Columbia River in the southeastern part of the province. New waters — decisions to make, what tackle to take? How large are the rivers?

I prefer to fish a dry fly or swing a wet using a floating line. I have a few bamboo rods made by Peter McVey, Ron Grantham, George Deagle and Bob Clay. They are special rods because they were made by fishing friends. I like to fish those rods suiting the length and rod weight to the size of a river and the target fish.

Three routes branch off from Highway 1 to get through the Fraser River watershed into the Columbia River watershed. In late August I headed up Highway 1 to meet Dan and Lynne Holder at Juniper Beach Provincial Park campsite, located near Ashcroft on the Thompson River. We intended to spend some time fishing that favourite river for trout before heading to the southeast rivers of the Columbia River watershed.

Ron Grantham and Peter McVey made fine bamboo rods, and both loved to fish the Thompson River for steelhead. The returns to that river are so poor that the river has been closed during steelhead season, but it is still a good trout fishery through the summer into the fall. The Thompson is a large river and it can be windy. I fished my Grantham 7-weight with a Hardy Zenith reel (owned by Ron and acquired from his estate) on this fishery. We didn't catch a lot on the Thompson — it was higher than normal and finding walk-in spots suitable for elderly guys to fish was difficult. But we did dance around on the slippery boulder-strewn river for a few hours and the trout we caught took hard and ran out a lot of line.

The next part of our journey would be over to David Thompson country. Simon Fraser, on his journey down the river later to be known as the Fraser River in 1808, named the Thompson River after David Thompson, a fellow employee of the Northwest Company. British Columbia has many mountain ranges and as we travelled down through the Okanagan Valley and through the southern route into the Kootenays it seemed to me we were either going up or down a mountain pass.

The Elk River in Fernie is a fairly large stream and known for its westslope cutthroat and large bull trout. My George Deagle British Columbia Jade 7-weight rod paired with Dan Holder's British Columbia Jade Perfect reel suited the size of the river and maybe the fish. We picked easy in and outs for our river drifts and for my spare rod I set up my Bob Clay 5-weight with my other Dan Holder reel.

The trout were not large but enough came to the fly on this heavily fished water. From our Fernie campsite I would wander upstream to a small pocket with my Grantham 4-weight set up with a 3-inch Hardy Uniqua reel and cast a Parachute Adams to westslope cutthroat.

Ron Grantam 7-weight bamboo rod with Hardy Zenith reel and a cutthroat.

Michel Creek flows into the Elk River at Sparwood. It is a small stream with abundant insect life and the westslope cutthroat grow large. My Grantham 7-foot, 4-weight with my Uniqua reel proved to be the ideal setup for this stream. Dan and I hiked into a run and the fish were busy rising to something, but no tentlike bugs floated down the river. Fish were active and rising throughout the run. I threw my size 12 Parachute Adams and watched it drift down stream towards me. It was taken by a nice trout that took out an amazing amount of line considering the pool was not that big. Lovely stream and pleasant to fish.

When we were in Fernie, Dan Holder wanted me to meet John Poirier, a bamboo rod builder. We visited him a few times and each time he wanted us to cast some of his rods. Besides building bamboo rods, John is an excellent fly tier and artist. A man of many skills. At one casting session he brought out two rods to try and then said he wanted me to have one of those bamboo rods. I didn't really know what to say to such a generous offer and chose the 8-foot, 5-weight built to Paul Young's parabolic taper. I wanted to try this rod before we left the area and contacted Bruce Kruk in Trail. Bruce asked me a couple times if I ever get up his way give him a call and he would take me fishing on the Columbia River.

We left Sparwood in the morning and were in the Trail campsite that afternoon. We did get a half day fishing with Bruce, and I christened the John Poirier rod with a Columbia River rainbow. On this trip, we did some sightseeing in David Thompson territory on non-fishing days. When Simon Fraser was exploring the Fraser Watershed (1806 to 1808) and journeying to the sea, David Thompson arrived in 1807 in the Kootenays. Thompson set up Northwest Company trading posts and through 1812 he explored and mapped the Columbia River to its mouth at Astoria. Thompson over his career travelled 56,000 miles and mapped 1.9 million square miles of North America. He has been described as the "greatest practical land geographer that the world has produced."

I enjoyed seeing the country and wondered what it would have been like when Thompson explored the area. But most of all the fishing experience was enhanced by catching trout using bamboo rods and reels made by friends.

Iron Gate Dam
Photo: Josh Deuplechian, TU

Conservation Corner

SAVING THE KLAMATH

Sam Davidson, Trout Unlimited

Historically, the Klamath River was the third most productive salmon and steelhead watershed on the American West Coast. Only the mighty Columbia/Snake Basin and the Sacramento River produced more fish.

It is an immense watershed, with headwaters and key tributaries in Southern Oregon and hundreds of miles of water in Northern California. Its rich waters have sustained tribal fisheries and cultures for thousands of years and supported extensive commercial and recreational fisheries since the arrival of European settlers. But the Klamath's salmon and steelhead populations are now tiny fractions of their historical numbers.

The primary factor in their decline is that, for over a century, the dams of the Klamath River Hydroelectric Project have blocked chinook, coho, steelhead, and Pacific Lamprey from reaching most of the best spawning and rearing habitat in the basin. These native fishes are now completely extirpated from the watershed above Iron Gate Dam.

The impacts of the Project's four dams were not limited to preventing fish migration to and from the Klamath's headwaters. The impoundments behind the dams cook in the intense heat of summer. When released, this hot water creates lethal temperatures for salmonids and perfect conditions for fish-killing bacteria which has in some years caused catastrophic die-offs of juvenile and adult salmon and steelhead below the dams. By late summer, the impoundments are filled with green sludge as poisonous algae blooms cover their surface, contributing to abysmal levels of dissolved oxygen in water sent downstream.

In 2002, as the operating license for the dams came up for renewal, potentially extending their lifespan another 30 to 50 years, the Klamath Basin suffered one of the worst fish kills in modern history. At least 35,000 salmon died that September when flows dropped too low and water temperatures soared. While the tribes of the basin had always opposed the construction of the dams, the horrifying fish die-off galvanized a new effort to remove the dams and reconnect the Klamath Basin.

Twenty years later, the broad coalition of Tribes, conservationists, nonprofit organizations, commercial fisherman and recreational anglers that came together in 2002 to restore the Klamath and its fisheries has a profound reason to celebrate. The dams of the Klamath River Hydroelectric Project are finally coming down. By the end of 2024, salmon and steelhead will regain access to more than 420 miles of high-quality habitat they have not been able to reach for over a century.

Reconnecting the Klamath

The road to removing the four Klamath dams has been long and difficult, with painful setbacks and critical breakthroughs along the way. There were many days in court; unrelenting efforts and protests by tireless advocates; countless hours of negotiations; and stacks of legal documents filed. Agreements were forged only to fall apart when Congress refused to act. But the advocates for Klamath dam removal especially tribes in the basin — never gave up. Each setback led to new negotiations and new proposed solutions, while the shared vision of a restored Klamath River never wavered.

Swing the Fly Anthology 2023

Habitat reconnected following dam removal

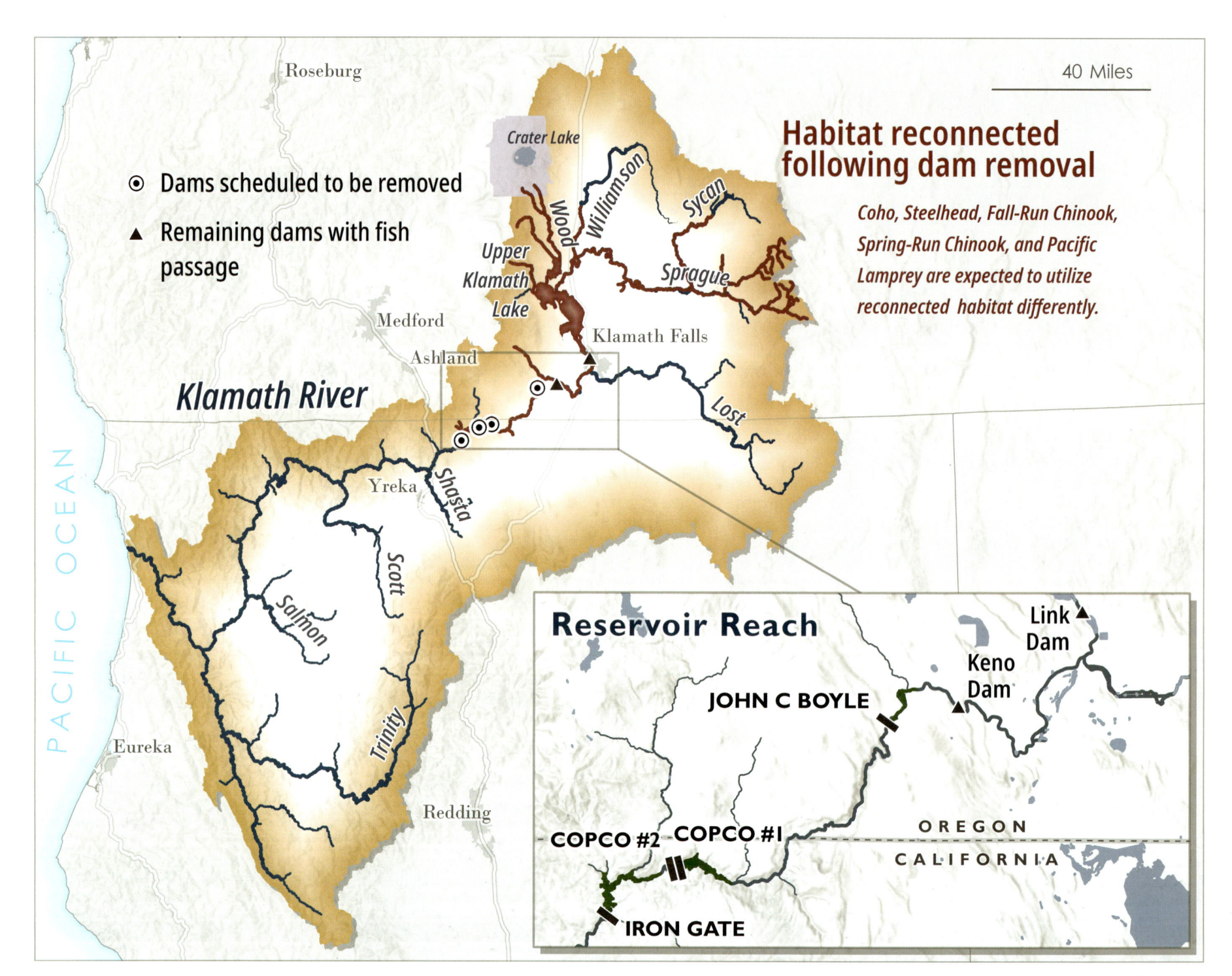

Coho, Steelhead, Fall-Run Chinook, Spring-Run Chinook, and Pacific Lamprey are expected to utilize reconnected habitat differently.

⊙ Dams scheduled to be removed

▲ Remaining dams with fish passage

Graphic courtesy Trout Unlimited

Ultimately, the fate of the Klamath dams depended on the Federal Energy Regulatory Commission's (FERC) approval of a comprehensive plan based on multiple environmental reviews, engineering studies, and funding commitments, developed by the Klamath River Renewal Corporation (KRRC).

On November 17 of last year, all the pieces finally came together. As Tribes held a ceremony on the river to watch the FERC proceedings, the commission formally blessed the KRRC's decommissioning plan when it issued the Final License Surrender Order for the Lower Klamath River Hydroelectric Project.

"The Klamath salmon are coming home," Yurok Tribal Chairman Joseph James said. "The people have earned this victory and with it, we carry on our sacred duty to the fish that have sustained our people since the beginning of time."

The KRRC, a not-for-profit entity created solely for the purpose of taking over the operating license for the Project and removing its four dams and related infrastructure, has now taken ownership of the Project. Planning has been underway for years, and the dam decommissioning process began immediately after FERC's final approval.

Copco II, the smallest of the four dams, will be the first removed. It will come out late in the summer of 2023. The reservoirs behind the other three dams will be drained the following winter, then removed simultaneously during the summer of 2024.

Altogether, this will be the largest river restoration project in history.

Once the impoundments are empty and the dams and their accompanying infrastructure are gone, the KRRC will oversee extensive replanting with a variety of native vegetation to restore the river corridor and riparian habitat of the former reservoir sites.

Brian J. Johnson, director of the Trout Unlimited (TU) California Program, and Chuck Bonham — now Director of the California Department of Fish and Wildlife and former director of TU's work in California — were key negotiators of crucial settlements and agreements between tribes, federal and state agencies, water users, commercial fishermen, and conservation groups that paved the way for FERC's approval of dam removal.

Johnson, an environmental attorney who started work on this campaign in 2005, brought all his skills to bear in working through the many funding, liability, and regulatory issues related to the dam removal project. Johnson's engagement in the Klamath campaign goes beyond back rooms to the board room — he currently serves as president of the board of directors at the KRRC.

"Our goal of reconnecting and restoring one of the most important river systems in North America for salmon and steelhead is now within reach," Johnson said. "TU is gratified and humbled by the unflagging commitment of our tribal, government, and conservation partners to this shared ambition. The license surrender order marks a profound turning point for the health of the entire Klamath watershed."

Preparing for the Fish to Return

Rebuilding durable populations of salmon, steelhead and other native fishes above the former dam sites requires dependable supplies of cold, clean water and intact, well-connected spawning and rearing habitat. The work that TU has led in the upper Klamath basin for the past 15 years to improve habitat, fish passage and water quality and to establish new water-sharing agreements is now poised to deliver on its full promise.

Much of the restoration work to date in the upper Klamath basin has been focused on protection and recovery of bull trout, redband rainbow trout and two species of native, endangered suckers in Klamath Lake. Now that the dams are coming down, there is new urgency to expand the restoration and monitoring work to include spring and fall run Chinook, coho, steelhead, and Pacific lamprey as these fishes begin to repopulate formerly inaccessible habitat.

Steelhead and spring run Chinook are expected to travel further upstream but the section of the watershed currently occupied by the four dams and their impoundments will provide the first available habitat for all returning salmon, steelhead, and lamprey.

To facilitate this restoration, TU partnered with the NOAA Restoration Center and the Pacific States Marine Fisheries Commission (PSMFC) to produce a report identifying and prioritizing restoration projects within the Klamath's reservoir reach.

After two years of work, the Klamath River Reservoir Reach Restoration Plan was released in early December 2022. This comprehensive report outlines the best habitat restoration and reconnection, fish-screening and flow restoration opportunities to help returning salmon and steelhead reestablish their populations. The report provides a comprehensive roadmap to all the agencies, Tribes, landowners and conservation groups working in the basin and will help guide federal and state restoration investments for years to come.

An Unprecedented Opportunity to Restore a River

Few things are worse for anadromous fish than dams with poor fish passage, or no passage at all. Conversely, it's increasingly clear that few things help salmon, steelhead and other sea-run fishes more than removing dams. TU's work to remove old dams on rivers such as the Penobscot in Maine and the Elwha on Washington's Olympic Peninsula has proven that, while bringing a river back to life is never simple or easy, fish return immediately to habitat above former dam sites.

On the Penobscot River, alewife, shad and Atlantic salmon numbers are growing. On the Elwha, rainbow trout trapped behind the dams immediately rebooted a historical summer steelhead run and winter steelhead and salmon

> RESTORING A RIVER MEANS MORE THAN SIMPLY GETTING FISH BACK ABOVE DAMS – IT MEANS IMPROVING THE WELL-BEING OF ALL THE HUMAN AND WILDLIFE COMMUNITIES THAT RELY ON THAT RIVER.
> - Chrysten Rivard, the director of TU's Oregon program

numbers are rebounding. Nearshore habitat is expanding and saltwater species at the mouth of the Elwha are thriving as sediment trapped behind the dams is once again delivered downstream by high winter flows.

Reconnecting and restoring rivers at a large scale requires many years of effort and investment to build the partnerships, trust, and funding that can deliver the outcomes that help fish and local communities. These rivers, and others where dams have been removed, affirm that this hard work is worth it, and lend greater impetus to ongoing campaigns to remove dams on the lower Snake River in Washington, on the Kennebec River in Maine, and the Eel River in California, all of which offer hope for recovery of some of the most legendary wild salmon and steelhead runs in the Lower 48.

The four Klamath dams will be gone by the end of 2024. The work of TU, tribes, resource agencies and other stakeholders to improve habitat, water quality and fish passage and to monitor the return of salmon and steelhead throughout the upper basin will intensify. Durable conservation solutions are not one-offs.

Chrysten Rivard, the director of TU's Oregon program, notes that restoring a river means more than simply getting fish back above dams — it means improving the well-being of all the human and wildlife communities that rely on that river. To that end, Rivard says, "TU will not rest until the Klamath dams are gone, the Klamath watershed is restored to good ecological health and function, native salmon and steelhead once again spawn and rear in the Klamath headwaters, and the cultures and communities of the Klamath Basin are vibrant and have improved water security for all their needs."

Additional Resources

Lessons from the Klamath
Brian Johnson joined Richard Harrington on The River Rambler podcast to discuss the inspiring dedication and partnership required to remove the Klamath Dams.
Find "Listen Now: Lessons from the Klamath Dams" on www.tu.org

Restoring the Reservoir Reach
Nell Scott elaborates on the habitat restoration work being prioritized in the portion of the basin where the dams and impoundments will be removed.
Read "Planning for the Klamath Dams to Come Down" on www.tu.org

The Return of Salmon and Steelhead
Haley Ohms outlines Oregon and California's plans for native fish to repopulate the upper Klamath watershed.
Read "Planning for Salmon and steelhead to Return as the Klamath Dams Come Down" on www.tu.org

The Klamath River Renewal Corporation
The nonprofit created to take ownership of the four dams and manage dam demolition and site restoration. klamathrenewal.org

Swing the Fly Anthology 2023   151

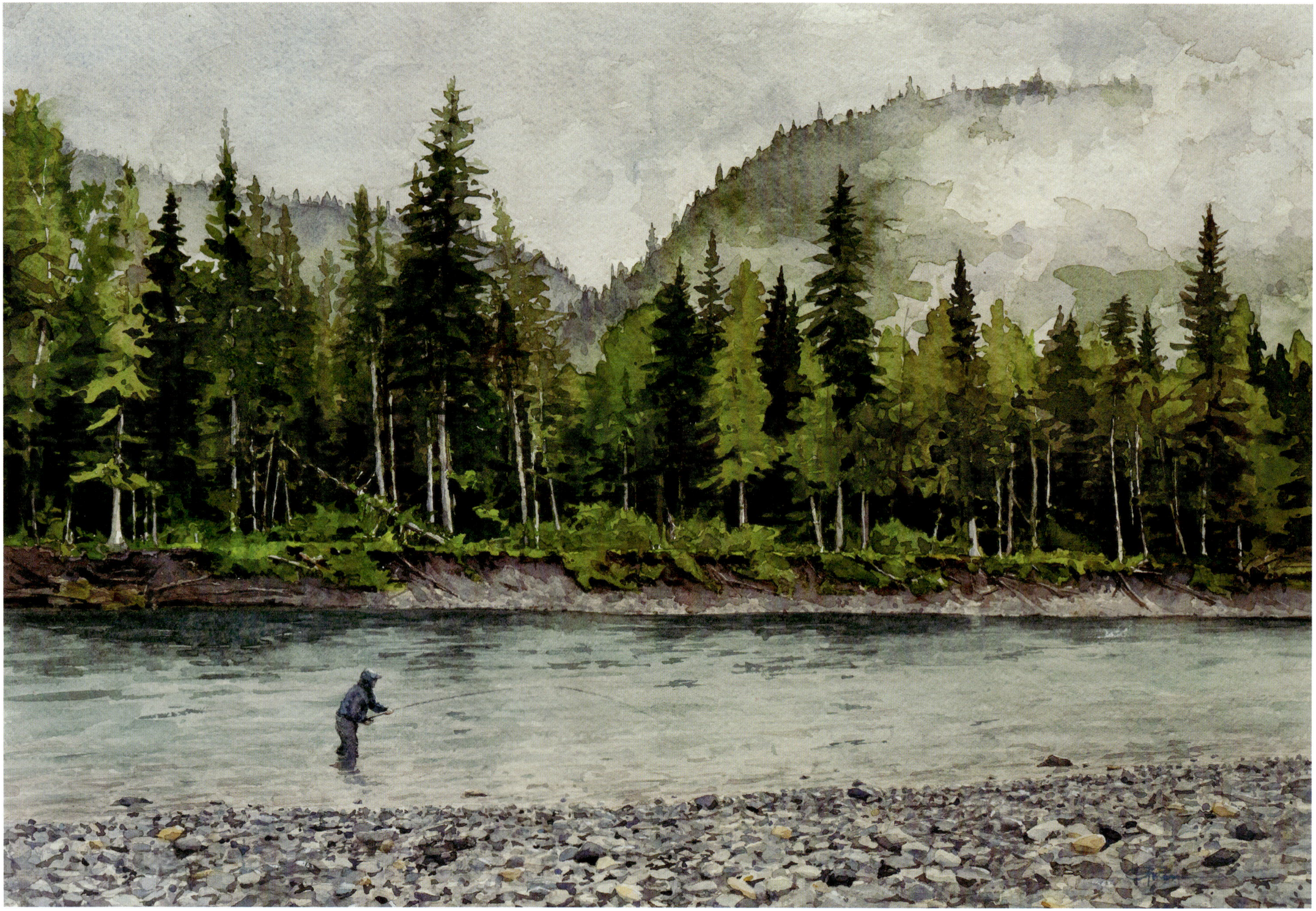

A FIRST SALMON TRIP

Greg Pearson

I don't speak French, so when I landed in Montreal and found a cab, there was some confusion as to where I wanted to go. Apparently there is more than one train station. Eventually I was dropped off at Montreal Central Station and had a few hours to kill before my 7 p.m. departure for the Gaspé Peninsula. I wandered downtown Montreal a bit and got a coffee. It's a beautiful city, but I was too excited to get to the salmon rivers and nervous I'd miss the train. So I sat in the corner of the station and tried to read a book but was distracted with the people watching.

Finally on the train and moving, I found my sleeper cabin, threw my pack on the bunk and headed for the observation car. I ordered a Molson from the attendant and watched the Quebec countryside roll by from the glass dome.

Thirty minutes passed, and I was still beerless. Maybe I was supposed to get it, and I had just assumed that the attendant would bring it up the stairs. I was a bit embarrassed if that was the case, so I went down to check. The attendant was in the same position as when I last saw him, smoking a cigarette, when I asked if I was supposed to pick up my order. "I bring it," was his reply after a lengthy inhale-pause-exhale. I tipped him a toony for his trouble when he arrived a bit later and reminded myself that not everyone was excited about a salmon trip.

The train rocked me into a deep sleep, broken when my 4:30 a.m. alarm chirped seemingly moments after my head hit the pillow. I sprung up and went straight to the observation car to watch the sunrise as we traveled along the Matapedia River.

The Matapedia was a classic Atlantic salmon river that I had read about many times. The same attendant as the night before cheerfully brought me a coffee and in quick order. He must be a morning person, I thought. As the filtered light brightened, I could make out the Sharpe canoes anchored along the bank, waiting for the day's anglers to arrive. The water was beautiful, and I wondered how many of the Matapedia's giant salmon were scattered about. How many would be hooked that day and on what fly patterns? What amazing battles would be fought in the high, tea colored water?

Topher Browne was waiting to pick me up at the train station in Bonaventure, greeting me with a warm smile and welcoming me to the Gaspé. He had invited me to spend a week with him, poking around a few of the rivers before he started his season of guiding at Camp Bonaventure.

We stayed at the camp and tried to stay clear of the staff as they hustled with their preparation. The camp staff were inspired and full of energy, knowing that the warmth of summer and fresh Atlantic salmon would soon be here. The kitchen was a popular hangout, and they stuffed us with fresh cookies, coffee, amazing

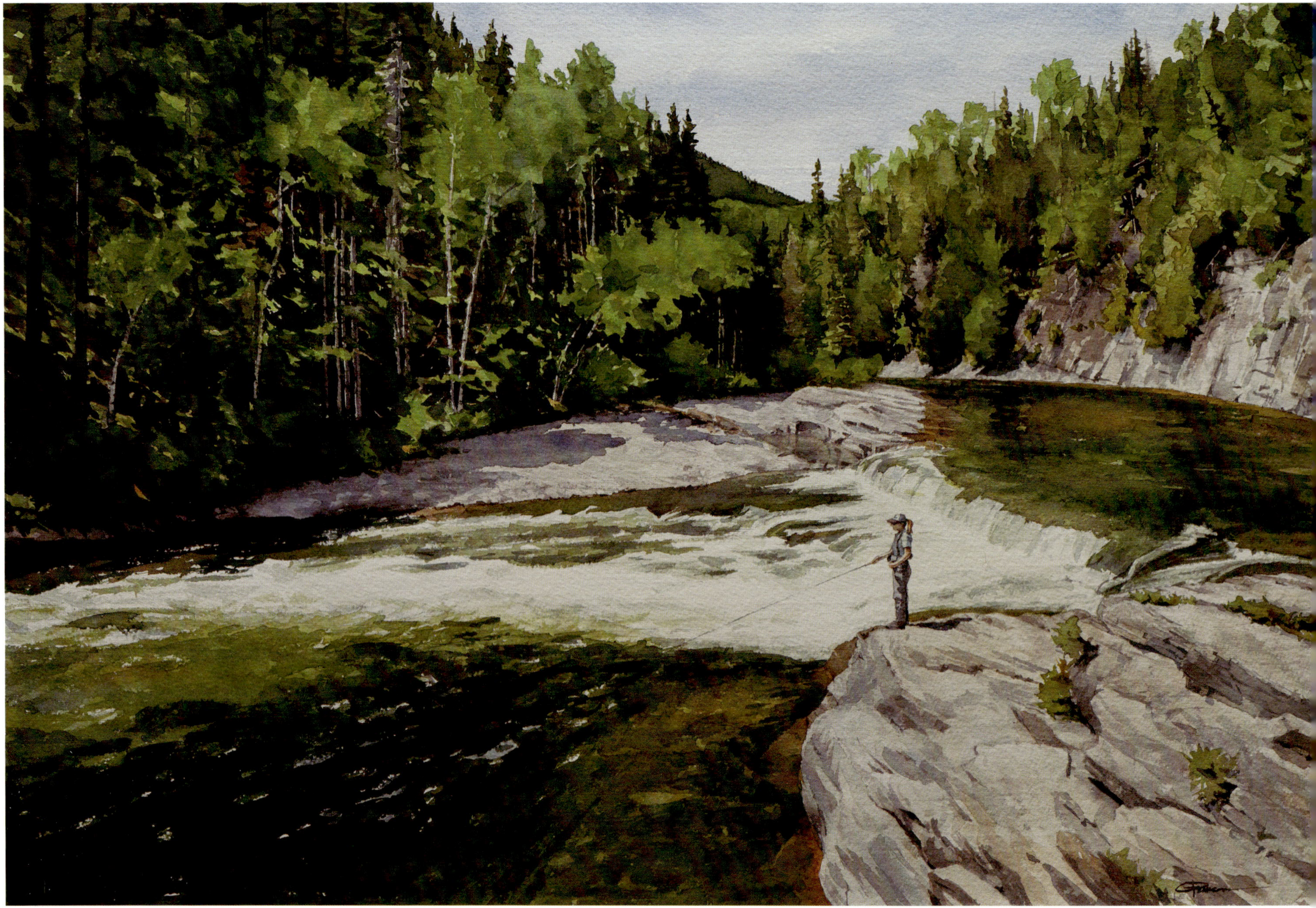

THE FLY WAS RIPPING THROUGH, THEN, HALFWAY THROUGH THE SWING I MENDED THE LINE UPSTREAM.

MARIO HOLLERED, "AND NOW YOU ARE BENCHED, FUCKFACE!"

meals and a lot of laughs and friendly banter.

The salmon camp is just above tidewater, and I could smell the Atlantic Ocean. It was early summer, but it was cold and damp; the sky was gray, and there was still some snow in the shady areas.

One of the guides, Mario Poirier, was there messing with boats and generally prepping everything for the season. Mario was a very friendly French-Canadian who chain-smoked and laughed just like 1980s Eddie Murphy, mostly at his own jokes. I was thrilled when he asked if we wanted to go for a boat ride and see if any early salmon had arrived to the lower river.

I had read every book on fly fishing for Atlantic salmon I could get my hands on and taught myself how to tie the classic flies. I could hardly believe it, I was now on an actual salmon river, just as fresh fish with chrome silver sides should be entering the river

Mario motored the 26' canoe up river a couple miles.

Looking at the cold, clear water I couldn't get the thoughts of fresh, 30-pound, aggressive and angry salmon out of my head and tried to temper my expectations. We went by a few pools and runs that I thought looked good, but Mario paid no attention to them. Finally, he slowed down and eased the boat up the right side of a rip of fast water and anchored, midriver, just below a rapid. He sat down and lit a cigarette. A minute or two went by and he said, "Are you going to fish or what?"

"Here?" I said.

"No over there" pointing at a log jam and then laughing. This water seemed so fast, but I did as I was told: stood up, unpinned my fly from the rods stripping guide, stripped out some line and made a cast, down and across and followed with a huge back mend to slow the fly down.

Mario looked at the line and then at me and then at the line again and with a confused look said, "What are you fishing for?"

"Well, salmon I assume," I answered.

"Not like that," was Mario's quick reply. "Cast more square to the current, and don't mend," Mario suggested. I cast closer to square and didn't mend, a large belly formed in the line and the fly raced in its swing. I couldn't help myself and I back mended to slow the fly.

Mario again said, "Don't mend."

Really? The water was moving so fast, and I really wanted a chance at catching a salmon. It didn't make sense to me, but I stripped out a little more line, made a square to the current cast and didn't mend.

The fly was ripping through, then, halfway through the swing I mended the line upstream.

Mario hollered, "And now you are benched, fuckface!"

After a few days of fishing with Topher and a couple of the other guides, I started to realize that I had wrongly assumed that fly fishing for steelhead and Atlantic salmon were the same thing.

Of course, there was crossover and common ground, but it seemed that the differences, some very subtle, would mean the difference in actively fishing for salmon or simply picking up the occasional fish.

I read a lot of books about salmon fishing and had applied the techniques to my steelhead fishing, but I didn't have a frame of reference until I stepped into an Atlantic salmon river.

For example, I would point to a fantastic piece of steelhead holding water and ask if they ever found salmon there. "Oh, maybe the odd fish," would be the reply — a polite way of saying no.

If I fished my fly at what I thought was a seductive pace, I was repeatedly reminded to speed it up. I would pick a fly out of my wallet and ask, "How about this one?"

And get a dismissive shrug and a reply, "Do you have anything a lot smaller?"

When I fish a dry line and wet fly for steelhead I very rarely mend the line, usually preferring to cast to the angle that the fly will fish properly right from touch down. I cast with just enough energy to turn the fly over with a straight line, at the proper angle for desired speed, and let the fly swim. I avoid banging casts that "bark the reel" and bounce a lot of slack into the presentation. So, if I don't normally mend why was I doing it on the salmon river?

It seems that salmon not only like a quicker paced fly; they will also hold in surprisingly fast water. Of course, a few feet down where the salmon or steelhead is holding the difference in current speed might not be as dramatic as it is on the surface. With salmon laying under the faster surface current, it becomes difficult for a steelhead angler to fight the urge to mend to slow the fly. But, if you don't want to get benched, called names and laughed at and hopecatch a salmon, from my understanding, it

Swing the Fly Anthology 2023

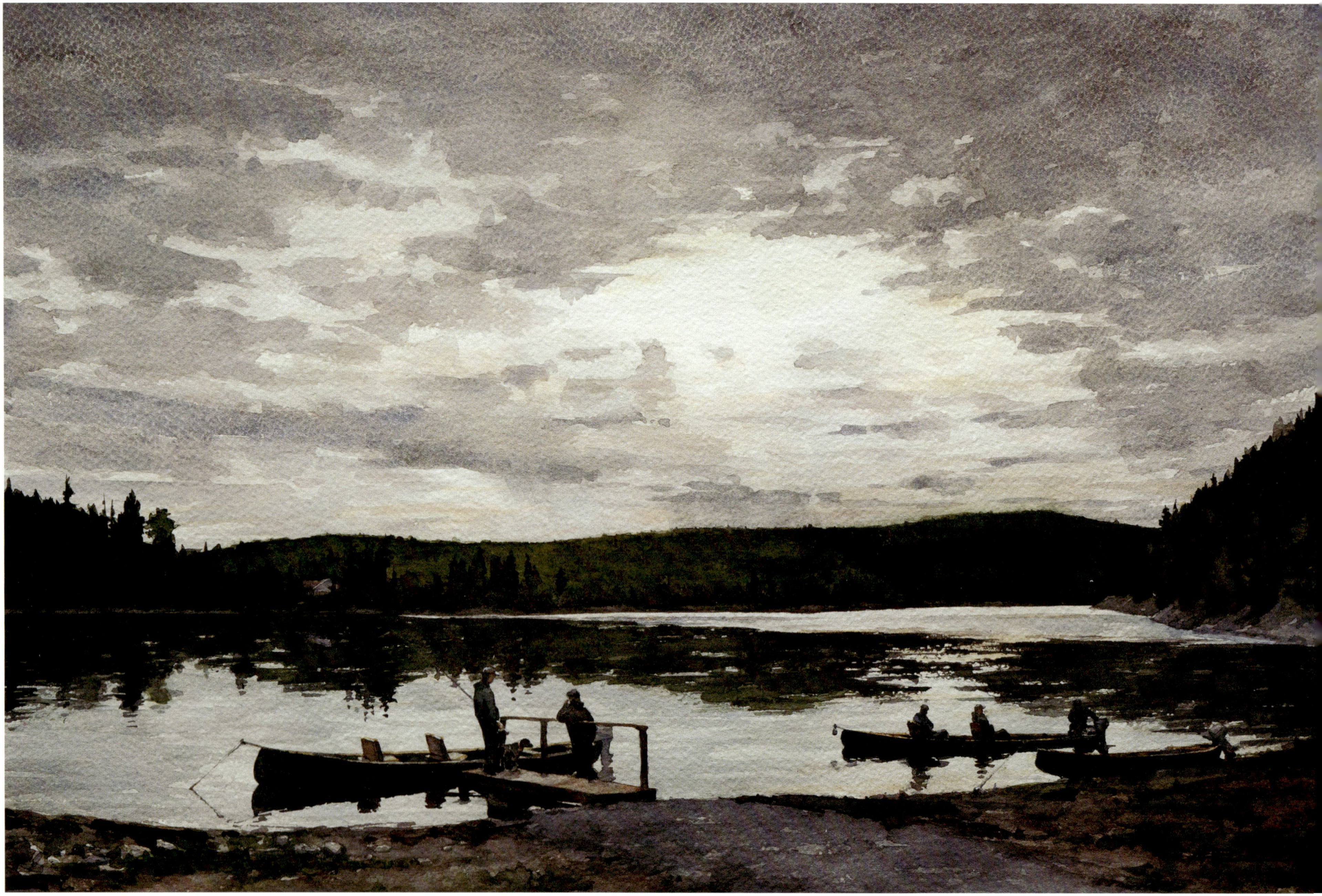

was best to let 'er rip.

After a few days I was no longer asking as many dumb questions, and I felt like I was in the game and covering the water well. However, it's all for nothing if there are no fish around. This was an early trip and summer was a bit late in coming. Wild animals, such as salmon, tend to show up right on time; that time doesn't always line up with our calendar, though.

Late in the fishless week, we found out that Topher and I would be fishing one of the branches of the Grand Cascapedia River. Topher told me that the Cascapedia typically got her salmon earlier than some of the other rivers, and that it was a "big fish" river. He said we would be the only two anglers with six pools to hike in and fish. I went to sleep the night before the last day dreaming of 40-pound salmon and jolting takes coming on a fast swing.

The next morning, hot coffee in hand, we made the drive, talking of course about all things salmon. We picked up our passes for the days fishing at the Cascapedia Society Office and drove the windy road upriver. Topher pointed out pools and famous lodges as we went and told stories of giant salmon landed and lost and the long history of salmon angling on the Cascapedia.

We ran into David Bishop, a famous Cascapedia guide, peering into water and waiting for his clients to arrive. He had seen a few fish around the last few days and was full of energy and encouragement. Adding to the refreshed hope was that it also seemed sunnier and greener here, with birds singing and the smells of summer had finally arrived.

The water of the Cascapedia flowed with the classic tea color, and the flies seemed to glow as they swam just under the surface. Topher and I had rotated through pools all week, but he insisted I fished first all day on my last day of a fishless week. He pointed out the usual taking lies of the salmon, but with each fishless pass I started losing faith. Finally, on the hike into our last run I came to the realization that although I had learned a lot, I would probably not catch my first salmon on this trip. I was no longer thinking of 40 pounders and was starting to think how a 10 pounder or even a grilse would be great. Halfway through the run and past the typical spot where the take should have been, I surrendered. My mind was starting to scheme how I could possibly make it back the following year. I noticed how slow my fly was fishing and thought about how to make it look livelier, but I was spent so what's the point? As my fly reached the hang down there was a giant boil on the slick surface.

I waited to feel the line go tight. It didn't. I couldn't believe it, I had a huge salmon follow my fly, swirl on it and return to its lie, no doubt bored with the slow, lifeless offering.

I could hear Mario's voice ... "Benched!" pinging through my head as the chug and rock of the train pulled me west.

COLORS OF FALL

Joe Janiak

It's always nice to get a fish during early season outings, but more often than not it's about working out the kinks and seeing how the pools have changed since the previous season. Angler: Nick Pionessa

If we are lucky, we have a home river. A river within a relatively short drive where we can escape for a few hours or a full day if life allows. A place that draws us back week after week, season after season — one we get to know intimately. We know which notch in the slate always holds a fish. We know the right sink tip for the specific pool at a specific flow rate, and we know the best spot for a sunrise or sunset.

Rivers we fish with friends and loved ones. The memories from these places go on for miles — mornings and evening, bluebird days and stormy ones. The memorable fish landed and the haunting ones that never came to be.

This is a series of shots from my home river at a really special time of year, when the fall colors are blazing and the river is electric with opportunity. Thanks for looking.

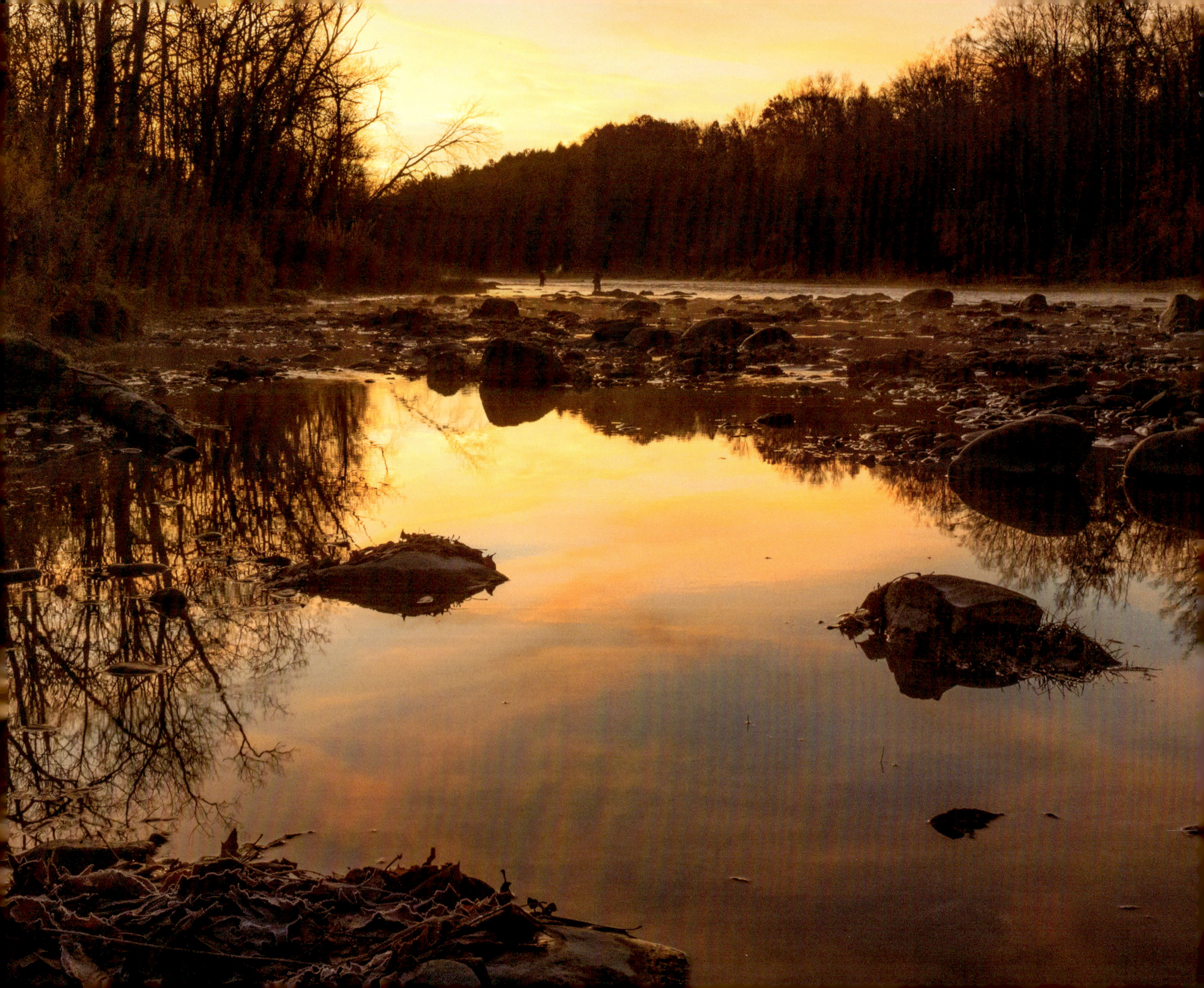

Bright sunshine and bright fish. Erin McGarry with the smile that every steelheader hopes to achieve on a day of swinging.

The anticipation at the start of a new day is what keeps us coming back time and time again. On this day our anticipation was fulfilled when we found a pod of bright fish more than willing to clober a swung fly in the bright sunshine.

Sometimes a fly chooses itself; other times the decision takes a little more consideration...

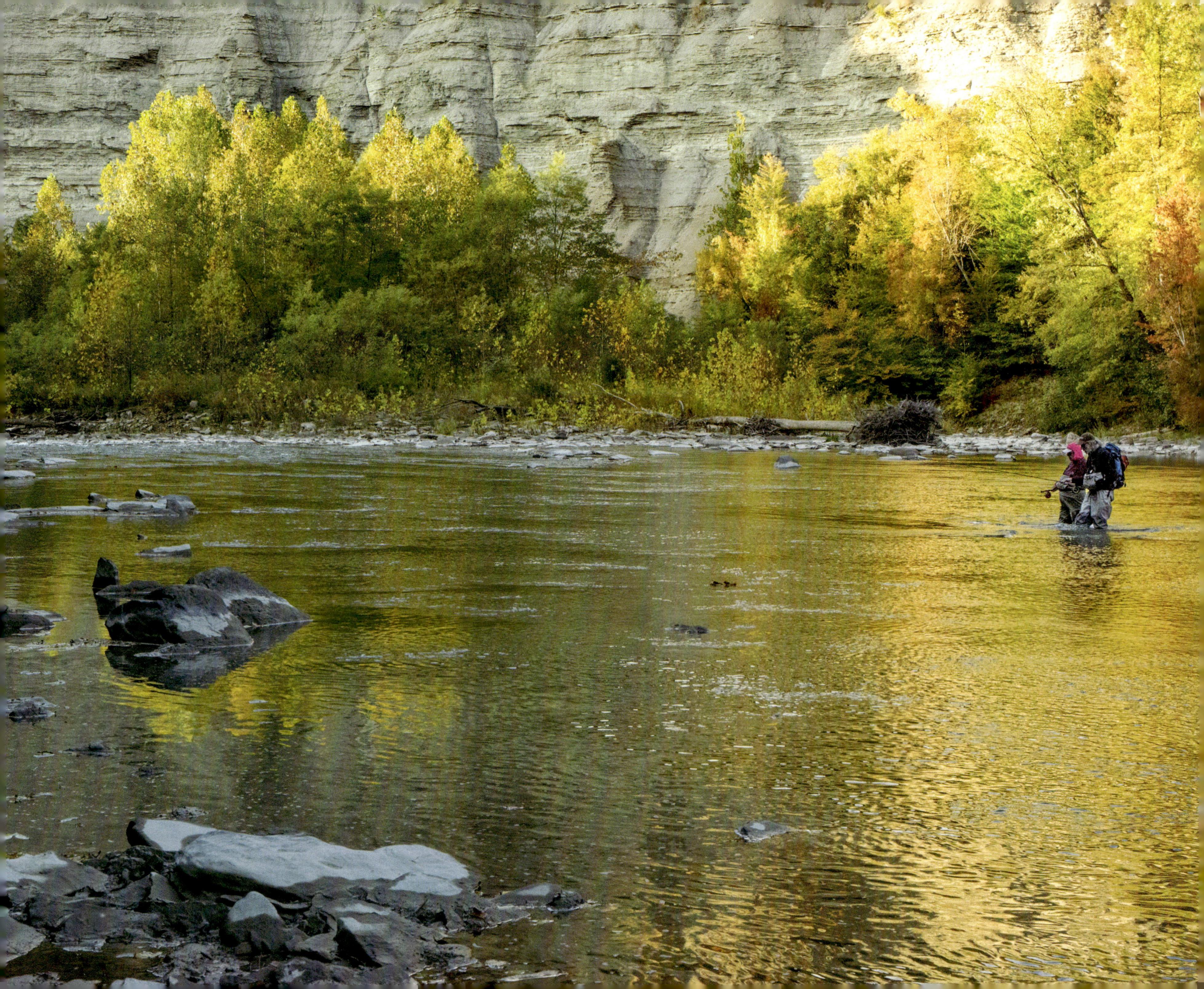

Facing page: Nick and Suzy Pionessa crossing the river on an early autumn evening. Zoar Valley, western New York.

Sunrise in Zoar Valley at peak fall color. I feel lucky to call this my home river.

Clearwater River by Richard C. Harrington

Stories to Tell

Green Ant by Anthony Perpignano

AFTER THE FLOODS

Sam Flanagan

Photo: Zack Williams

Haggard men linger outside the roadside market,
Sneaking in their early morning tallboys
Telling stories of floods,
Over the tired sighs of late winter,
Before the wind comes up again,
And the hard line of rain,
Fetches the closure of another day.
.
They will part with reveries
Of the old years,
When the river spoke clearly.
.
Down below the bridge,
Most saw this water too slow.
Before the tedious slog of rain and wind,
Churned up this long bend in waiting.
.
None of this morning will be neat,
Finding this way,
Or that,
Through winter's expired larder
Of sticks and stones,
To some slick tailing water.
.
Most will still avoid this place,
Because nothing will get figured out down there.
Despite February's candied green waters,
The cigarette boils and streaked lies
Will teach hard lessons:
Fraying rain-wearied marriages,
Neglected chores will linger,
Entire days will be lost there.
Just one more pass.
.
Goosebumps throughout.
.
Standing knee-deep begs a presence,
Found,
And then lost,
A long time ago.
.

The south wind comes for a second day,
Hastening late afternoon
Into another dark oblivion.
The last struggles of fall leaves still dangling,
Reminders of the miseries,
And toils, of summer and drought:
Long gone.
.
Welcome, again, to the electricity of flood,
And the cruel work of renewal to follow,
Beckoning easy days,
When the sun is,
Once again,
Kind and welcome.
.
Eventually,
The wind will release,
To the streaming, blue sounds overhead,
Where the tops of trees talk
To quiet shadows underneath,
And green cobbles return,
Telling secrets
To the passing ghosts
Sliding through emerald velvet mysteries.
.
Now, this watery cradle,
Cold, almost soured and softened,
Returns as an old friend.
.
I cannot step far this morning,
As the smooth lines
And hot shivers of hope
Bear witness to this slickened water,
Moving in a long, silent hiss of purpose,
As the first willow buds
Shudder in the currents.

Harpham Flat

THE CADDIS, THE FLY, THE FISH, AND THE BIRD

M. Robbins Church

Harpham Flat, a/k/a Dutchman Flat (take your pick) on the Deschutes River — I was there mid-November 1988. I had driven over from the Willamette Valley for another shot at summer steelhead. It had been a good year, and I couldn't resist one last fling. I had arrived late the evening before. Mike and Gloria McLucas had left cabin #7 of the Oasis open for me.

I liked that stretch of water along the long reach of Harpham. Earlier that year, I had taken a fish at the upstream head of it and, later, another fish midway down the long slight curve. I worked those pieces this November morning with no takers, then moved on to the stretch at the bottom of the flat, just above the curve to the downstream rapid. There, I ducked into a gap in the alders above the faster water.

A few October caddis were still in the alders and on the water, and as I surveyed the slick near the bank, I saw one quietly taken off the surface by a large but unidentified fish. This is great, I thought. I had been swinging a black wooly bugger down the river, casting as well as I could single-handed with the trees as a tight backdrop.

I snipped off my streamer, added some lighter tippet, and tied on a bushy #10 October Caddis. Here we go, my chance to get a Deschutes steelhead on a dry fly!

Even with the slight gap in the alders, there was no room for a backcast, so I slopped some line out about a dozen feet, straightened it with a roll cast and swung it downstream under the overhanging branches. The still unseen fish rose and sipped in the fly, then came fast as it dropped back down to its lie. I grinned as I snugged it up and braced for a run.

Nothing happened. Nothing. Nada. The fish was on, but not moving. I leaned hard on the 8-weight bamboo rod, placing an impressive bend in it. Still no response. I lifted the rod straight up and pulled. I flattened it to the upstream side and pulled. The fish stayed put. Although part of my leader was out of the water, I still couldn't see the fish.

I had been dissed before in my life, but never by a fish. I stood there, perplexed and pissed. Something had to give — I couldn't stand there all day. I shifted the rod to my left hand, held it as far up in the air as possible, reached out with my right foot, and kicked where my leader disappeared into the murky water.

That is when something happened. Fast. The fish, still not showing itself, bolted downstream into the rapids like an attack submarine at flank speed. The drag on my Hardy St. Aidan reel made a sound like a blender about to explode, but had no effect on the direction or velocity of the fish. I stood there stunned — nothing to do but watch the line and backing disappear, praying that there were no tangles that would rip the guides from my rod. In desperation, I lurched

Swing the Fly Anthology 2023   169

A solitary angler fishes Moss Hole on the Deschutes.

A cabin at the Oasis Resort, late '80s

along the shore downstream, but there was no way I was going through even the edge of the fast water at any speed that would help me.

Then, with just a few loops of backing left on my reel, the fish stopped and turned into a back eddy far downstream. The line went slack. It's running back at me, I thought. With a hint of hope, I reeled as fast as I could, then realized that the barbless fly had come free.

As I rewound a couple hundred yards of backing, my fly line, leader and fly, thoughts of new equipment entered my mind — large arbor spools, maybe multiplier reels, bone-fishing type drag. All the male fly fisher's equivalent of "bigger hammer."

The next day I was back, not with new equipment, but with renewed hope and burning curiosity. This time I did not go to the head of Harpham — I started at The Place. Same fly. Same drill. Slop out some line. Roll cast. Swing it.

Then it happened. My first drift brought a strike! Wait a second, why was my fly still there on the surface? Missed it, I guessed. I gathered myself and cast again. Another rise! But no. Was that a tail? One more time, the charm, right? With total focus, I tracked my fly. Yes, there it was — another tail slap. A few more casts brought no more responses. Laughing, I reeled in, stepped from the river, and went to search for friendlier fish. I knew when I was beaten.

Later that day, during my midday lunch break, I ran into Mike in the Oasis Cafe. I told him my story of the monster steelhead and its remarkable behavior. It was his turn to laugh as he informed me he knew the spot well and, *That my friend was no steelhead. It was a fall Chinook, fresh into the river. Having some fun with you. Pulling your chain. Flipping you off!*

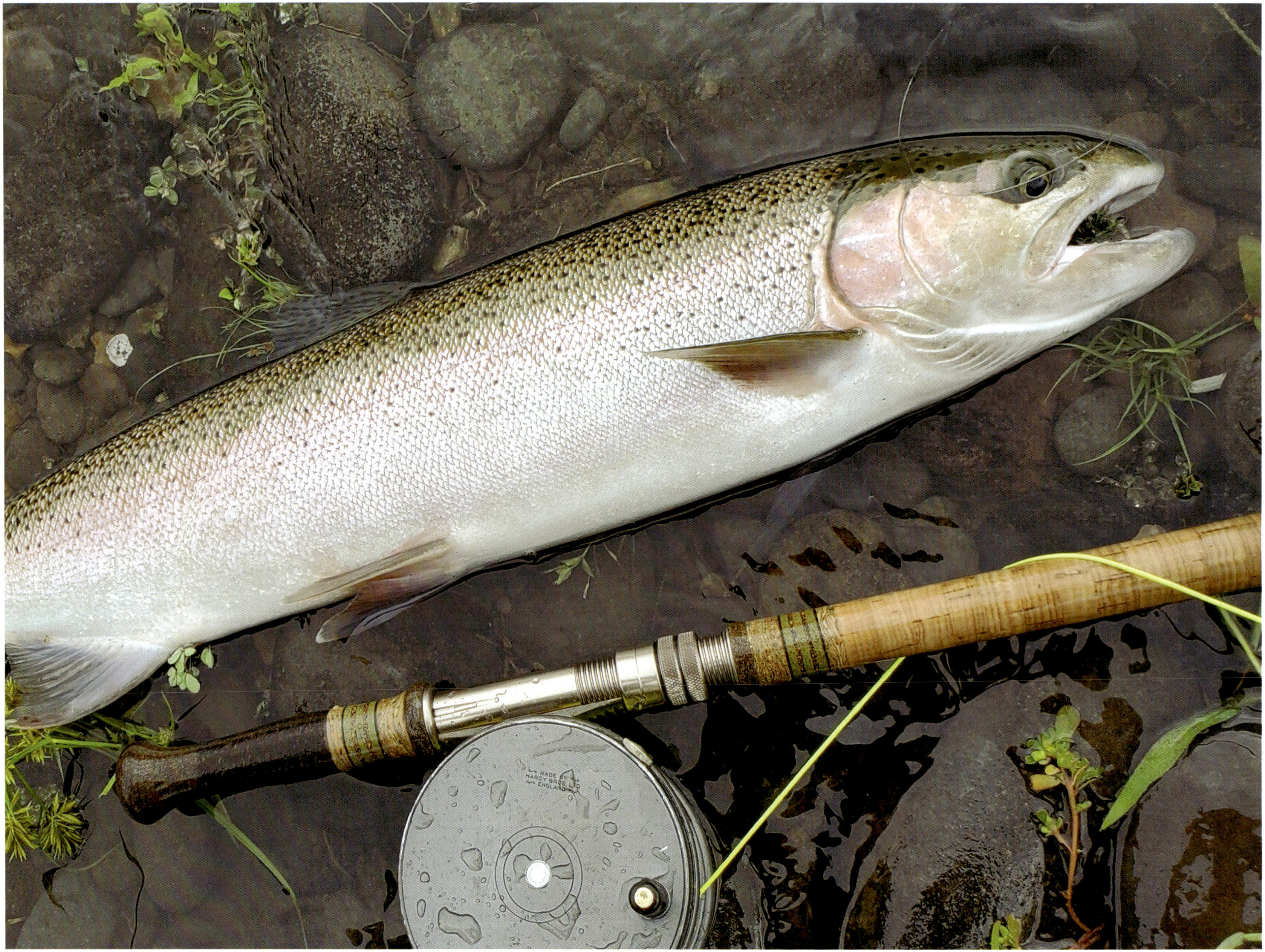
MADE BY
HARDY BROS. LTD
ENGLAND

THE LONG JOURNEY

Todd Hirano

My interest in two-handed rods began in 1994, when I briefly resided in Bozeman, Montana. I frequented the River's Edge Fly Shop, and a couple of the shop employees took annual trips to Skeena River tributaries each fall. As I was beginning to plan my first trip to Skeena country in the fall of 1995, one of the shop employees suggested that I try a two-handed "spey rod."

The thought of utilizing 14- to 15-foot rods for steelhead seemed like overkill, but I had just heard about the use of two-handed rods in fly fishing magazines and in Trey Combs book *Steelhead Fly Fishing*. Along with Bill McMillan's emphasis on line control in his book *Dry Line Steelhead,* my mind opened to the possible advantages of fishing the long rods.

I ended up purchasing my first two handed rod, the Sage 9140-4 "Brownie " in 1995 at the advice of John Hazel, who was working at Kaufmann's Streamborn shop in Tigard, Oregon. I was initially considering the lighter, 7136-4 Brownie, but John advised with a tone of final authority, "If you will do any winter fishing at all, you need the 9140." In the interest of staying within the budget of a family with young children, I purchased the rod in kit form and built it myself.

Lines for two-handed rods were limited in 1995, so I started off by using a Cortland DT-9F line on my newly built rod. Two-hand casting instruction was also limited at the time, so I purchased a Mel Kreiger video from Kaufmann's and later Hugh Falkus's book on spey casting. I was able to conceptually grasp some of the mechanics of the single spey and double spey from the learning materials I had on hand, but my on the water performance of these casts was lacking. My inexperience and attempts at teaching myself to cast the two-handed rod left me frustrated with only the occasional cast going out with any semblance of elegance. I was also beginning to realize that using a standard double-taper line was doing me no favors, either.

My first session of using the two-handed rod took place on the Bulkley River in late September 1995. I had just checked into the Douglas Motel in Telkwa and had several hours to wait until my father-in-law Jim Jones and his friend Toby were to arrive from Bozeman, Montana. I figured to practice my spey casts until evening arrived.

I was able to make modest single speys when I was taking things slow and not aiming for distance. I worked through a couple runs and as evening approached, then returned for a second pass. As I reached the lower section of the run, a steelhead came up for my modified Waller Waker in three consecutive rises and was then solidly hooked and off to the races. Upon landing the spirited steelhead, a friendly kid came over to chat and was kind enough to snap some photos of me with the steelhead. I marveled at the multiple firsts I had just accomplished: my first steelhead on a fly, my first steelhead on a dry fly; my first British Columbia steelhead; and my first steelhead on a two-handed rod. At that moment my fate was sealed as a spey casting, dry fly steelheader.

Since my early days of using two-handed rods, I have gone through various phases with preferred setups for spey casting. I fished my 9140 Brownie exclusively for close to a decade before adding the 8136 Sage IIIe. I then began following a trend of going to shorter rods for a few years. I then went to a phase of using vintage glass single-hand rods to spey cast Wulff Ambush lines. In 2014, I then went to using inexpensive Cabela's switch rods. Years later, I returned to using the longer rods in my collection. Whenever I was fishing my 9140 Brownie, I felt like I was fishing a "long rod."

I had no interest in rods longer than 14 feet as I never felt limited with the capabilities of my already massive gear collection. Well, in the spring of 2021, a young guy named Calem had been reaching out to me through social media about the equipment he had been cycling through. He was looking for the "silver bullet" of rods and lines that would make casting easier for him. He would try out something new and then soon sell it if it wasn't suiting his needs. He was routinely giving me lines he had tried and didn't like — which I happily accepted.

He began telling me about a 16-foot 7-inch, 7-weight rod that was built by Steve Godshall of Central Point, Oregon. Calem talked me into meeting up with him on my local river to "test cast" the long rod. At first glance, the sheer length of the rod seemed outlandish, but I caught a glimpse of the amazing aesthetics of Steve's workmanship — I marveled at the beautiful handle and feather inlays. Even though I could not imagine the usefulness of such a long rod, I entertained Calem's insistence of having me cast the giant rod. I figured he just wanted to show off his latest toy.

Incrementally lengthening line until I had the head and a few strips of running line out on effortless cack-handed single speys, I realized that I had a big smile on my face. I commented to Calem how cool the rod was and that it did not feel out of place on my homewater at all. I loved the ease of casting and found myself readily adjusting to the extra length. Calem also noted my delight with the giant rod, then slyly says, "You wanna buy it from me?" Calem already had his mind on the next best thing, so he offered me the rod at a price I couldn't refuse. Thus began my passion with the long game.

Ownership of the rod led me into contact with its builder, master craftsman Steve Godshall. Steve and I became fast friends and I found every excuse to make the three hour drive to Central Point to visit with him, talk rods, and drop off/pickup rods that I had Steve working on. I love Steve's custom handles so much that I have retrofitted many of my older rods with his exquisite handiwork.

Steve's shop is close to the upper Rogue and there have been times when I would drop something by for Steve to work on, then hit the Rogue for a session of dry fly steelheading. On occasions Steve would text me that he was done working on the rod I left with him. The second 16-foot-plus rod that I obtained was a custom built 16-foot 7-inch, 5/6-weight that Steve asked me to "try out." Of course, anytime I "try out" a custom rod from Steve, I always want to buy it. This long, light rod is a delight to cast and fish with. However, I realized that available long lines in the lighter weights are limited. Casting a 5/6 Vector XL at only 50' line on that long a rod is akin to a mega sized scandi setup. Although it is a fun, comfortable combination to fish with, wind can bring challenges with the light line.

I had purchased an inexpensive Orvis Streamline 15-foot, 10/11-weight a few years ago from a friend who bought the rod at a local fly fishing club auction. I experimented with casting this rod with the heaviest lines I had on hand, none of which were rated for a 10/11-weight rod. The firm, progressive action of this rod just didn't respond well to being under loaded.

I purchased a heavier line that I hoped would properly load this powerful rod. I got a hold of the 10/11 Beulah Aerohead (810 grains @ 62') and found that this line made this rod come alive. I had the opportunity to bring this rod/line combo out to the Clearwater, and it felt right at home. The mass of the heavy line cut the wind and the firm power of rod gave direct feedback on what I wanted the line to do. I later purchased the longer 10/11 Ballistic Vector XL (870 grins @ 75') through Steve Godshall and found this line to also perform well with the bargain Orvis rod. I grew to love this humble, entry level rod enough that I got a Steve Godshall custom handle retrofitted to it. This modification always transforms the performance and feel of any rod.

I had not previously imagined using rod/line combos in the heavier weights until I stumbled upon that Orvis 15-foot, 10/11-weight, but I realized that I liked the performance of long lines in the heavier weights. I discovered that there needs to be more weight in lines where mass

Swing the Fly Anthology 2023

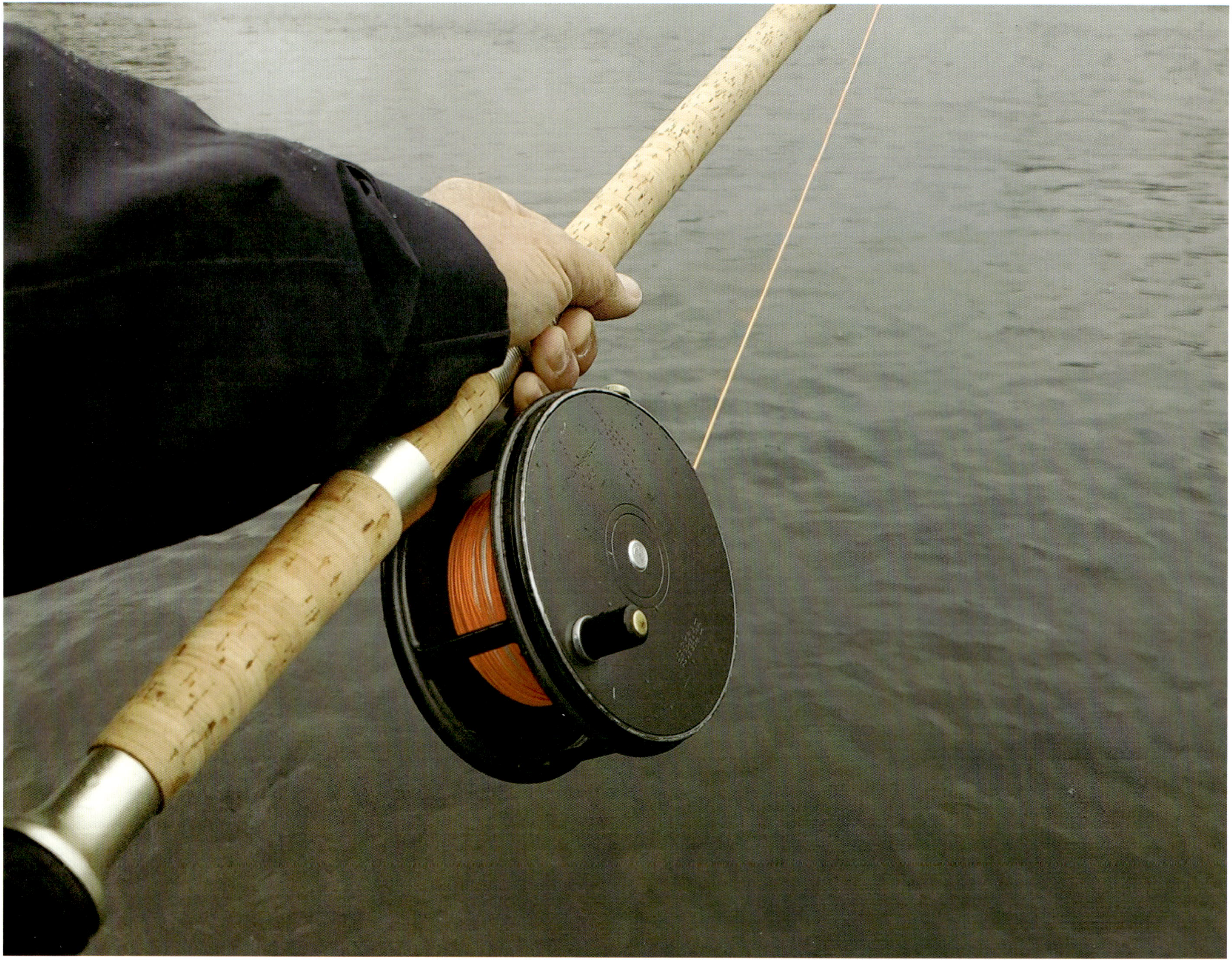

is stretched out over a longer span. I began to think if a 15-footer is fun — what about a 16-foot-plus, 10/11-weight? Calls were made to Steve Godshall and to my surprise, he responded that he does not build and sell very many rods in the heavier line ratings, but he was wanting to help me out.

After some brainstorming, Steve called me back and said he had a couple options for me to look at. I made the drive to his shop to look at what he had. One option was a 17-foot, 8/9/10-weight Meiser Highlander CX that was a built as a loaner for potential customers to try out. Only a few of these blanks were built due to very small demand. Another option was the 16-foot, 8/9/10-weight Meiser Highlander CX loaner, and the other option was a blank that Steve mocked up with a tip top for me to try out for feel before building it out.

I immediately fell in love with the Meiser 17-footer and found the 10/11 Vector XL to be a perfect match. The 16-footer also felt great with the 10/11 Vector XL, but I figured if was going big, I might as well go with the 17'er. Bob Meiser kindly finished it off with his trademark scripting and feather inlay.

The blank that Steve mocked up didn't have the progressive power profile that I wanted so we continued problem solving on another rod that he could build for me to cast 9/10 lines. The solution Steve came up with was taking a 15' blank with the power profile I liked, then extending it with a 2-foot-plus handle section. The end result was a custom built, 17-foot, 2-inch 9/10-weight that loves vintage CND GPS lines and the Gaelforce Equilizer 83 9/10. I also recently came upon another unexpected opportunity when a Speypages member reached out to me to sell his Bruce and Walker 16 1/2-foot, 9/10-weight "Walker" at a price I couldn't refuse. This is a sickness.

What I have discovered with the use of long rods over the past couple years is how versatile they are. I always thought that the mega-sized rods were only at home on big waters like the Clearwater or Snake Rivers. I have found the long rods to be right at home on the Oregon rivers I fish which are often many times smaller. With the long rods and lines, I am able to cover larger swaths of water, often from bank to bank. I am also able to cover lies at a steeper angle more easily when necessary. I remember the first time I took the 16-foot 7-inch Quantum to the North Umpqua a couple years ago and felt a bit ridiculous being on a intimate river with a giant rod. However, when I fished the famous Swamp Creek run with the long rod for the first time, I was amazed with how easy it was to cover the holds along the opposite bank with a steep angle that allowed for slow swings over prime structure.

Casting the longer rods and lines can seem intimidating, but with practice and adjustments in technique, there are great joys in laying out a long line across steelhead waters. Bruce Kruk has been incredibly generous in sharing tutorial videos on casting on forums like Speypages and Swing the Fly. Bruce's demonstrations and explanations on casting have been incredibly helpful to me. The use of the longer rods and lines has also called me back to utilizing left hand up casts when necessary and this has been another learning curve with the "Long Journey", but the efforts have been worthwhile.

It has never been my goal to be able to cast record distances and enter competition at Spey-O-Rama. Thank goodness for that, because my modest casting capabilities still allow me to see my dry flies when an aggressive steelhead attacks.

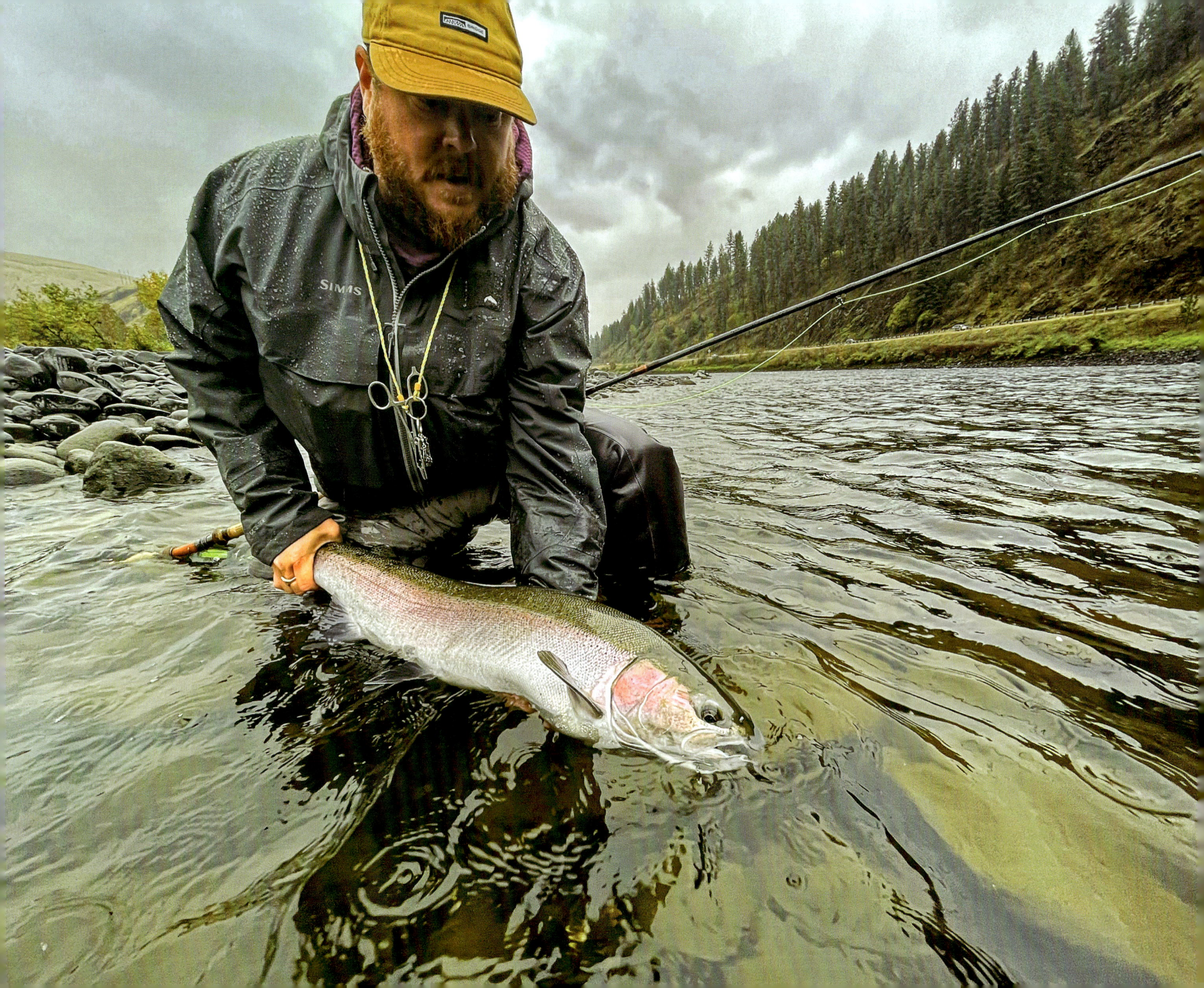
SIMMS

NAMING RUNS

Bill Pfeiffer

We gazed downriver past the tailout and saw the deep green of the slot at the start of the next run beaconing to us, like the Sirens, calling in a couple of lost sailors.

"You ever see anybody swinging this spot?" my fishing partner asked. "It looks pretty juicy."

"Nope." I replied. "But we're definitely gonna!" You know the feeling when you hear that voice saying, "Now that I look at it, this place looks like a steelhead hotel."

We slipped our Watermasters softly into the eddy at the top of what looked like a wading nightmare, a 100+ yards of riprap that dropped straight into the abyss of the river channel. It left little room for error, and that was simply wading it; not fighting 18 pounds of raw muscle, straight from three years in the North Pacific. We knew it wasn't going to be easy to even cast here.

"Well, as they say, if it's hard for anglers to fish, it probably holds big fish," I said, scrolling through the fishing advice encyclopedia in my brain. "I'll take the top. You start at the meat."

About a dozen casts later, I heard the scream of his reel and saw the water erupt below me as a gorgeous bright hen steelhead made her first valiant run for freedom. I reeled up and started to think about how in the hell I was going to get down the rocks in time. Like Gollum on meth, I scrambled my way, counting the bruises and scrapes. Gradually, he brought the fish under control, I tailed it, and we basked in the glory of her magnificence as she finned gently between us for a few seconds.

"What an amazing fish!" my buddy stammered, shaking and blown away by her power.

"Incredible," I replied. "Let's let her go. Maybe I can finally find one of my own here, too. She's got a buddy out there." We watched her vanish, celebrated with some tobacco, and I slunk my way back to my rod on the bank.

My emotions were split evenly down the middle, joy for him, with a good helping of self pity for the long dry spell I'd been on. I peeled some line back out and gruffly started back to my perceived futility. Why the hell didn't that fish eat my fly? No sooner did this thought cross my psyche than I felt the strong grab and pull of a large steelhead.

"Fish!"

My buddy frantically reeled in his line as we watched the giant buck take to the air, cartwheeling higher than any I'd ever seen before. Soon after it splashed down and turned, the hook came free, and I sat back on a slightly less sharp boulder, like a plastic bag full of Jell-O.

"Dude, I'm so sorry," my buddy said, just getting back up the hellish bank as I got out another smoke.

"What can you do, man? That was the greatest jump I've ever witnessed from a fish."

"Agreed. Well, one thing's for sure: I bet we'll be fishing this run a lot more often," he laughed.

"CALL 'EM WHATEVER THE FUCK YOU WANT TO."
                    -POPPY CUMMINS

Photo: Nick Halle

"You caught the first fish. You should get to name it." And so our brainstorm began for the rest of the day, as we tried to encapsulate the past few hours into a label unique to only us.

Naming runs is something fly swingers take particular joy in. All anglers like to name their fishing spots, even guys plunking for catfish at the "Honey Hole," but spey people are especially fixated on giving a place a moniker to pass along to their friends, and if you're lucky, the greater community. If you know the name of a particular run on a famous river, you know something that not everyone in the world knows. You are, effectively, in the club. When you visit new water and meet new anglers, evenings chats around the campfire are in a secret code only the initiated can understand. But after a few years, you're a code talker, too, with a whole new language that's only known to a few, the ultimate inside joke.

My home steelhead river is the Clearwater in Idaho and many of the runs are famous to the fly swinging community. From the Miller Hole to the Stink Hole, every spot with walking-speed current and a few boulders seems to have a name between Kooskia and Lewiston. Not all the names are imaginative or creative. Every river I've fished seems to have a "Powerline" run. Some have several. (I was recently told about a scientific theory that sea-run fish get confused by the electrical field near high tension power lines, causing them to rest.)

As all steelheaders know, whether you're swinging Camp Water, Eagles Nest, or Leaning Tree, we don't always have a scientific reason why a certain spot is a good one. Sometimes it's the angler known for always being there, sometimes it's a particular instant in time, or plain convenience, but every run name has a story behind it.

I asked Poppy Cummins at the Red Shed what he thought about all the different names for the Clearwater holes. I originally thought I'd make this bit about all the folklore surrounding the river. We talked for a few minutes about all the history, but in the end I think he said it best: "Call 'em whatever the fuck you want to."

It dawned on me that it really didn't matter. Names are for you. So if you ever find yourself swinging Indiana Jones on a cool October day, count yourself in the club. And no, I'm not going to tell you where it is.

Photo: Zack Williams

TUNING THE DESCHUTES WITH A *NINE*

John Barratt

I awakened to a nagging headache requiring two pills. The sun had risen, though the canyon was still cloaked in shadows. I remembered parts of the 14-hour drive, nothing about setting up camp. I really wanted to be on the Olympic Peninsula or in British Columbia, but with only four days off, traveling that far was unrealistic. Plus, I knew this river, or so I thought. My memory was no longer reliable strokes will do that.

The campground was largely empty. I lingered over breakfast, savoring the warmth from the compact stove. On the ground nearby, a pair of scrub jays fought over a food wrapper left by a previous camper. When I flattened my right palm on the picnic table, I could feel the vibrations made by the tiny avian feet. Contrary to Nate's insistence, I still do not think he cautioned me about how much the surgery might enhance my sense of feel.

The staff at DeserTech call me a NINE, short for "neural interface no electrode". I live in Palmdale, north of LA, a short drive from DeserTech's offices. Nate assures me I grew up in Portland.

When I checked yesterday, the Deschutes River flow near Madras was 3600 cubic feet per second. I still have balance issues. To be safe, I brought a wading staff. There are no fly shops in Palmdale, so I ordered a few items from an outfit in Bend. When the package arrived, it also contained a colorful, adhesive-backed sticker from a local brew pub. The decal struck me as a surprisingly kind gesture. Random things like that affect me.

I chose the 13-foot, 6-weight spey and devoted almost 30 minutes to preparing my gear. The steelhead runs are so low, I reluctantly decided to target only trout.

The water was far colder than I expected and the riverbed a maddening jumble of moss-covered rocks. I moved tentatively, relying heavily on the wading staff. I forgot to set my anchor point on the initial casts. On the third attempt, the nerves in my right arm twitched. I pulled upward and felt an opposing tug before the line went slack.

I felt my confidence growing as I swung the heavily-weighted sculpin pattern over a mid-channel shelf, casting, moving and recasting. Something caused the fly to pause, I immediately lifted the rod tip and was rewarded with a clump of green debris.

When Nate, the chief science officer, explained the implant procedure, complete with a slick animation, it seemed simple enough — a miniscule stent threaded into my cortex and another device, implanted in my upper chest. Signing the consent form, I ignored the lengthy risk section and my doctor's cautions, and instead thought only about restoring feeling to my right side.

A loud splash, no more than four rod lengths away, drew my attention. An osprey straddled a large trout in the shallows. Nate constantly

Photo: Zack Williams

> THEY ARE NOT CONNECTED IN ANY WAY, AND YET THE DEVICE IN MY CHEST SENDS SIGNALS TO THE STENT IN MY BRAIN. I OFTEN ASK NATE TO EXPLAIN THIS; BUT HE ALWAYS TELLS ME THE SAME THING – THAT INFORMATION IS PROPRIETARY.

encourages me to focus on the nerve impulses, the twitches. He calls it tuning. I crouched, grasped the nearest exposed boulder with my right hand and closed my eyes. Nothing. The distance was too great. I couldn't feel the wriggling fish or the osprey, just the relentless current. Disappointed, I returned to my fishing.

After missing two likely takes, I realized I wasn't doing it correctly. The next time my right arm tingled, I swung the graphite downstream, parallel to the current. Eight redsides later, I wished Nate could see me. I was becoming skilled at differentiating inanimate objects from fish.

They are not connected in any way, and yet the device in my chest sends signals to the stent in my brain. I often ask Nate to explain this; but he always tells me the same thing — that information is proprietary.

I waded into deeper water, immersed myself in the vibrations, and began catching or, at least, hooking fish at will. I had no idea the Deschutes River was so productive.

"Wow, it looks like you've got it figured out. Is that one of those fancy spey rigs? What flies are you using?"

Startled, I turned to face the voice. Minutes must have ticked by because the stooped man felt compelled to repeat himself. I furrowed my brow, mentally assembling potential replies. I wasn't trying to be evasive or rude, just accurate in my response.

My questioner shook his head and muttered something inaudible. I knelt, clasped the wet surface of the nearest boulder, and felt his retreating footfalls.

Original artwork: Richard C. Harrington

"SON, YOU CAN BRING WHATEVER KINDA RIG YOU WANT TOMORROW MORNING, BUT IF YOU WANNA CATCH JUNGLE TROUT, I'D TAKE THE OFFER."

JUNGLE TROUT & JUNGLE RODS

Robert Meiser

I grew up in an area of the country that never lacked in finny diversity, nor in devoted sportsmen. The upper Great Lakes is just plain loaded with an incredible variety of game fish. Between friends and family, I was constantly exposed to one kind of fishing trip or another, on a year-round basis. We fished the same waters whether they were encased with three feet of black ice or mirroring the calm of a midsummer sunrise.

The crew I fished with knew their home waters well, and we had a seasonal routine of fishing trips that were as diverse as the critters we were after. The decision of where to go for a three-day holiday weekend, and what to fish for, was always decided by the older and wiser guys. There always seemed to be an endless amount of data that needed to be fed into the formula before a final decision was made — things like advancing storm fronts, wind direction, safe ice, stream levels, weed growth, post-spawn, pre-spawn, boat ramp crowds, peppermint versus ginger schnapps, first shift and second shift work schedules, grandkids, wives, power augers, Zebco 33s, Mitchell 300s, or tip-ups, leeches, crawlers, shiners, Rapalas or Mr. Twisters. All very complex stuff that warranted serious discussion. Most importantly, though, was which resort nearby had the best polka bands, Pabst on tap and Friday night fish fries! These were all important considerations, and these sage decisions had to be made by our most experienced souls.

As a boy, and beyond, one of my favorite summer weekend camping destinations was a small primitive campground on the Mt. Morris chain of lakes. Located in Waushara County, the tiny community of Mt. Morris is in the middle of central Wisconsin's legendary Sand Country. These lakes are typical for the area: ultra clear, spring fed and tucked into the beautiful surrounding oak and pine hills. Their shorelines are fringed by towering stately groves of white pine that shade modest, well-kept summer homes and a few youth camps. These are very pleasant, quiet lakes, whose silence is usually broken only by nothing louder than the mellow grumble of a 5-horse Evinrude outboard motor or the distant laughs and giggles of the church camp kids from across the lake. A thick layer of long, soft, white pine needles covers the floor of sand country, and it seems to muffle the sharp edges of most sounds. I've always loved this place. My parents and a couple of friends got together and set up a little 16-foot Mallard trailer on this small campground in Mt. Morris. Between work vacations, holidays and weekends, we all kept the trailer occupied for several summers.

As a grade-schooler, I spent two summers there myself, and I got to know the lakes pretty well. The Mt. Morris chain of lakes were not really targeted by many serious fishermen. You occasionally heard stories about some camp kid being nearly yanked from the dock by some monster Northern that decided the kids' nearly landed pumpkinseed was breakfast! But, if you knew where to find them, the chain was loaded with big bluegills, crappies, bass and a surprising number of 36"-plus northerns.

The number of these stuffed leviathans hanging above the back-bar mirrors of the local resorts testified to their healthy existence, and over the years we caught a few of these big guys, but come the full moon of June, we were after bluegills on the beds. They were my earliest fly rod experience, and armed with my first store bought 8-foot fiberglass Heddon Pal, a size HDH floating fly line and a foam-body Dickey Spider, I'd load up on these little brutes. I swear, if bluegills got to be ten pounds, it'd take a come-along to bring em in!

One late morning while cleaning a mess of these guys, I noticed a new camp set up across from ours. Leaning over a big cooler mounted on the open tailgate of a rust bucket Rambler station wagon was a newcomer to the park. He was an old guy with a rumpled felt hat, a pug pipe and a severely patched pair of canvas hip boots. On his camp stove was a cast-iron skillet full of nice-sized, sizzling brookies and a couple cobs of steaming sweet corn. He noticed my interest, and invited me into his camp with a nod. I couldn't refuse the invite — he had trout, and hopefully he'd share a few secrets with an anxious kid. He certainly looked like a wise old fisherman to me, like one of our own elders.

Waushara County is laced with miles of little sandy bottom spring creeks: Willow, Mecan, Pine, White and a few others. All chuck full of browns and wild brookies, but at this point I didn't have much knowledge of these creeks, and was anxious to learn. Once I got close enough to this old gent checking his cooler, I knew I'd really hit pay dirt, because within it was the most beautiful batch of brookies these young eyes had ever laid on! My intense stare obviously did not escape his notice, as he offered me a place at the fire to join him for breakfast. We talked, drank coffee and ate trout, but more than that, I got invited to join him on a section of a nearby creek he called "The Jungle." He said, "This is where these trout were caught, and the recent rains put the fish on the bite." We'd fish together the following morning.

It turned out that compared to this guy, we were the newcomers to this campground, as he had been using this area as a mid-way camp en-route from Chicago to the trout streams of Michigan's Upper Peninsula for over 25 years. He had a brother that lived in Mt. Morris, and the trout that he had on ice in his cooler were destined for his brother's freezer. He would pick them up on his return trip and, along with the accumulated keepers from the U.P., would return home for an annual 4th of July trout fry with his friends and family. Sounded right to me.

As I was returning back to our camp, he asked about the rod I'd be using in the morning. I returned to my new pal. "Nice rod," he said. "Any flies?" I showed him what I had. "Good, but you won't be using them tomorrow; too much brush; they don't call it the Jungle for nothing! We'll be using garden worms and crawlers, you can borrow one of my cane poles."

I was fine with this, as I had been fishing every hand-me-down bamboo rod I could get my hands on since I was knee high to a piss ant. But, I was proud of my new fiberglass fly rod, and asked him if I couldn't rig it for worms and pass on the cane pole offer.

He said "Son, you can bring whatever kinda rig you want tomorrow morning, but if you wanna catch Jungle trout, I'd take the offer. Your rod won't get you into the really brushy, deeper, dark water shadow holes and undercuts where the bigger brookies are. Let me show you a few of my cane rods. You'll see what I mean. I got a few started at my brother's place, and I need to get them done for him before I leave for the U.P.; he fishes the Jungle too! Go ask and see if you can drive over to my brother's place with me."

This Jungle business was sounding more intriguing all the time, especially the "deep, dark hole" stuff. I definitely had to do this!

I was introduced to his brother and family and was led to a well weathered fieldstone, wood-clad building on the lakeshore that served as a boat house and workshop. Its sun lit wooden plank floor was full of benches strewn with mountains of cantilever metal tackle boxes and assorted fishing gear. There were various hand tools, a small metal lathe and a jointer. A free-standing band and table saw filled the middle spaces. The exposed ceiling joists above us supported assorted lengths of 1"- to 2"-thick, air curing, rough-sawn pine and oak planks, ancient wooden landing net frames, bags of duck decoys and well-worn wooden oars. The exposed interior wall studs displayed a fine selection of buxom calendar girls. Cobwebs stubbornly held sawdust-covered clusters of browned pine needles suspended into every nook and cranny, and in the afternoon heat, the building gave off the friendly smells of old outboard motor gas, Borkim Riff pipe tobacco and pine shavings.

On one cleared bench top were three bamboo cane poles, each about 6- to 7-foot long. Not split cane rods, but cane poles, like no other I had ever seen before. The old guy called them "Calcutta" cane and said, "For this purpose, Calcutta is the best cane to use. They have smoother nodes, are straighter, have flater tapers and are lighter and stronger than the regular cane poles one can buy at most any tackle store."

He was right, I was very familiar with the tackle store variety of cane poles, and these looked more like a stout piece of tapered oat straw. I didn't really know what a 'node' was at the time, but I got the idea. These poles were arrow straight, and the node segments were spaced much further apart. The three poles he had on the bench were in various phases of construction, with one nearly finished.

It was this one that he handed to me. The rod was very light and had a gentle flex to it. It had a highly polished oak wood seat milled and glued into the hollow butt end of the cane pole. On

Original artwork: Richard C. Harrington

the seat were two simply milled and polished locking bands made from ½-inch-wide sections of brass pipe. These held the legs of an old single action Pfuelger skeleton frame fly reel in place. The grip area above the reel seat was formed by a varnish-covered winding of cured rawhide strap, of which each end was lashed with a 1/2-inch-long wrap of fine, single-strand copper wire. The rod had only one agate guide on it, and it was located just above the grip. Just above this single guide, was a smooth, feathered back, tear-shaped slot, bored through the rod's surface. The tip of the rod was fitted with a milled brass collar with radiused and polished edges that went slightly proud of the rod's tip top edge. The whole rod length was incrementally thread wrapped to add strength and varnished. A fine braided casting line, with an attached section of mono tippet went from the reel, through the guide, and entered the inside of the rod at the lower slot. It exited the rod's interior at the tip of the rod, where it went through the smoothly milled, brass tip top collar.

I had never seen anything quite so impressive, nor so confusing! My first question was: "How does the line get through the inside of the pole?"

"I burn out the node membranes with red hot steel, then finish the inside with extended rat tail files and reamers," was his reply. "That's what we're gonna do this afternoon, and you're welcome to stay and watch if you wish."

This I had to see!

The steels used to burn out the membranes were in various lengths and diameters, made from 1/2" to 1/8" diameter round stock. They were heated on the burner of a white gas camp stove until the tip glowed and then quickly plunged into the interior of the pole. The membranes burned out quite easily, and a smaller diameter stock was used as he progressed towards the tip. The membrane edges were then cleaned up on the inside diameter of the pole by using extended series reamers or files. The reamers were made from square stock steel, with the edges ground and sharpened. For this purpose, various sizes of square stock were used to match the inner diameter of the pole. They were set up with a 'T' handle and turned by hand. Very simple. The tips of these poles were perhaps a shy 3/16-inch in outer diameter, the butts maybe 3/4"-inch or so. He made the rod in two sections, cutting the pole at a mid-length node. The sections were then scarff jointed and outside sleeved with a milled and polished brass collar. The rod was as finely made as any split bamboo rod that I have ever seen. It was beautiful in its simple elegance.

Upon completion of the nearly finished rod he'd shown me earlier that day, he handed it over to me and said, "Here you go laddy, the perfect jungle rod; if you wish, you can use this one tomorrow." I didn't bother to ask him why he went through so much trouble to build a rod with only one guide. I felt sure he had his reasons, and I also figured that it surely had something to do with this mysterious jungle trout business. I'd find out about this stuff tomorrow.

As instructed, I met him at his campfire at sunrise. His breath was visible over a hot cup of coffee, and little was said as we both waited for the sleep to leave our eyes. When we finished our coffee he said, "Let's go

Brook Trout

Original artwork: Richard C. Harrington

son; the trout await us."

The creek section we drove to was not on public land, and I will say no more (as a solemn oath I made to him then and still hold to this very day), other than that it is a section of stream between Mt. Morris Hill and Lake Poygan. We parked the car well off the road, hidden from the view of any passersby.

When asked why he did this and chose to walk down the road for nearly half a mile before we crossed the bridge, his answer was, "Sometimes people follow me or my brother to see where we're gonna fish!"

Now, I've heard stories of guys like this. Seemingly paranoid guys, who leave their driveways before sunup with their lights off, so as not to alert the neighbors of their departure. Guys that when followed enroute to their favorite fishing holes, lead their uninvited guests on a merry chase throughout the unlit back roads of rural Wisconsin, for miles on end, only to return them back to their own driveways! Could this old coot be one of these legendary guys?

There was no visible trail as we left the road to enter the brush that engulfed the creek. My guide and mentor carried two items in his hands — a trout rod and a machete, which lent an ominous twinge to this sketchy ordeal. I had never seen such a thick jumble of buck brush and tag alder. In fact, I don't think I could have even imagined it. It looked impenetrable, in every sense of the word! We entered the brush on our hands and knees and tediously crawled our way back towards the creek.

At one point, what I now considered to be my quite possibly crazed and seriously deranged trout guide said, "I have a trail blazed through this thicket just ahead. I don't cut the trail right to the road, because if I did every local within 50 miles of here would be sneaking in and following me and my brother's trail to our best holes."

I remained unresponsive to this explanation. At a minimum, I just wanted to see a trailhead, or at least be able to proceed vertically. At maximum, I considered the fact that I might be on the verge of becoming some weird tabloid statistic!

As foretold, the trail did begin just a short distance ahead. It was a narrow, barely shoulder width, winding passage, with thick edges reaching well above our heights. The alder branches had obviously been pruned back for years.

Shortly, the trail led us to a small sun brightened opening, filled with an untrammeled, high ground grassy meadow, flowered with patches of cowslip and wild iris. The meadow framed an alder-free section of our creek, as it slowly meandered its way back into the jungle. The creek was all deep, dark, full of shadow holes and undercuts ... just as promised. And it was beautiful!

"This," he said, "is where we'll begin. Most of the holes that we fish will be like this one. But this one is deep, so don't use a little garden worm, use a big crawler to get down deep enough. Go off to the side, way up to the top of the hole, and weasel your way into the brush. Don't spook the hole. Poke that rod right through the brush, and feed out line downstream into the undercuts, and watch the line closely. If it even twitches, set the hook. If it stops, or starts moving up stream, set the hook; if line suddenly starts screaming off the reel, and heading downstream, don't bother to set the hook. It's a big trout, and he's yours!"

I did as instructed to the letter, and immediately realized the advantage of this rod. The line never got tangled in the brush as it was fed out, nor did it tangle up as the line raced through it with a good fish on. And boy, I hooked a beauty on that very first drift. In fact I hooked several that day; all thanks to the fact that the old guy let me have first crack at nearly every hole we came to.

It turned out that he and his brother had been grooming this trail for many years, and in fact, they each lengthened it a bit every year or so to open up new holes. The trail followed the creek for more than a mile and a half through the entire length of the jungle. The trail never really went right to the creek bank. They cleverly placed secret trail markers, so you knew where the cut offs were that led you on hands and knees to exactly the right position above each hole. In many places, you could be literally six feet away from the creek bank and not see it. For this reason, jungle trout rarely saw a hook. They grew bigger than the average brookie found in the nearby public waters, and there were greater numbers of them.

Over the following years, I, too, with their permission, cut a few lengths of my own trails down to the hidden, tangled banks of the jungle and told them what trail markers to look for. This went on for many years, and I don't think more than three people actually fished this creek section on a regular basis.

It was an incredible day in the jungle. Woodcock could be heard making their cheerful whooping serenades far above our heads. And in the high grass of the meadows, ultra-protective male red-winged blackbirds aggressively dove at us when we dallied too long or too close to their mate's nesting sites. Bobolinks sang their impossibly complex, melodious tunes for us, and many fat, brilliantly colored wild brookies were brought to the grass with our jungle rods.

We fished until the nighthawks started to show and the twilight air started to fill with the drone of countless hordes of thirsty mosquitos. We swatted our way back through our narrow, now dimly lit hand carved hallways through the jungle, and reached the road's entrance just at sunset.

I know both brothers are now gone, as this was over 60 years ago. But I do return to this neck of the woods every few years, and I still fish these same secret holes. The creek is still full of nice brookies, and it's now the only stream left on which I will allow my over-inflated fly fishing ego to use bait. The jungle trail is now in the hands of a loyal, unnamed guardian, and I trust its whereabouts will always remain a secret, except to a chosen few. I don't think it's possible to fish this water with anything other than a jungle rod, and I know that its present riverkeeper fishes with one of his own. A Jungle Trout rod made in the traditional Jungle fashion.

Three cheers to our clever, departed rod builder and his wonderful jungle trout rods.

May his legacy continue forever!

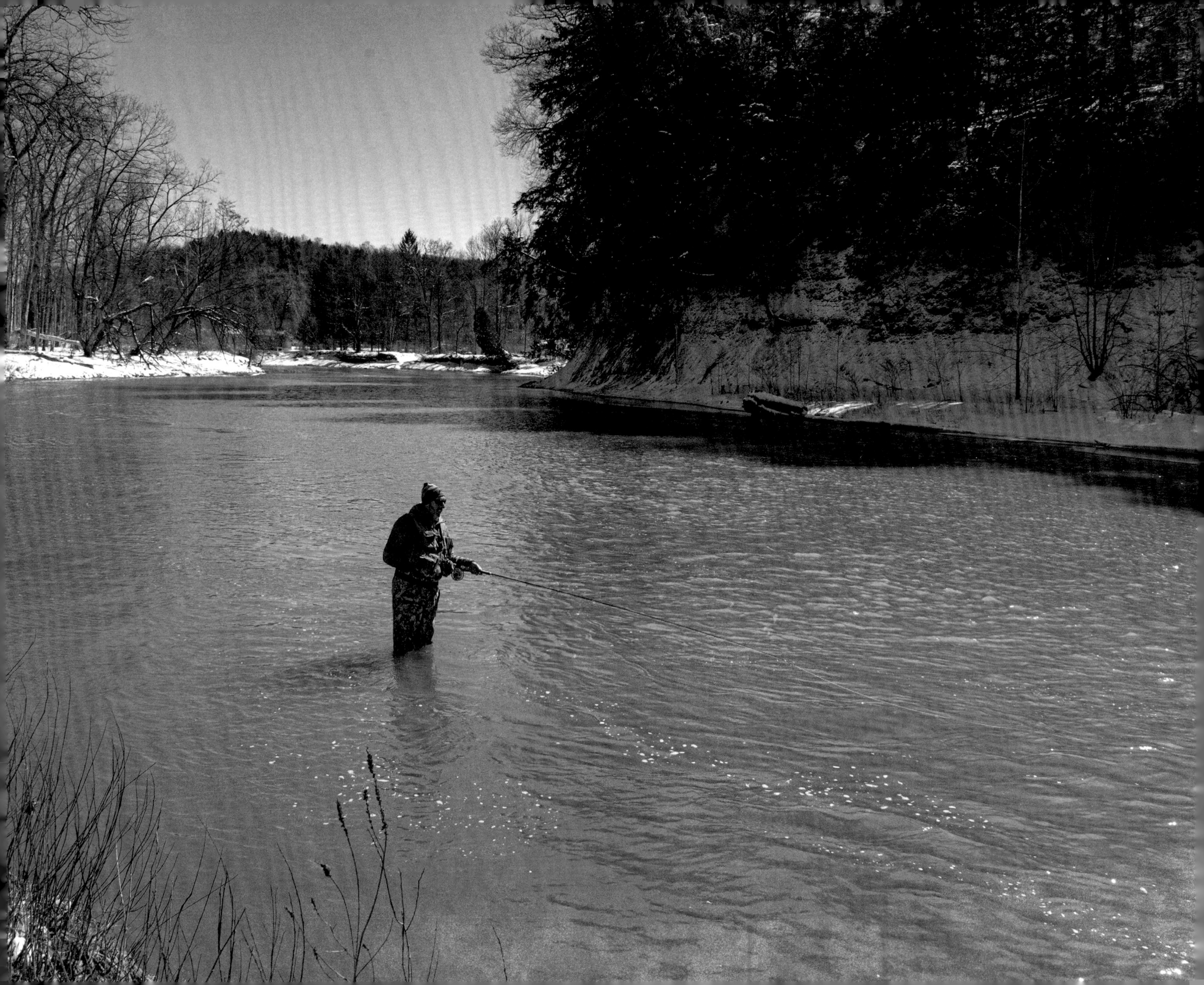

REFLECTIONS ON WINTER

Rick Kustich

Growing up near Buffalo, New York, I learned at a young age to embrace the winter or else too much time was spent staring at inside walls. Sledding, pond hockey, skiing and other activities made wintertime quite fun. We actually hoped and prayed for cold and snow to enhance the winter experience. And we never seemed to give the cold much of a thought. Frostbite wasn't in our vocabulary — it was simply numb fingers and toes.

I guess it's easy to develop an adverse relationship with winter, especially as you get older. The cold can wear on the psyche. Drab skies that don't reveal the sun for weeks takes its toll. Clinical depression rates rise, and a general malaise seems to develop among the masses.

Fortunately, I found winter fishing in my early adult years. It wasn't all fly fishing at first but quickly moved that direction through a time of great discovery. I dived into a developing fishery of large lake-fed steelhead and brown trout. Weather was never a deterrent back then as cold, snow and wind were part of the package. Often much satisfaction was found in just beating the elements.

I still enjoy immersion into the winter conditions. Somehow there is empowerment within standing thigh deep in bone chilling water while others find their place indoors. But with age comes discretion by now searching for winter's slightly softer side. Instead of fighting it, I seek to be absorbed by it. The revitalizing forces of a flowing river give hope that this dark, dank season is only part of a progression that makes living in the Great Lakes region unpredictable and ever changing.

A river looks different in the winter. Snow and ice choke down its size and attitude. Flows are slowed by the lack of runoff from its feeders meandering through the earth's frozen surface. A river in winter looks dark and foreboding in contrast to the brightness of snow packed banks. But the currents are often gentle, readily accepting a visitor for the day.

Almost immediately legs are cooled as water barely above freezing moves around waders with the effects penetrating the body. There is a sense that a river in winter is at rest or in limbo, waiting patiently for the replenishing qualities of spring. Going in I know that fish metabolism is slowed in such cold conditions and that finding active fish is most difficult in the winter. But what I seek has less to do with catching and more to do with simply saying "no" to the confinement of indoors. Cabin fever won't control me. An act of defiance.

Senses seem more alive and aware in winter with a feeling that no other time of year garners the same respect and awe of the natural world. Winter leaves us pondering the force of nature's extremes. But when the winds have died, and the snow squalls have passed, a serene hush surrounds a river in winter. The snow absorbs ambient noise allowing for escape into a peaceful trance. It is then that I am so pleased to be a part of the day as opposed to merely observing.

Everything is slower and takes more effort. Walking snowy, icy trails require focus to not end the day early with injury. Heavy snow bogs down each step, quickly taxing stored energy. Extra layers of clothing weigh on the arms and body during every cast. But it's a small price to pay. Maintaining nutrition and hydration is key for both enjoyment and safety but packing in a day's worth of supplies along with camera gear and extra clothing only adds to the necessary effort.

Slow is the approach to fishing as well. I suppose there was a time when I didn't believe a steelhead or trout would chase down a swinging fly in cold winter water — buying into fake facts distributed by those lacking enough patience to uncover the truth. Chase and eat they do, but often on the fish's terms. A fly fished deep and slow usually fishes best. Soft inside seams and slow tailouts tend to hold the most fish and allow for the deliberate presentations that give a predator plenty of time to take advantage. Grabs can be firm and obvious reminiscent of warmer days. Fish that have just entered in the winter months pull with authority. But others are quite subtle requiring a more direct reaction for a firm hookup. While a passive hookset is my usual response to the obvious grabs in fall and spring, a pull back on the rod creating an effective strip set can connect to a subtle grabber before the fly is dropped.

The one thing that doesn't seem to change in winter fishing is the never-ending internal struggle wondering if the right combination of fur, feathers and synthetics is attached to the end of the tippet. Too big? Too small? Not enough flash? Not enough weight? The questions are endless. But striving for a level of simplicity there is reliance on big and dark, black and purple in stained water and smaller muted olives and browns in clear water. A splash of fluorescent pink or chartreuse seems to do the trick at times and I have become fond of a little more flash than in the past. Going with tried

HEAVY SNOW BOGS DOWN EACH STEP, QUICKLY TAXING STORED ENERGY. EXTRA LAYERS OF CLOTHING WEIGH ON THE ARMS AND BODY DURING EVERY CAST. BUT IT'S A SMALL PRICE TO PAY.

and true helps to eliminate the voices of doubt. In the end, fishing a fly that instills confidence almost always seems to work out.

In recent years my connection to winter fishing has never been stronger. I appreciate the quiet and solitude like never before, shutting out the noise that has become all too difficult to avoid. And the opportunity for winter fishing seems to have grown over the past five years. Weather windows can be found regularly — between wide and wild fluctuations — to fish rivers that had been mainly too frozen to fish from December to April in years gone by. The climate and world around us are changing. Good for winter fishing? Perhaps. But at what cost? I sometimes feel guilt. My Catholic upbringing? Possibly. But more likely that great winter fishing may just be another canary in the coal mine. Even a slight increase in summer temperatures threaten the survival of the region's naturally spawned smolts on some river systems.

Walking back to the vehicle it's difficult to not to be impressed with the advancements in clothing and equipment. In comparison I laugh at my attire from the early winter fishing days. But even with technology on your side a full day of standing in the cold fighting off various elements leaves your being in a completely exhausted state. The body craves a reward for accomplishing the challenge. And a big bowl of hot chili or greasy cheeseburger never tastes quite as good as when enjoyed after spending a full day on a river in winter.

Swing the Fly Anthology 2023

TRESPASSERS WILL BE OFFERED A SHOT

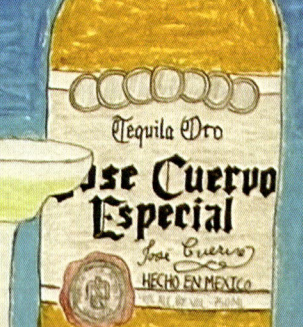

ACCOMMODATIONS

Luke Probasco

"Are you sure this place isn't a former crime scene? I can almost see a chalk outline," said my good fishing partner, Nanney, when we stepped into our room for the night.

While I don't think there were any dead bodies in the room, I could almost guarantee there was some illegal activity here over the years as hinted by the "if you see something, say something" signs in the hallway. Our accommodations for the night were just a skosh above what you'd find at a place that rents rooms by the hour. The sort of place where you don't take your shoes off and you sleep on top of the bed with all of your clothes on.

We were on a 16-hour road trip to meet up with our buddy Dan on one of the famed western rivers. When you can barely keep your eyes open, periodically letting one eye rest while the other pays attention to the road, your standards diminish faster than a lonely bachelor's at last call. I suppose we should have been thankful to find a bed. The chain motel, across the street with a brightly lit parking lot, had their fancy "No Vacancy" sign illuminated.

Four hours later, with energy drinks in each hand, we were on the road again. No rest for the wicked — or the angler. The night at the no-tell motel got me thinking about the places that anglers stay in the name of fish.

The closest I have ever gotten to staying in a lodge is when I shack up in Nanney's garage for a week every winter to swing for steelhead. Our steelhead crew descends on his place from all over the country every February when the run is at its peak. He lives on the river and is a gracious host. A welcoming sign outside his shop says "Trespassers Will Be *Offered a Shot*."

In the last couple of years Nanney has brought in a port-a-potty for the week. I'm not sure if that was to save his own bathroom or to torture his guests — probably both. The air in an outhouse gets pretty heavy after a week of steelhead bums eating semi-warm breakfast burritos.

Since Jonathan and Dave have been coming to steelhead camp the longest, they get dibs on Nanney's travel trailer. After many years of running into them on the river, trading embellished steelhead stories and sharing conservation efforts, Nanney offered up his palace on wheels.

Turns out the place they had been staying at before Nanney extended an invitation was super sketch but also the only place to stay within a 30-mile radius. Jonathan would wear his wading boots in the shower. Dave would bring a burner sleeping bag from his home in Nashville, just so that he didn't have to sleep inside the bed. The rooms came complete with a sign at the bathroom sink requesting that guests, "Please do not clean fish here."

Being the new kid, I get the couch in the shop. This allows me to test the temperature rating on my down sleeping bag. (Side note: In what universe have those ever been accurate?) After a late, glutinous dinner of local crab, oysters and steak, and generous pours of bourbon, slumber easily sets in. The pellet stove's fan hums me to sleep. Occasionally I wake up to see the flames of the fireplace dancing in the dark, reminding me it isn't time to get up yet.

This last year, Jonathan and I worked hard with the Washington Department of Fish and Wildlife on the Coastal Steelhead Advisory Group. Knowing how dire the steelhead runs are, we suspected there might not be a season. When word finally came out that there would be a season, Nanney sent out a group text that simply said, "Guess this means you assholes are coming again this year." Yep. Wouldn't miss it.

As steelheading goes, there is never a sure thing, but there is certainty that we'll be at Nanney's house every February to try.

Four walls and a roof are nice for an angler, extravagant even, because for my crew, more often than not, we are sleeping in tents, usually on hard, unlevel ground. I still don't know how it happened, but a buddy once managed to roll to outside of the tent, with just his head inside the door, when he woke up.

Usually though, we are in too much of a rush to hit the water and defer the un-fun stuff — like setting up camp, until it is pitch dark. And after a day of toasting to fish landed, putting up a simple dome tent is akin to building the Taj Mahal. More than once my good friend Justin has slept on the hard ground rather than going back to the truck to get his air bed. As he justified, "I'm talking in cursive. Not feeling too uncomfortable right now."

One night, after the campfire took its last breath, we collectively decided it was time for bed, as the morning rise would be in just a few hours. Minutes after settling in our sleeping bags, the lullaby of the breeze was interrupted by a maxed-out bluetooth speaker screaming Tom Petty's greatest hits.

"What the deuce?" questioned Justin.

"I'm pretty sure that is coming from Nanney's car. He's sleeping in the back," I groaned.

It was. And it did.

All. Night. Long.

By sunrise, as we were getting ready for the day, Nanney rolled out of the back of his SUV, completely refreshed, and chuckled, "Hey, were you guys able to hear my music last night?"

Just as he asked this obvious question, our neighbors from across the campground decided to march over. Watching them navigate the sagebrush and rattlesnakes, it was obvious this wasn't a "how's the fishing?" sort of visit. More than slightly perturbed, they told us, "Don't come around here no more."

I'm still not sure if they thought they were being punny and quoting the Tom Petty song or if it was just a coincidence. Either way, they were gone the next night. And more importantly, the batteries in Nanney's speaker were dead, allowing the rest of the campground to get some sleep.

That same trip I learned that rainflies just keep rain out. When the wind picks up in the desert, sand finds its way everywhere. I forgot about this minor detail.

While planning for the trip, I opted to sleep in an all-mesh tent, thinking to myself, "No rain in the forecast. Clear desert skies. I'll count stars instead of sheep!"

Just after setting up camp, a breeze came up. Blurg. When sleeping outside in the desert, a little wind goes a long way. You know things aren't going the right way when sand starts collecting in your beverage and that Lagavulin 16-year-old scotch that you saved for the trip is no longer enjoyable. By bedtime, everything had an ⅛-inch of sand on it — my pillow, sleeping bag, water bottle. Everything.

For a quick minute I thought about relocating to the back seat of my truck, but remembered the last time I slept there my back hurt for a week. It would work in a pinch, but I ultimately decided to rough it out. There are probably people that pay good money to have their face sand-blasted at the salon. Sort of like a mud bath, right?

I'm not gonna lie. Wind and sand make for a long night. It was one of those nights where you dust off your phone every hour to check the time. The sunrise coming up from the hills was a welcome sight, even though it meant an exhausting, slightly hungover day was ahead. At least I didn't have a sore back from sleeping in the fetal position all night in the back of my truck.

As far as accommodations go, the closer proximity to water, the more forgiving I am — and it seems to be the same for other anglers. A few gems that have been found written in guestbooks along the way:

"Sure, all the silverware was in plastic bags due to a cockroach infestation, but it was on the lake. Five stars!"

"My kid refused to brush his teeth after looking at the bathroom sink, but I could hear the river. Will be back!"

While not all places I spend the night are this memorable (thankfully!), I welcome a little discomfort on my adventures. Plus, it makes for great memories and a good story.

If you ever are doing a little dusty parking lot camping and hear Tom Petty all night long, come on over. Trespassers will be offered a shot.

Photo: Zack Williams

THE TEMPTATION OF LILITH

A tale of continuity, of sorts

Steven Bird

I suppose you could say the kid's fishing pole is a bad idea. A Snoopy pole — picture of Charlie Brown and Snoopy on the package, fishing. I don't know. It might not be that great of an idea for a gift. Even if there is a kid, it would only be three years old and no three year old can operate a Snoopy pole, not without help anyway. But there's really nothing I can provide, realistically, so I guess the gift is just my way of being a dad, if by chance I am a dad, and a way to show my appreciation on the anniversary of our meeting.

I didn't get her name. Not sure she had a name. She never spoke. Not in the way most of us speak. Though she was a master of body language, able to get her point across alright. I call her Lilith.

It was high spring and such a fine day I was compelled to get out and fish. It'd been warm the past few days, triggering hatches and mating swarms of grannom sedges. Love was in the air alright. I hiked a mile upstream of the trailhead before starting to cast. Wild country up there, and I had the stream all to myself. It felt good to be in the back country. Sometimes when I'm by myself and feeling good I sing out loud, and I sang: "Do not forrr-sake meee Ooooooh my daarrrliiiin...."

The fishing was good, but, weird, I had the feeling I was being watched. I chalked it up to the energetic nature of the day working senses that'd been shut in the cabin most of a long winter and now a bit overwhelmed by Mother Nature's unfolding charms. I concentrated on casting and minding the drift. Like I said, the fishing was good, I was leaning over the water releasing my seventh cutthroat when I caught a flash of movement.

There. I saw a patch of auburn showing through a break of scrub cedars. Fur. A big animal, I was sure. Then, higher, another patch of fur. I thought I saw it jiggle.

It wasn't an elk. An elk would make a mad dash out of there with a nose full of human at this range, I reasoned. A bear. Had to be a bear. Okay no big deal. Outfitting, I encounter them on occasion. Not grizzlies. Black bears. Unlike grizzly bears, black bears are fairly shy and will avoid you if you respect their space, usually. The jiggling color patch was a concern. I estimated it to be about eight feet above the ground, which meant the critter it belonged to was taller than any standing black bear. I figured: yup, shit, a grizzly, and a big one, stalking me, standing over there behind that bush inhaling my scent and licking its nose.

HEY YAH YEEAH! I made a two-step false charge toward it waving the flyrod over my head.

I held my breath. I thought I saw it move but my yelling and stomping hadn't come close to producing the effect I wanted, which was to get it to flush and run. At this point the smart thing to do would've been to ease back out of there, but I'd already thrown down a territorial challenge, so I figured the stalking bear might interpret my retreat as a sign of weakness, inspiring it to more aggressive stalking. While I swirled in the conundrum, the cedars quivered and out into full view stepped Lilith.

She was striking. Fully eight feet tall, and not thirty feet away, looking at me. My mind couldn't allow it. Oh no. This was a thing that did not fit my reality frame. I turned my head and looked toward the water, considered making another cast and just carrying on with the fishing like she wasn't there, then looked back to see her still standing by the cedars. Obviously female. She stood straight, not bent forward like an ape. Other than being eight feet tall and entirely covered with red fur except for her pink face, she looked human. Well, closely related to human, a kissing cousin, forgive the pun. The gold, almond shaped eyes possessed intelligence and purpose, and something else I couldn't immediately read. The mouth was straight and broad, showing just a hint of lips spread across the slight protrusion of a muzzle — not much of one — but a muzzle, no getting around it. She was not altogether unattractive. Her breasts? Not the shoe-sole breasts of an ape, but round, glorious basketballs capped with distended pomegranates. Her head was crowned with a maelstrom of red hair, a shade redder than the auburn tone of her fur, matted to dreadlocks, looping to below her waist.

I was in shock and off guard when she rushed me —

Stupidly, I tried to fend her off with my 3-weight Granger, and even though the rod was imbued with the mojo of a thousand rivers and easily worth a thousand dollars, it proved useless, a limp reed disintegrating to splinters against the impact of Lilith's swift charge. She snatched me up, tucked me under her arm like a football and ran upstream covering impossible lengths of ground in a stride while I kicked and flailed like a crazy man — which served to bring rib-breaking pressure from the giant arm, forcing me to stop.

Caught, crushed, terrorized, I flopped and dangled like a half-dead carp fated for the stewpot. Hooking up a spur canyon, she proceeded uphill never breaking stride.

I was in a bad dream and couldn't wake up. I pissed my waders.

Lilith stopped at a rock overhang near the top of a ridge. A bower of cedar branches arranged like a large nest had been laid beneath the overhang. She dropped me into the center of it then scrambled back to study me, the prize.

I dared not move.

She squatted there for a long time, watching me.

I began to get my legs back and started to think. I determined that she didn't mean to kill me. If that'd been her intent she could have easily done it by the river and saved herself the trouble of hauling me to the ridge top.

Then, slow, deliberate, she rose to full height, stretched her arms to the sky and put her palms together. She smiled. I think. I interpreted the expression to be a smile. Then she swept her arms out to her sides, each hand assuming a strange, delicate mudra, and she began to dance, graceful as any hula girl, her hands like bird wings opening and closing, shifting through a series of mysterious poses. Something about her … she was entrancing. I couldn't look away. She was seducing me. I'm not completely thick, I know when I'm being seduced. The notion was terrifying, yet the urge to jump up and run seemed to be dissolving, somehow.

Then a thought struck me and I tensed, imagining a ten foot tall jealous buck sasquatch busting from the bushes in full-cry fury, grabbing me between his thumb and forefinger and pinching my head off, then pulling off my arms and legs, and then all the other grippable appendages, easy as plucking petals from a daisy - he loves me, he loves me not … Any sparking aspiration to romance I might have been entertaining, maybe somewhere in some secret backroom of my mind, was iced.

Lilith began to sing as she danced, a song without words, melodic inhalations and exhalations of breath, rhythmic sighs punctuated with low whistles: Hih hih hih sweeeeeee - all the while her eyes pinning me.

I tend to reason in phases. First, the reactive, presumptuous monkey mind phase: I was past that one, I figured that she wasn't going to kill me, at least not right away.

Then the pragmatic phase: I reasoned that the beguiling Lilith was under the influence of her biological clock, 'in season', if you will, and, possibly, there was no male sasquatch available in the territory, so I was to be *that guy*.

That lead to some considerations regarding taxonomic boundaries, transitioning me to the meeting house filled with morally traumatized Puritan ancestors who stood me on the precarious fulcrum between a sense of Darwinian duty rooted in the pragmatic phase, and an ethical dilemma, which always precedes the final phase: in which, I transcend reason and surrender to The Flow.

Lilith ceased her song, stopped dancing, and stood giving me the soulful eye. Then she stepped to the bower demure as any maiden, turned her back to me and sank to a prairie hen pose on the cedar bed, her twin haystack bottom looming inches from my face. She smelled like a honey-glazed baked ham. The pink bud between her legs blossomed to a chaotic rose before my eyes. This girl was good to go no doubt about it. My call. I possessed the key to my own salvation. My only hope was to place it into the slot and do my level best. And I did need to get out of those wet waders…

There's no good reason to relate the intimate details. I've probably divulged too much already. For you who are dying of curiosity, I offer that it is an actual fact that the higher primates really do practice every type of pleasuring enjoyed by folks. We shared the granola bars from my fishing vest. I was secretly proud when the energetic Lilith, finally sated at the end of my third day of captivity, succumbed to sleep. That's when I made the getaway.

I hike in every year on the anniversary. This year I'm bringing the Snoopy fishing pole and the usual bags of frozen berries and granola bars. I know she likes granola bars. I'll leave the stuff at the old bower under the ledge. No, I've never seen any sign of her since that time. Love? Well. Hard not to feel something.

the RIVER RAMBLER

Like steelhead camp in your car.

Available at TheRiverRambler.com or wherever you find your podcasts.

©Richard C. Harrington 2020

CUSTOM CANE RODS BY DAVID L. REID — Hand Made in the PNW

You Only Live Once, Fish Cane

DAVIDLREIDBAMBOO.COM | 208-207-6749

Clockwise from top left:

Nineteen-year-old Charles Lingren and me. C.T. wanted to catch a coho on the Fly. He came, made a couple of casts and accomplished his goal with a 9 lb. Tlell River coho.

Eleven year old Charles Lingren with a Copper River trout about to be released.

Art Lingren guiding a coho closer to shore for release. September 2022.

Art and Charles Lingren with a Copper River steelhead, spring break, 1988.

THE TIDE TURNS

Art Lingren

Spring break was a favourite time of the year for me and my son, Charles (C.T.), when he was young. Some spring breaks we spent on Vancouver Island camping and fishing for steelhead. One place, Haida Gwaii, became a favourite place to go. Charles and I made our first trip to Haida Gwaii in 1988, when he was 11 years old.

My guide friend Mark Walsh in Sandspit had a two-for-one package for steelhead, and Air Canada had a $99 flight, making it a reasonably priced trip. I thought it a good place to get Charles into some trout and steelhead. Mark had a Labrador dog, and my son liked being around it as much as he liked the fishing. Over the years we did other trips, some in the summer where I went ahead with the truck and camper and Charles, often bringing a friend along, would fly up and spend a week or two then fly home. On those summer trips we fly fished for pinks and coho salmon and did a little bit on the lakes. We camped, and the kids loved the campfires on the beach.

One of most memorable Haida Gwaii fishing moments happened when Charles was 19. University was to start on Monday after Labor Day in 1996. Bob Taylor, Ron Schiefke and I were on a multi-week trip to Haida Gwaii with my truck and camper. Charles contacted me from home saying he wanted to catch a coho on the fly and asked if he could fly up and meet us.

We picked him up at the Sandspit airport and headed to the Tlell River on September 6. None of us had fished the Tlell. We went down the road along the river towards Tlell River House. The tide was out and the river looked good. When I saw a nice looking run, I parked the truck set up a rod and reel with a floating line and tied on a red and white, polar bear-winged, silver-bodied fly. I told Charles to go and fish the tail out of the run. Three casts and he was into a coho that tipped the scale at nine pounds. Shortly after Charles landed his coho, a fisherman hiked upriver and told Charles that he saw him catch that fish after three casts. The fellow was from Europe and had spent five days on the river without a bite.

Charles wanted to see some of the places we visited on earlier trips but returned later to the Tlell. He had one more day, and with good tides to fish, he caught a larger coho. He flew back to Vancouver pleased with himself. He wanted to come catch a coho on the fly and managed to land two.

For many years we didn't fish much together. Charles was at university, then taught English in Japan, then worked toward a master's degree in Alberta. During his summer months he guided at salmon lodges. He still liked to fish and now he is settled in his career. He is able now to get away more, providing he has access to the internet and cell phone coverage.

September fishing in Haida Gwaii has been an annual trip for me for many years. In the last few years Charles would fly up for a long weekend. However, in 2022 the tide changed. I didn't want to do the 1,000-mile drive from my home to the Haida Gwaii ferry at Prince Rupert, then a seven-hour ride across Hecate Strait to Skidegate, and a further drive to the Tlell River. Charles rented Grandpa's House at the Richardson Ranch for a week, booked airline tickets, rented a car and paid for the works.

Yes, the tide changed, and he now organizes the trips and I tag along.

SILENCE OF THE LAMM

Pete Bodo

My eyes were slow to adjust to the darkness as I walked into the hotel bar in Maupin, on the banks of the Deschutes River. The watery sunlight of the autumn afternoon in the high desert pushed against the mullioned windows overlooking the river at the back of the pub but failed to brighten up the heavily varnished, knotty-pine paneled walls inside.

I was hoping to run into a guy named Sean Lamm. Guide Chris O'Donal, the go-to guy for many of my fly-fishing buddies, was all booked up when I reached out to him on short notice, but he asked his client, Lamm, if he would be willing to partner up for the days in question on an overnight trip swinging flies for steelhead. Lamm did me a solid by agreeing to share the trip. A single patron sat at the bar, slouched back against the wraparound backrest of his stool, half of a shit-eating grin on his face, a ball cap pulled down over his brow and a heavy pour of some brown liquor in a glass before him.

The bartender was a man of indeterminate age in a black Harley-Davidson t-shirt with the obligatory ponytail. Blonde heavily streaked with gray. He stood with a leg up on an aluminum beer keg, and said, "So, the bear says. . ." The patron finished for him "... You don't really come up here to hunt, do you?'" The bartender guffawed. I leaned out over the bar and had a closer look at the other customer.

"Fallon?" I said. "Jon Fallon?" He turned to me leisurely, eyebrows arched. "Afraid not, but I get mistaken sometimes. I have that kind of face."

"Of course, my bad," I said. I don't know why I thought the guy was Fallon, not least because he was dead, and those folks tend to stay that way. But there was something about that weathered, angular framed by a trim salt-and-pepper beard, and those sunken blue eyes, that triggered a memory of that bon vivant Fallon, with his jelled hair and bespoke brogues.

I ordered an Olympia draft and was about to offer to buy my neighbor a drink when a generic ringtone interrupted. The stranger fished a cell phone out of the pocket of his blue chambray shirt, excused himself, and left the bar by a side door, taking his whiskey with him. I nursed my draft, thinking he might return. The bartender asked if I'd heard the one about the two nuns that were ordered to paint their room without getting any paint on their habits. "No, but who was that other guy, the one who just left?" I asked, finishing my beer in one long swallow. "Got me," the bartender said, shrugging, "but I guess it ain't Fallon."

Fallon. I never really knew him, or even exchanged words with him. But I knew of him — everyone did. Rich, handsome, a womanizer, he was the subject of endless gossip and speculation. He occasionally showed up at a fishing-related social occasion or fundraiser in New York at the fishing club I belonged to, where I was the long-time conservation committee chairman.

Fallon gave generously, but he was all about the fishing. Rumor had it that Fallon was one of the very first westerners to fish Mongolia, where he caught a 30-pound taimen on a size 18 Parachute Adams. He was allegedly so well-connected that he had a standing invitation from the Queen of England to fish her beat on the River Dee at Balmoral Castle — famously declining to take her up on it because he didn't like that they killed fish over there. He reportedly quipped

"Morning on a Desert River" by Richard C. Harrington

HIS DEMISE WAS A TRAGEDY IN A TIGHTLY-KNIT COMMUNITY THAT SKEWS MORE TO TRAGI-COMEDY ON THE ORDER OF CLOUSER MINNOWS BURIED TO THE BEND IN EARLOBES, OR THREE-THOUSAND DOLLAR BAMBOO RODS SPLINTERED BY CEILING FANS.

that his stand caused no hardship, because he stood a better chance of taking a 25-pound-plus Atlantic salmon fishing among the bozos on the public water of Quebec's Matapedia River than the tweedy boys on the Dee.

Everyone wondered how Fallon's comely wife Nina put up with him. His wealth may have had something to do with that. Still, some suggested — only half-kidding — that it was a good thing Nina had an airtight alibi for the day Jon Fallon went missing. As the story goes, Fallon took his 24-foot Contender out of Montauk Harbor in New York one late October day to fish bluefin during the herring run. The weather turned ugly. The Contender was found some 48 hours later, bobbing around on heavy swells near Block Island, trailing 30-feet of Rio Outbound fly line and an 11-inch articulated herring fly made mostly of craft fur. The boat was loaded with gear but empty of humans — including Fallon.

His demise was a tragedy in a tightly-knit community that skews more to tragi-comedy on the order of Clouser minnows buried to the bend in earlobes, or three-thousand dollar bamboo rods splintered by ceiling fans. At his memorial service, one eulogist fondly recalled that the deceased would often kick off a fishing adventure at some posh lodge with the same toast: "Gentlemen ... as Henry David Thoreau once said, 'Many men go fishing all of their lives without knowing it isn't fish they are after.' Bushwa, I say. We know what we're after. Big fish ... and lots of em!"

Someone else at that service also remarked: "Dying at sea, man. That's next level."

I ate dinner alone in the busy hotel dining room among groups of beer-drinking, racoon-eyed meat-eaters swapping fish tales. Anxiety and anticipation kept me tossing and turning all night, partly because I had yet to catch a wild, sea-going steelhead. If I made up a bucket list, this would have been right on top. In the morning, a hard-used Chevy Silverado with a cap, towing two drift boats stacked one atop the other, stood growling under the porte cochere of the hotel. It was still dark, with chilly October drizzle beating a tattoo on the truck. I introduced myself to Chris O'Donal and Nick Rowan, who would precede us down river in his own boat containing the camping gear. A figure in a rain jacket with the hood up over his cap appeared next to me and said, "Howdy. I'm Sean Lamm."

"Oh hey. Tom Merino," I said, absurdly adding, "That's Merino with an 'e'."

"Like the wool," Lamm said, grinning. "Could be useful today."

"I think I saw you in the hotel bar yesterday."

"That's right. Boning up on stupid jokes."

Lamm told me he was a transplant from Rhode Island, now living in Idaho's "steelhead country." He grinned when I said I was from New York and asked, as many often do, "How are things in the Big Apple?" It was hard to tell if he was being sarcastic, but something about Lamm struck me as a little off — nothing unusual in the fly-fishing crowd.

We talked about fishing with the two-handed

rod. I explained that I was fairly new to the spey game — "work, kids, mortgage, etc.," but hoped to take my first wild steelhead on the swing.

"Should be doable," Lamm said, "if we don't get blown out by the storm headed our way." Chris emerged from the tailgate and greeted Sean with a man hug and small talk. Nick closed the cap window. Soon we were traveling in a caravan on the washboarded gravel road to Mack's Canyon, where we would leave our rental vehicles and the truck for the shuttle service to move down to the takeout.

A few miles downriver, Chris pulled hard at the oars and nosed the drift boat into a small backwater at the head of a juicy-looking run. The light was still poor, the water opaque, with an oily sheen. The glassy surface where the riffle petered out was broken here and there by a push of water from a subsurface rock, often with a seam trailing. "Head or tailout?"

"Your choice," Lamm said.

I chose the lower half of the run. Chris organized my Skagit setup, tying on an Intruder-style tube fly with small bead chain eyes. Lamm's gear put my utilitarian outfit to shame. The handle of his two-handed rod was as ornate as a scepter. I lusted after his gorgeous reel and told him so. It was black, with a graceful, S-shaped handle. Lamm decided that he would fish a waking fly, the most exciting — as well as least productive — technique. It came as no surprise.

The drizzle stopped soon after we'd combed through the first run without moving a fish. By then, a warm but gusting wind was breaking up clouds as big and gray as an elephant's ass, revealing swaths of hard blue sky. Lakes of sunlight moved across the enormous hills. Drifting downriver, we saw mule deer, and three bighorn sheep high on a hill. Lamm and I switched it up at the next run. I started in the choppy water at the top. Lamm stepped about 75 yards below, where the current slowed and spread into a tailout. I got into the familiar step-cast-step rhythm of swinging, relaxed. The sun popped out and lit up the tight loop of Sean's shooting head, and the bright red running line unfurling in the air. He was a superb caster.

Neither of us had a grab. Nor did we move a fish in the next run. "It's going to happen," Sean predicted as we drifted down to the last run before lunch. "That rain water and some sun is going to warm up the river and get the fish active. That's just what we need. It's got to turn things on." But it didn't happen.

We ate sandwiches in the boat. I felt like I was listening to a Ted Talk as my companions compared notes on steelhead fishing. A jet sled roaring upstream slowed down. The guide cupped his hands around his mouth to overcome engine noise and said his clients had hooked three and landed two. Lamm looked like he had indigestion and muttered a word that isn't easy to forget.

"Bushwa."

The fishing was challenging. Late in the afternoon we pulled in at a long run full of boulders and boils. By then, dark clouds were moving swiftly, accompanied by occasional gusts of wind, the beginnings of the expected stormfront pushing through. I wanted to finish my cigar and watch Lamm fish his skater, so I stayed in the boat while he clambered out to try his hand. The riffle-hitched, purple muddler was zigging and zagging erratically, leaving a pronounced wake on the surface as it swung around in the current. Suddenly, it was engulfed in a big boil, the kind you get when you flush one of those train-station toilets that has no tank.

It was magical. Lamm played the fish expertly, handling it with loving care. He never took the fish fully out of the water to remove the fly and had no interest in having his picture taken with it. As the fish swam off into deeper water, Lamm took a deep breath and sighed. Turning to me, he said there were bound to be more fish in that area. Why didn't I try them, maybe with a skated fly to avoid hanging up in the rock garden.

"You sure?" I waited a beat then jumped to my feet. Imagine, taking a steelhead on a skated fly. I managed to interest a fish that chased the muddler, boiling and slashing at it, cast after cast, some six times without ever grabbing hold. My hands were shaking, but I managed not to yank the fly away. When the fish appeared to lose interest, Lamm tied on a different skater, an October Caddis.

The fish crushed it on the first swing, sending a spume of spray high in the air. "He's on," I yelled as the rod bucked in my hand and line melted off the reel. I stumbled after the fish, downstream. Excited, Lamm talked me through the struggle, sometimes grabbing the top of my waders, like a father helping his kid as I negotiated the slippery river rocks. I don't know who was more pleased when I eventually landed the fish.

My first steelhead. A wild one. At an estimated 12-pounds, it was large for a Deschutes fish. Caught not just on a swung fly, but a skater. I whooped with glee. The fish was a gorgeous specimen, thick-bodied and blue as a rifle barrel on top, with silver sides and a hint of rose on her gill plates. "Just look at her," Lamm said, standing over me, arms folded. "She's so pretty. Just like a little person." I held her gently by the wrist of her tail, head pointed upstream, while she recovered from her exertions. "Turn her a little left," O'Donal said, snapping a final picture. The steelhead flipped her tail, slid free of my hand, and evaporated into the emerald-tinted flow. We watched in silence as she disappeared. Lamm would take another fish out of the run in the fading light.

Our campsite was among some cottonwood trees. Nick had pitched the tent Lamm and I would share amid sagebrush on a little flat behind the open-sided mess tent where Chris quickly set to work to prepare dinner because the wind was picking up. Nick announced that he had just gotten engaged, so we drank a toast to that before we dug into our chili and cornbread.

I picked my companions' brains about casting, Lamm explaining the mechanics with the precise language and certainty of a physicist. I was outgunned when the talk turned to past fishing trips. "I don't mean to be nosy, Sean," I said. "But what do you do, that you get so much time in all these cool places?"

A cagy look flickered in Lamm's eyes before he quietly said, "I hit the mother lode with some investments, including Amazon. Yeah, just lucked out. You?"

Songwriter and studio musician, I told him, adding that I had never "lucked out" with a big hit. We talked about music while the wind grew more insistent. The propane lantern above the table was beginning to sway noticeably, moths still dive-bombing it.

In addition to my lingering elation, I was feeling sentimental and quite buzzed. The bottle of bourbon I broke out to celebrate had started full but now, thanks in good part to Lamm, it was getting perilously close to 'E.' The guy even drank better than I did.

I poured the last of the hootch into our glasses. I lifted mine in a toast of thanks to my companions, impetuously adding, "Give a man a fish and you feed him for a day. Teach him to fish and you never know what the hell he's going to do!"

As if on cue, I tipped over backwards in the folding camp chair. Everyone cracked up. Lamm stood, hunched over with an arm over his stomach, trying to contain his glee. He held his glass up at a crazy angle (fortunately, it was already empty), and barely got the words out, "He may end up... catching ... big fish ... and ... lots of 'em!"

A fierce gust set the rolled-up sides of the mess tent flapping. Some of the pots in the kitchen area went bouncing and clanging across the rough ground. Giant raindrops exploded, sending up puffs from the fine sand. It cut short the levity. We lurched around, securing stuff and weighing it down, then hightailed it for our tents.

Alone, I tried to read a bit under my headlamp but I was too tipsy. So I watched the sides of the little tent swell and contract in the wind like a giant lung — cozy in my sleeping bag on the folding cot. I finally dozed off and fell into a heavy sleep.

"Tom?"

"THEY ALMOST GOT ME DOWN IN PATAGONIA, OF ALL PLACES, WHEN I WAS THERE FISHING THE PANCORA CRAB HATCH ON THE COLLÓN CURA."

Hearing my name woke me up. "Sean?" The only sound was that of the rain, lashing at the tent in waves driven by the wind.

"You know, don't you?" he said.

"Yes, Jon. I know."

"How?"

"Bushwa."

"It is, admittedly, an odd word. You knew about the toast, then." he said.

"You were famous for it."

It was silent. My head was clearing. The rain, so powerful just minutes ago had ceased. Fallon — Lamm — quietly said: "They're going to kill me, you know."

"Who is?"

"The guys I took the money from. Bad actors."

"What money?"

Lamm laid it all out, calmly and briefly. Lamm took a great deal of the money he was managing in New York and, after making sure his wife Nina would be well provided for via an offshore account, he disappeared. "She was becoming a colossal pain in the ass, always with the sailing or ski vacations," he said, as if vanishing off the face of the earth were a reasonable option to spending snowy weekends kicking back in a Deer Creek condo.

"She never understood me. And frankly I was getting bored babysitting heaps of other people's money." Lamm explained those "other" people included some sketchy South American operators. Now they, along with the IRS, were hunting Lamm and closing in.

Lamm had a mole at the FBI, a guy he met while the two of them were on a musky trip, pioneering the art of fishing articulated streamers. He tipped Lamm off that the feds were prepared to move on him, hoping to bag the gangsters at the same time. Lamm explained, smiling beatifically at the memory, "They almost got me down in Patagonia, of all places, when I was there fishing the pancora crab hatch on the Collón Cura. But the owner of the estancia where I was staying, good friend, smuggled me over to San Martin de los Andes in an ox-drawn cart."

He paused. "I wouldn't recommend the trip. Bumpy as hell."

"So now what?"

"I have a friend who has a cabin way off the beaten path up on the OP, near the Sol Duc. That should start fishing well pretty soon. Just a hop, skip and a jump to British Columbia from there." It was silent for a while. Then Lamm said. "Funny, all this fuss, when all I ever really wanted to do was fish."

I was awakened by sunlight beating on the little tent, and the smell of frying bacon and fresh-brewed coffee. There was no sign of Lamm or his gear, just an empty cot. When I crawled out, I saw that someone had broken down most of the camp. Chris was at the cook stove. The air was cleansed and still. I wandered over to the guide, helped myself to a cup of coffee, and blew on it before I sipped.

"He's gone, isn't he?"

"Yep, He was damned lucky the storm pushed through so fast. They took Nick's boat and a lot of the gear. We'll take the rest, plenty of room on the boat. Oh, and Sean covered your tip. Generously."

I thought for a moment, and said, "You knew, didn't you?"

"Yeah, I did. But not until yesterday." Chris smiled and passed me a plate with breakfast. "I'm thinking he recognized your name or something. He must have had some kind of plan, but all he told me was not to worry. It would be cool."

What was in all this for Lamm? Maybe he just missed home. Thought I would take a message back to the "real" world: Fallon lives! The legend grows! He's a rogue, not a tragedy. People will talk.

"He told me something last night about some

guys looking for him," I said. "Maybe I was his cover in some way I don't understand.."

"Something like that," Chris said. "I think he felt whatever happened, you could be trusted. Fallon is one strange cat."

It was all crazy, but still — the morning was gorgeous, and we would have most of it to fish. The river was up and still rising, but not blown out yet. The conditions were anything but optimal, and skating flies was out, but I was thrilled to land another lovely steelhead — and lose another.

We hit the take-out ramp at around 1 p.m. I grabbed my stuff and jumped out of the boat while Chris went for his truck and trailer. I fished inside my waders for the keys to my rental. I walked up to the parking area, but I didn't see the generic, maroon rental Chevy anywhere. Exasperated, I hit the automatic door lock and a navy Ford Taurus nearby chirped twice, lights blinking. As I glanced at the vehicle details on the plastic key fob, two black SUVs came roaring into the lot, heading right toward me — followed by three gray, nondescript vehicles that could only be government. The truth dawned. Lamm had switched out our keys at night, He was now in my rental — and in the wind. Even as the doors slammed all around, people yelled, and government agents advanced toward me, guns pointed, I had to smile. Then I began laughing. The Thoreau quote rattled around in my head.

What a trip. Nobody would believe it back home. At least not the part about me catching my first steelhead on a waking muddler.

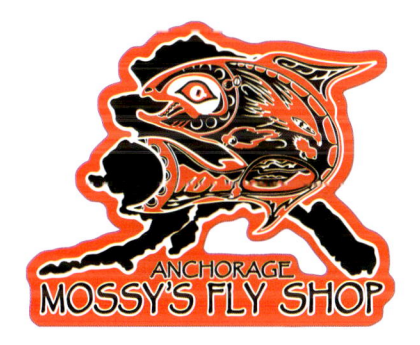

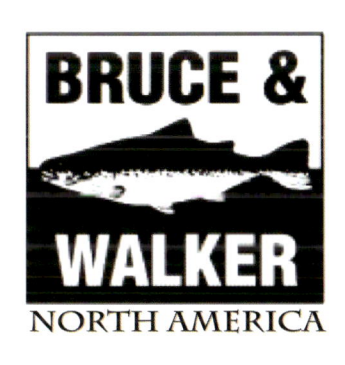

John Alevras has been a dedicated steelhead angler for 39 years. He is the author of *Leaves From a Steelheader's Diary* and *Building a Collectible Angling Library*. He also edited and published *A Guide to the Haig-Brown Fishing Tackle Collection* and collaborated on the publishing of *The Greased Line, Selections From Four Decades of the Washington Steelhead Flyfishers*, both limited edition publications. He has also had articles published in English and American angling journals.

Mitch Baker (editor) is a budding spey enthusiast, a former human resources bureaucrat with the State of Washington and a part-time school bus driver with a full time need for calming hobbies. He lives south of Olympia with his wife, Susan, who flyfishes infrequently but casts consistently better, and a pint-sized Senegal parrot named Tazzie who has yet to produce any feathers suitable for being affixed to a steelhead hook.

John Barratt is an avid fly-fisher residing in Central Oregon. After retiring, he began writing about fly-fishing. One of his stories, "Goose Creek," appeared in *The FlyFish Journal,* and *American Fly Fishing* has accepted two of his humorous pieces for their Fish Tales section. He recently completed a literary fiction novel titled *"A Startup on the Henry's Fork,"* which explores the myriad lessons entrepreneurs can glean from fly-fishing. He is also working on a collection of fishing-related, humor pieces for inclusion in a future book.

Steven Bird is a lifelong flyfisher living beside the American Reach of the Columbia River in northeast Washington, where he writes, guides and gardens with his best friend, Doris, his live-in caretaker and illustrator, and their two cats, Stinky and Sundown. Steve is the author of *Upper Columbia Flyfisher*, the publisher of the now-in-print *Soft~Hackle Journal* and works as trout spey editor for *Swing the Fly*.

Kirk Blaine is the Southern Oregon coordinator for the Native Fish Society and resides in Roseburg, Oregon, 20 miles downstream from the famous fly-only section of the North Umpqua River. Kirk is an avid angler spending countless hours on the North Umpqua River pursuing steelhead and salmon. Outside of angling, you can find Kirk hiking the trails, whitewater rafting, or skiing the peaks in the North Umpqua Watershed.

Pete Bodo chose not to pursue fame and fortune as an Instagram influencer or a Tik Tok "creator" with three million followers, happily settling for life as a family man and bourbon abusing coast-to-coast steelhead and Atlantic salmon nut. Pete is a former principal Outdoors columnist for the New York Times and wrote the Home Pool column for the *Atlantic Salmon Journal* for a number of years. He is the author of, among other books, a novel (The Trout Whisperers; Stackpole, 2006) and The Atlantic Salmon Handbook (Lyons Press, 1997). His three favorite flies to swing are the Hoh Bo Spey, the Hoh Bo Spey, and the Hoh Bo Spey.

Glenn K. Chen is a federal fisheries biologist with over 34 years in researching and managing Pacific salmon. He has been an Alaska resident for more than two decades and avidly pursues anadromous salmonids in the Great North at every opportunity.

M. Robbins Church holds a bachelor's degree in analytical chemistry and a Ph.D. in aquatic ecology from the University of Virginia. Now retired, his research with the U.S. EPA focused on effects of acid rain on lakes and streams, hydrochemistry of forested catchments and stable isotope ecology of salmon streams of the Pacific Northwest. At age 74, he no longer wades to Station on the N. Umpqua – well, most of the time, anyway.

David Conrad is a lifelong outdoor enthusiast and conservationist who grew up in the mountains of Idaho, Montana and Colorado, where he spent most of his formative years chasing snow to feed his snowboarding addiction before finally landing in Seattle, WA. His arrival to the world of steelhead was late but decisive, and he's used that late arrival as an opportunity to bring new perspectives in advocating for wild fish and the habitat they depend on.

Trey Combs needs no introduction. He is the author of three landmark books on steelhead flies and fishing—and now one more.

Adrian Cortes finds amusement in tying classic fly patterns in hand. He prefers the dry line for winter steelheading and exclusively fishes dry flies for summer-run steelhead. With complete confidence in the dry fly, these days he is more apt to encourage others to fish a dry pattern than he is to fish himself. In his words: "In 2019, my 15-year-old daughter Emma landed two dry fly steelhead on the North Umpqua. I'm playing with 'house money' 'til I'm dead."

Sam Davidson grew up near a steelhead stream, which wrecked his chances of living a normal life. A lifelong outdoorsman, he has worked on policy and communications for Trout Unlimited for 20 years. His writings about conservation, fishing, and other outdoor pursuits have appeared in a variety of publications.

Kevin Feenstra resides in Newaygo, Michigan, guiding around 200 days per year on the Muskegon River system. His flies have been published in books, magazines and online, and he has written articles for international, national and regional fly fishing magazines, and he recently authored the book *Matching Baitfish*, a must read for all swung fly anglers. Find out more at feenstraguideservice.com, kevinfeenstra.smugmug.com, swingabigfly.com and at his Instagram handle: @kevinfeenstra

Sam Flanagan's year along the far Northern California coast revolves around three key events: the late summer return of steelhead to the Klamath, the first Fall rains to get it ALL going, and, finally, the return of the Swainsons's thrush in late Spring to reset the clock all over again. In between, he is an avid forager, gardener, homesteader and dry fly trout purist. Just as salmon and steelhead are products of landscape and climate, Sam's writing is continually trying to record our own human experience of climate, place and time.

Aaron Goodis is a freelance photographer and fly fisherman living in Vancouver, B.C. He currently runs his freelance photography business shooting for magazines and brands in the outdoor industry. He also works at Michael & Young Fly Shop in Vancouver. Aaron has been a dedicated spey casting enthusiast primarily fishing for winter steelhead in the Pacific Northwest. His work can be seen at @agoodisphoto; @flyfishing_photography; www.aarongoodisphoto.com

Richard C. Harrington is a painter, printmaker, podcaster, fisher and river rat, living life curiously, in Oregon. His work can be found at www.richardcharrington.com, www.southlimasteelheadsociety.com and www.theriverrambler.com

Al Hassall's work has been around a long time, gracing the pages of magazines, journals, books and book covers, and various environmental causes for over 40 years. He recently retired from *Fly Fisherman Magazine*'s Seasonal Angler after 42 years, freeing him up to fish more and further explore his watercolor and ink techniques. For Al, it's always been the journey, and the destination will come in due course. If you haven't already, check out his work – it might bring a smile! He can be contacted at alhassall@trillium-studios.com.

Todd Hirano is an avid steelheader from Springfield, Oregon. Todd's biggest influence in steelhead fly fishing has been Bill McMillan. Since his early reading of *Dry Line Steelhead* in late 80s and ongoing friendship and communication with Mr. McMillan, Todd has been a disciple of dry-line methods. He can be found fishing surface flies most of the year, with some brief interludes wetfly/dry line fishing in winter. Todd's blog Dry Line Steelhead-Oregon chronicles his obsessed fishing life.

Dec Hogan began his lifelong obsession with steelhead fly fishing during a historic era: He was there when steelhead were still relatively plentiful and two-handed rods were a new and exciting tool to the Pacific Northwest steelheading community. He's taught thousands the way of steelhead and the two-handed rod. Dec is the author of the acclaimed book *A Passion for Steelhead* and coauthor, with Marty Howard, of the tome *Steelhead Fly Tying Art and Design*. Dec lives with his wife Amy and black Lab Raven in Midway, Utah.

Marty Howard Absorbed by fishing from the moment he laid cast with rod and fly, Marty Howard is a driven soul. His first steelhead fly produced at the vise, a California wet fly, prompted a lifelong consuming addiction. His desire to master every aspect of the sport has yielded opportunities throughout the fly fishing experience. His early goal to attain expertise in macro photography is clearly evident within the pages of *Steelhead Fly Tying Art and Design*. He and his wife Christine reside in Heber City, Utah.

Joe Janiak makes his living selling architectural coatings, but his passion lies in photography and outdoor adventures. Based in Buffalo, New York, he spends three quarters of the year swinging flies for Great Lakes steelhead and the remainder in search of wild trout or paddling and hiking the backcountry. Joe's work has been featured in *Swing the Fly*, *The FlyFish Journal*, *The Drake* and *Eastern Fly Fishing*. Joe has also worked with Galvan Fly Reels and McFarland Rod Company and is always looking for new photographic projects.

Rick Kustich began fly-fishing nearly 50 years ago on the lakes and streams of upstate New York. He has since traveled extensively to experience the finest fly-fishing throughout North America but continues to find that some of the best fishing often exists in your own backyard. He is author of *Hunting Musky with a Fly* and *Advanced Fly Fishing for Great Lakes Steelhead, Modern Spey* and more. Rick's work has appeared in numerous national and regional publications and websites. He has also spent time as a fly shop owner and fly-fishing book publisher.

Art Lingren is a Vancouver, British Columbia, born and raised fly fisher, flytier and author of over 20 Pacific Northwest-related fly-fishing books. He is a member of the Totem Flyfishers, a past president and historian of the British Columbia Federation of Fly Fishers and an honorary member of the Loons Fly Fishing club. He is primarily a steelhead fly fisher but likes to fish for other cold waters species as well.

John McMillan is the science director for The Conservation Angler. He has worked as a fishery scientist for 26 years on the Olympic Peninsula and has published numerous scientific articles on topics ranging from steelhead life history diversity to the effects of hatcheries on wild salmonids. John is also a life-long steelhead angler and spends the majority of his free time either fishing or snorkeling and taking underwater photos of salmon, trout and steelhead.

Bob Meiser dearly loves the poetry of fishing the two-handed fly rod on all levels. He has always enjoyed the personal reward (and sometimes elusive pursuit) of performing the "perfect delivery" with the two-handed rod and has always appreciated the amazing beauty of the gamefish that we are allowed to pursue, and venturing into the equally beautiful environments that they are found. Above all: he has always enjoyed the two-handed rod itself.

Jeff Mishler is the producer of the best selling Skagit Master DVD series and a published author in *Swing the Fly*, *The Drake* and *Gray's Sporting Journal*, to name a few. A former wildlife cinematographer, television commercial director and producer of marketing media for brands like Nike, Columbia Sportswear, Adidas, Microsoft and Intel, Jeff now lives near Bend, Oregon, with his family where he is either working up a quirky plot line, tying flies for an upcoming adventure or booting spammers off Skagitmaster.com.

Tony Perpignano Artist, architect, husband, father, grandfather, steelhead whisperer, Tony Perpignano, lives in Montana and has been enchanted with western rivers for most of his adult life. The energy, and sensory overload of rivers that creates these unique time capsules, recharges his lifeblood and is the focus of his artistic muse. More of Tony's work can be found at www.floriantrout.art.

Bill Pfeiffer grew up chasing wild brook and brown trout in Williamsport, PA, before packing up his car and blindly moving to Missoula in 2001 to fully embrace his passion for fly fishing. He has been a licensed fly-fishing guide and instructor since 2006 and continues to lead trips and teach new anglers when he can find the time. Bill works for Montana Trout Unlimited as their Outreach Coordinator. When he's not looking at a screen or teaching kids to fish, you can usually find him swinging flies on the Missouri or doing some old fashioned bass fishing.

Greg Pearson started working in a fly shop 30 years ago while studying fine art at the University of Utah. Guiding, teaching fly tying and Spey casting, hosting trips to British Columbia, Quebec and the Bahamas and working as a manufacturers rep has finally led him back to full time art. Greg has illustrated several fly fishing books and magazine articles and now focuses on painting sporting art and landscapes. GPearsonArt.com @gpearsonart

Luke Probasco is a fly fishing writer/photographer who plays bass for Brothers and the Beat when he is not chasing fish. You can follow him on Instagram at @flyfishnw for embellished stories, fly patterns and all things fly fishing.

Armando Quazzo started his fly fishing and fly tying career nearly half a century ago. He has had articles published in Italian, Spanish, English and U.S. magazines, and he has co-authored a novel on Atlantic salmon. He tied professionally while a university student and still ties flies by the dozen for his own boxes (@aqflies on Instagram). He is a double-handed rod casting addict and plans to retire in Norway in order to swing flies on a regular basis for salmon there. But, except for the cat, his family is not aware of this. Yet.

Jim Ray began his (almost) lifelong fishing addiction at the age of 4, fishing with his Father and Grandfather in a farmer's pond with earth worms for horn-pout. While enthusiastic, he was at best an occasional fisherman until 2000, when a fishing friend suggested taking his wife to a flyfishing school. She took to it immediately, and the rest, as they say, is history. Since the mid 2000s, Jim has become a passionate devotee of the two-handed rod and swinging flies for anything that will eat them.

Swing the Fly Anthology 2023   215

Daniel Ritz is *Swing The Fly*'s Conservation Field Editor. A recovering journalist turned outdoor writer and conservation communicator based in Idaho, Ritz moonlights at his local ma' and pa' fly shop when he isn't swinging a fly through one of his favorite Columbia River tributaries.

Joseph Rossano is a multidisciplinary artist, environmentalist and outdoorsman. His work explores themes of natural history, extinction, taxonomy and conservation in the genres of assemblage and installation art. Rossano is known for manufacturing environments incorporating wood, photography, technology and glass. Through the creation of collectives, including artists, scholars, scientists and industry, Rossano presents contemporary histories, revealing human interaction with species throughout recorded time.

Kait Sampsel is a native Oregonian who loves anything to do with the outdoors; however, fishing and dancing with the river's creatures has completely captivated her, propelling her into stewardship and community inclusiveness. She is a mother, wife, full-time guide, member of the editorial team at *Swing the Fly* and co-owner of Humble Heron Fly Fishing and Fine Art in Southern Oregon. Her goal is to create innovative, meaningful and long-lasting relationships through the connection driven by wild rivers and their inhabitants.

Marcel Siegle is an award-winning professional photographer. Originally from Germany, he has been living in California since 1989 and now lives in the Sonoma Wine country adjacent to a steelhead spawning habitat. Besides being a commercial photographer, he also creates fine art photography, with a heavy emphasis on fly fishing. He has been chasing steelhead on the swing for 25 years. Some of his fly-fishing work can be seen at www.flyfishingjunkie.com.

Thomas Wöelfle was born in Wolfrathausen, Germany – a small town near Munich, where he now lives with his family, just 10 minutes away from the River Isar, his home river to fish and swing for trout. As managing director of a modern, high-tech dental lab, fishing and taking pictures is his holy ground and way out – a fine and good compensation to this stressful job. Thomas likes the art, the approach and philosophy behind the spey community.

Glenn Zinkus is an outdoor writer and photographer from Corvallis, Oregon. When not engaged in piscatorial pursuits or shooting outdoor photos, he is likely to be traveling or finding upland birds behind his Brittanies. Glenn writes on fly fishing, conservation, upland hunting, and worldwide sporting and travel experiences. Glenn pens pieces for a wide range of outdoor publications. More of his work can be seen at www.glennzinkusoutdoors.com.